MR ONE HUNDRED BILLION

Gavin Weir

PART ONE

Prologue

Exciting news! An email dropped into my inbox this week from the Office for National Statistics: apparently they've worked out exactly how many humans have walked this earth, from the dawn of time, and they've used some kind of algorithm thingie to trace the precise time and place at which the 100 billionth person was born. And that person, it turns out, was me!

I can hardly believe it – me! I'd always hoped that someday, somehow, I'd discover I was special but until now there's been very little evidence of that. For 60 years I've been Mr Nobody. Now I'm going to be Mr One Hundred Billion.

All I have to do is reply to the email with a few details such as my home address, telephone number (home and mobile), bank account (branch and number), NHS number, social insurance number, passport number and copies of my driver's licence and birth certificate and they'll send me an official diploma authenticating my claim. Once they've received the admin fee of £1,000 in Bitcoin, of course.

The email is signed by a Professor JRR Madoff, and he says I should keep the news to myself until they're ready to announce their big statistical breakthrough to the world at a press conference, and I completely understand the need for secrecy at this stage. I myself am a journalist – well, a sub-editor, not a reporter – but it's the same thing. Almost.

By which I mean we're all on the same team. After all, it's me and all the other faceless subs who prevent those squawking infants in the newsroom embarrassing themselves and the newspaper on a daily basis; we're the ones who pick up on the factual errors they make, who write in the dates and ages they're too lazy to write in themselves, who translate their lame, incomprehensible intros into actual English.

We make them look good while we go unrecognised, toiling

away unrewarded in the background, working shit shifts and odd hours while they pick up their Journo of the Year awards and visit exciting places and meet beautiful people and … and … but I digress.

What I'm trying to say is that I know how the newspaper world works, and I know the sort of media feeding frenzy a story like this will spark. I'm going to be famous, so I'll probably have to learn how to use Twitter, and sign up to TicketyBoo or whatever it's called, and WassupDude and maybe even LonelyFans so I can take selfies of my bare bum and withered thighs while bending over, arching my spine and pouting back at myself in the bedroom mirror.

Not sure who'll actually pay to see that – especially if my bad back twinges at the wrong moment and my pout turns into a wince – but apparently it's the sort of thing you have to do when you become an influencer, which I almost certainly will. In fact, don't be surprised if by this time next year millions of British teenagers are suddenly dying their hair grey like mine and buying Skechers extra-wide-fit shoes to handle their prosthetic insoles. Ha!

Anyway, the bottom line is the public is going to want to know absolutely everything about me, so I've decided to write it all down here before the madness begins; to share some of the significant milestones along the life path that Mr One Hundred Billion has trodden. Trod. Trodded. Treaded. Whatever. You get the picture.

Future generations will need to know the nitty gritty. So here goes:

The story begins in Paisley, Scotland on XXXX X, 1962 (and if you're wondering why I've blacked out the exact date, it's because you don't want to be giving away too much info online. So many scams! You can't be too careful these days!).

It was a home birth, and I'm told that my mother endured a gruelling labour, cursing me for a solid 20 hours before I eventually dragged my reluctant bare arse into the world, and that my father then had to hold me upside-down by the heels and slap me around a bit because I wasn't breathing. Also, I was apparently born with my face on the side of my head – true story; something to do with my mother having fallen down a flight of stairs a couple of weeks earlier – and that barely six hours after the birth my skew face started turning a sickly shade of blue due to a lack of oxygen as my lungs filled up with gunk, and my father had to do the piñata thing again, thumping my back and chest until the pipes were cleared.

Either that or he was thinking that any boy-child would have to be accustomed to senseless violence if he were to have a chance of survival in Paisley, so he thought he'd give me a head start.

Survive I did, skew face and all, but the Grim Reaper was apparently still hanging around hopefully, waiting in the shadows for his chance, and he nearly got it when I was 18 months old. My sister, who would have been about three-and-a-half years old at the time, was carrying Baby Gav around when she dropped me on my head on the stony kitchen floor. Butterfingers!

She tried to pick me up but slipped on a patch of water, this time catapulting me into the side of the stove, hitting the *other* side of my head, the one where my face used to be. (My face, by the way, had at some point in the previous year naturally gravitated around to the front, where God had intended it to be. I know this because I was, of course, able to walk by that age – and if my eyes had still been pointing permanently to the east I wouldn't have been able to see where I was going, would I? I might even have fallen down the same flight of stairs my mother did before I was born, and there's no record of that ever happening!).

Anyway, the second fall fractured my skull just below the right ear and I apparently spent a miserable couple of weeks sitting upright in a hospital bed, my hands tied to opposite ends of a metal cot so that I didn't inadvertently lie down on the broken bits of bone.

I must have decided at that point that Paisley wasn't for me, because the records show that a few months later, soon after my second birthday, I decided to emigrate to South Africa. I was gracious enough to take my parents with me, along with my elder brother and even my clumsy sister – on the understanding, of course, that there would be no further subtle attempts on my life.

My father left in May 1964 and got settled in his new job in Johannesburg and found a home to rent in the nearby town of Benoni, and only then, six weeks later, did he send for the rest of us. My mother, who had never been outside Scotland before, said her goodbyes to family and friends and set off with a brave smile, a couple of suitcases and three small children – aged five, four and two – on what was apparently an absolutely hellish 48-hour odyssey down the African continent.

There were no direct passenger flights in those days so she had to change planes several times along the way before, late in the afternoon of the second day, her ancient DC-6 finally spluttered into the pale blue skies over Jan Smuts international airport, midway between Joburg and the town we would call home for the next couple of decades.

It was late June, wintertime on the Highveld, and that first bird's-eye view she had of Benoni from the small window of the plane was one that stayed with her forever after, because it was so very different from the damp, cramped Scotland she was used to. She saw below her a neat town centre ringed by clean and meticulously planned suburbs, dotted with swimming pools and sports field and schools, interspersed with dams and patches of open land and … and what where those strange mini-mountains scattered all around the town? Mine dumps?

All of it was surrounded by tinder-dry, straw-yellow grassland stretching as far as the eye could see: the veld. You'll be hearing a lot about the veld in these pages, because I would grow to love it with a passion – though that didn't stop me and my fellow juvenile delinquents burning it to the ground, year after year, just to see how many times in a day we could get the fire department out to the scene.

But let's not get ahead of ourselves; we'll get to The Troubled Years soon enough. Let's try to stick to some sort of timeline. Tradition dictates that we start with The Early Years ...

CHAPTER ONE

The first memory I have, of anything at all, concerns food – which makes sense because, as will became apparent in these pages, I've always been a glutton, a human gannet, a walking foodtrash compactor who can eat his own body weight in a day without any of that nutrition ever seeming to filter down to his skinny legs. This memory is just a brief flash: I'm maybe three years old, and I'm sitting out in the sun-soaked back garden of the first house we lived in in Benoni. I have an apricot jam sandwich in my hand and lordy it is good, it is so-ho-ho gooood! If I could fit a soundtrack to this memory it would be that 1980s Yello tune with the thumping bass and the guy with the deep voice saying just two words over and over again: "Oh yeah" – doof, doof, doof, doof – "Oh yeah!" – doof, doof, doof, doof – "OH YEAH!"

To this day I enjoy an apricot jam sandwich, but like everything else in life, it's never as good as the first time.

The second memory I have also concerns food: the delivery man from the local shop has arrived on his bicycle and is holding out a roll of butterscotch sweeties – for me! What did the man look like? Can't say. I was focused on the butterscotch sweeties.

The third memory? Also food, but this one has a touch of the traumatic: I'm standing at the window of my mother's bedroom, peeking through the venetian blinds to the street outside. The ice-cream man is waiting patiently out there for me to return, because I'd flagged him down a moment earlier when I saw him cycling along the road with the big icebox mounted above his front tyre.

In this memory I'm crying hard, because my mother has said no, it's almost dinner time and I'm definitely not having a stinking Eskimo Pie ice-cream!

"Wah!"

"No."

"Wah-hah-hah-haaaaah!" Great jagged sobs they were, tearing my little body asunder.

"NO!"

Deep, deep breath. "WAAAAAAAAH!"

"Bugger! I'll give you something to cry about –"

Pitter-patter of tiny steps as I run for my life. Not for the last time. Not by a long shot.

Memory number four is neither happy nor sad but is equally brief: I'm standing atop the low wall at the front of the house watching as my sister Christine, a few steps in front of me, bends down and points her bum at the Afrikaans kids who live across the road. She is chanting: "Afrikaner, vrot banana! Afrikaner, vrot banana!"

Vrot, for the benefit of non-South Africans, is the Afrikaans word for rotten. Rotten banana. So there's that food theme again.

My wife Asha is a psychologist, and a very good one. She tells me that there's something very, very significant about the fact that every single one of my early memories concerns food, but she refuses to elaborate. There are times, however, when I glance up unexpectedly to catch her giving me a lingering, sympathetic look.

One thing I should mention about that first house we lived in is that it was haunted; genuinely infested by some kind of angry, malignant spirit. Personally, I can't claim to have seen anything weird there or even vaguely supernatural – maybe the ghost should have tried taunting me with a doughnut if it wanted to get my attention, or maybe I was simply too young to think it odd that my toy cars used to occasionally go revving across the floor by themselves – but my father used to tell some scary stories about our home in Ewing St, Rynfield, Benoni, and he was a quiet man, not given to sensationalism nor fabrication (I'm withholding the street number, out of consideration for whoever lives there now). So what follows next is not so much a personal memory, but a memory of one of the stories my father used to tell, when pressed on the subject.

We had visitors over for the evening. It was mid-winter, and at some point the cheery fire in the hearth began burning low so my father stood and gathered up the scuttle and went out to the back yard to fetch some coal. This was 1964, or maybe 65, and most houses in those days still had a separate lavatory just outside the back door.

My father, over at the coal shed, looked up in time to see a shadowy figure step out of the house and into the lavatory, pulling the door closed behind him. One of the visitors, he assumed. But when he walked back into the house a moment later, well, all the visitors were still sitting in the chairs where he'd left them.

A burglar – had to be! Everyone went rushing out to the lavatory. They flung open the door but there was no one there. Our family dog, a fearless Rhodesian ridgeback, started barking like crazy at something it could see but the humans could not, edging away wild-eyed, snapping at my father when he tried to push it forward into that small lavatory. I'm told those visitors never visited again.

Of course, there has to be some rational explanation. That's what I normally say when presented with tales such as this; either that, or the story has grown as the years go by, with the teller exaggerating a bit here and a bit there.

Well, maybe … but there are a couple of things to take into account. This happened at the height of the apartheid era, and even cash-strapped immigrant families such as ours were expected to have a black maid and a gardener – but this was apparently well known as The Haunted House, long before the unsuspecting Weir family arrived from Scotland and decided to rent the place, and it was months before my folks could convince one of the women from the nearby black township to set foot inside, despite the scarcity of jobs.

More compelling for me is the fact that, long after we'd moved to another house, maybe a decade later, we met another family who coincidentally had also lived there for a brief time (a very brief time!) – and they too had a bunch of scary stories about the odd goings-on.

Me, I'm not sure I even believe in ghosts, but I do wonder sometimes what I would find if I were to revisit Ewing St today. The house is still there; I know, because I've looked it up on Google Streetview. I've compared it with some old family pics I have, and it looks a lot like it used to 60 years ago. The low wall in the front has been replaced by a steel-rail fence, and the roof has tiles now instead of tin, but the window where I stood howling in vain for an Eskimo Pie appears to be exactly the same.

Is the ghost still there, I wonder? How long do ghosts 'live'? Do they fade away after a certain time? Go senile? Get transferred to a new town; get promoted to a castle rampart somewhere if they can scare the living bejaysus out of enough people?

Some things are best left unknown, I think. So let's get back to the trials and tribulations of the young Mr One Hundred Billion, already at this tender age saddled with a variety of unkind nicknames: Hungry Haggis, Locust Boy, Dances With Sandwich. (OK, I made that last one up, right now, and I copied it from the Kevin Costner film about the Native Americans and the wolves. As far as I know, there were no Native Americans in Benoni in the 1960s to bestow tribal names on me or anyone else, and it would be a couple of decades still before the movie came along. But the name would have fitted like a glove).

CHAPTER TWO

A keen student of world history will know that South Africa in the Sixties was a nation divided; a society in which everything was black or white; a land of plenty for some but deprivation for most. I don't pretend to be any kind of political analyst, and you're not going to find on these pages even the suggestion of a deep dive into the roots of apartheid nor its ultimate demise. I'm no academic (as will became glaringly, comically apparent later in this tale). But the complex situation did throw up some unintentionally funny moments, and I can share one of those with you here.

We'd been living in Benoni for perhaps a year when Granny Weir, my father's mother, decided to pay us a visit. I have some old cine-film footage that shows her being greeted at Jan Smuts airport after a long flight from Scotland. The shadowy, flickering images cut to our new home in Ewing St, where Granny Weir – a bit of a battleaxe, let's be honest – is stepping out of the family car to be welcomed by a small group of friends and neighbours, and even the black maid we'd finally been able to persuade to work in the haunted house.

This was long before the invention of video, and there's no soundtrack, of course, so the whole thing feels a bit like a Charlie Chaplin silent movie – especially when the stout, bespectacled old lady gives all the kids a manly hug, then shakes hands with all the friends and neighbours, and then the maid too.

Shock and horror from the friends and neighbours! You don't shake hands with the black maid! Not in Benoni! Not in 1965! But Granny Weir, oblivious to the scandal she had provoked, was just getting warmed up.

One of those friends and neighbours was a Mrs van S, from the house next door. She and her husband were proud, elderly Afrikaners; good neighbours and solid citizens, and when she asked my mother and Granny Weir to pop around for afternoon tea in the days that followed, they were happy to accept the invitation. Granny Weir baked a batch of her finest scones to present to the host in a Tupperware bowl, and the host reciprocated with a tray full of homemade koeksusters.

Briton and Boer were getting along swimmingly until old Mr van S arrived home from work. His wife had told him that the loopy Scot who'd shaken the hand of the maid was coming for tea, and he was eager to join the conversation and put the case for why she shouldn't have done that.

He began with a brief history of his people, telling how his Voortrekker ancestors had broken free of British tyranny in the Cape of Good Hope and headed north, up into the wild, uncharted country. He himself could trace his lineage to the great Andries Pretorius, hero of the Battle of Blood River and the man who gave his name to the city of Pretoria, he said.

As the Voortrekkers pushed up into the continent they ran into a bunch of black tribes already living there – the "Kaffirs", as Mr van S put it; a highly derogatory term, of course, and the equivalent of the N word so hated in the United States, but a word that was pretty much commonplace at the time.

Anyway, to cut a long story short – which Mr van S apparently did not do – Granny Weir's attention wandered at some point in the presentation and she appears to have lost the thread. Blame it on the tasty koeksusters, or perhaps the first hint of senility; whatever the case, she became aware at some point that the room had fallen silent, and that Mr van S was looking at her expectantly, obviously awaiting some sort of response.

She cleared her throat. "Och aye … um! So … so yer a direct descendent of tha Kaffirs?" she asked hopefully.

There was quite a bit of shouting at that point. It was all in Afrikaans, but Granny Weir and my mother were able to sense a certain hostility in the air and left soon afterwards. Later, my mother was able to recall three words which had cropped up repeatedly, and with great vehemence.

One was "bliksem", which in this context can be translated loosely as "bastard". The second was "rooinek", a throwback to the Anglo-Boer War, which had ended more than 60 years earlier but which remained a source of lingering resentment for many Afrikaners; "rooinek" translating as "red neck" – a dig at the pale-skinned British soldiers who always turned a bright shade of red under the harsh African sun.

The third word was "soutie" – short for soutpiel, or salt penis, another common term for us British immigrants. A soutpiel has one foot in the UK and one foot in South Africa. With his penis dangling in the salty waters of the ocean between.

Granny Weir was supposed to visit for a month but ended up staying for six. I can't say whether that was because she was loving life in Benoni, or because the people back home in Paisley were enjoying a bit of quiet time in her absence and had started collecting money in the churches and at county fairs to pay us to keep her there for as long as we possibly could. Either way, she made her mark, and the stories she left behind are legion. Her broad Scottish accent plays a role in all of them.

Her stout walking stick was her constant companion, and she used it to help her shuffle down to the local grocery store one day with my brother, Graham, to pick up a few things for dinner. At some point after they'd reached the store he turned left into the toys aisle and she turned right to find the tinned peas, and when she looked again he was nowhere to be seen. She brayed his name a few times, loudly, and was starting to panic when she spotted him over in the corner where the fresh produce was kept.

"Graham! C'mere, son! GRAHAM! Are ye deef!" she called, but there was no response. She hobbled forward again, and as she came up behind him she could see him at one of the stalls gathering up handfuls of something that didn't look at all healthy.

"GRAHAM!"

Still no response. She hoisted her walking stick like a shepherd's crook and hooked him around the neck, and as he spun around to face her she hollered: "Pit doon tha chocolates, son! Kin ye no see they're aw foostered!!!"

But the chocolates weren't chocolates; they were hazelnuts still in their shells, and there was no indication they were foostered, or rotten. More to the point, the boy handling them wasn't Graham! Whoever the lad was, he wrenched free of the walking stick and went running off shouting for his mother, who came storming over a moment later demanding an explanation.

Graham had returned from the toys section by this time but as Granny Weir and the irate mother exchanged mutually incomprehensible insults he sidled away again, pretending he wasn't with her. Which was something we all learnt do many times over in the six months before she finally boarded her flight back to Scotland.

CHAPTER THREE

I met a surprisingly large number of natural-born psychos growing up in Benoni. I can't say if that would be true of any town; if the ratio of bad kids to good kids is the same the world over, or if there was something in the Highveld water that brought out the worst in so many young boys. Whatever the case, there was an elemental savagery to those early days that had a real *Lord of the Flies* feel to it.

Take Arthur R. He was maybe three years older than me, and he lived a couple of doors up the road from our new house, at 88 Honiball Street. I like to think that Arthur, if he survived into adulthood, was later shanked to death in a third-world prison somewhere, and that the rest of the inmates held a little party afterwards with illicit alcohol and marijuana muffins to celebrate his passing. He really was a mean bastard.

He bullied and humiliated all the neighbourhood boys who were smaller than him and he broke our toys just to see us cry, but the incident that stands out most in my memory involves another of our family dogs, Champ. She was a German Shepherd bitch with a gentle nature and none of the aggression you might expect from her breed, and when Arthur came calling one day and discovered that Champ was heavily pregnant – well, that seemed another excellent opportunity to spread a little sadness in the world.

He grabbed a nearby broom and used the handle to prod hard at Champ's distended belly, searching out the unborn puppies inside with ever-more violent thrusts. Champ tried to take cover under a bed, but Arthur's long broom handle could reach her there without any problem, and she was saved only by the timely intervention of the maid.

Arthur was banned from our house after that but, this being *Lord of the Flies* country, another bully quickly rose up to take his place, and within a couple of weeks I was being beaten up on a daily basis by the boy next door, Archie G. He was about the same size as me, but older – he was five, I was four.

My mother took exception to this: she was Glasgow born and raised, after all, and if anyone was going to beat up her kid on a daily basis it would be her, not some snot-nose amateur from next door.

I have very clear memories of the cold and frosty Highveld morning when Archie G came knocking as usual, asking for Gavin to come out to play. My mother had other plans: she surprised us both by grabbing the pair of us by the wrists and dragging us over to the double garage around the side of the house. She opened the side door and pushed Archie G inside, then she knelt down and shoved her face into mine and said through gritted teeth: "You get in there and you hit him so hard on the nose with *this* " – she scrunched my right hand into a fist – "that he comes out crying. Got it? If you don't, I'm coming in after you – and you're going to be the one crying! GOT IT?"

I got it. I stammered out a yes. She opened the door and shoved me inside, where a terrified and bewildered Archie G was already close to tears. I stepped forward hesitantly and threw my still-scrunched up right hand in the general direction of his face with all my might – and lo, his nose exploded in a shower of red, and he fell back on his bum and started wailing at the top of his voice.

The door flew open and my mother came rushing back in. She took Archie by the hand and shepherded him over to the garden tap, guiding his nose to the flowing water and holding it there until the water ran clear.

I stood watching, genuinely dumbfounded, trying to understand what had just happened, holding my fist up to my eyes every now and again and blinking at it and thinking: "Wow. wow. Wow!!!"

Archie G never bothered me again.

I'm re-reading what I've written so far and thinking that things have taken an unexpectedly dark turn: near-death experiences, ghosts, animal torture, psycho kids and Glesgie mothers – and we haven't even reached my sixth birthday yet! So let me try to lighten the mood with a few happier memories.

White Benoni in those days was something of a melting pot; a mix of Afrikaners and English-speaking South Africans, along with huge numbers of European immigrants drawn by the African sun and the lucrative jobs associated with the thriving gold-mining industry in and around Johannesburg. There were Scots, English, German, Greek, Lebanese, Portuguese, Italian, Dutch – you name it, we had it, and Honiball St was a microcosm of all that.

The houses were new or still in the process of being built, and the gardens were big. Archie G's father had erected a couple of wooden goalposts in the back yard for his two boys, and I have some cherished memories of me and a bunch of other young Pelé wannabes kicking a cheap plastic ball around that makeshift pitch, dribbling and diving and shouting for hours on end.

We'd carry on late into the evenings, when the air was cool and the mosquitoes were out and it was so dark we could only see each other by the light spilling from the kitchen window where Archie's mother was preparing another fragrant Greek dinner. We'd stop only when one of the other mothers came out and started yelling up the street for her sons to come in to eat. Magical times.

If there was one small criticism we had of the goalposts Archie's father had constructed it was that he had failed to secure the heavy wooden crossbar to the supporting poles, and at least once a week it would come crashing down on the head of whoever was playing goalie. Which was a great time to dart forward and slip the ball into one corner, I found, until that particular play was outlawed.

Other memory flashes from that time are less detailed but no less treasured. In one I'm on my bicycle, riding solo for the first time as one of the other kids – Archie's big brother Angelo, I think – holds the saddle steady from behind and then lets me ride free along the sandy road. In another, I'm standing barefoot on that same road, watching a cloud scudding by overhead and marvelling at how fast the shadow on the ground is going (I'm wearing shorts; that much I know. No shoes or shirt. Was I wearing briefs underneath? Just how feral was I? The world may never know).

I can remember me and half a dozen other kids galloping around in the garden of the Afrikaner family two houses up, the Van Z's, all of us pretending to be horses in the Rothman's July Handicap (I was Sea Cottage), and there's one other incident that springs to mind, also involving running.

All of us English-speaking kids went to the same school, Rynfield Primary, and every September they used to stage the annual school sports day. I remember waking up at the crack of dawn on one of those early summer mornings and getting kitted out in my white shorts and vest and Bata plimsolls, and then racing up and down the dirt road, over and over again, with all the other boys; warming up, as it were, for the main event later in the day.

Only one boy didn't turn out that morning: Alistair N, the new kid on the block, who lived three houses up, on the other side of the road. He was also the only one of us who actually won his race that afternoon.

Alistair N and his family were also Scottish. They moved into Honiball St maybe six months or a year after we did, and they took a while to adjust to life in Africa. The thunderstorms were wilder and the hailstones a hell of a lot heavier than the ones back home. The garden ants were redder and more aggressive. The spiders were bigger and uglier and way more venomous. But it was the snakes that struck true terror into the heart of Mr N.

He'd heard that the virgin veld that still surrounded the houses in those days was infested by tens of billions of spitting cobras – which, of course, was a long way from the truth. Yes, there were snakes out in the veld, but they generally got out the way of any approaching human long before we crossed paths.

Some cruel practical joker, however, had told the new Soutie that there was only one way to stop the deadly rinkhals slithering into your house while you slept at night and spitting lethal venom into your eyes just as you were waking up: you had to dig a trench at least a foot deep and a foot wide all the way around your house and fill it with table salt.

And that is exactly what Mr N had started doing one Saturday morning when Mr van Z, who lived opposite, looked out his window and realised what was going on. He ambled over and introduced himself, and convinced Mr N to step away from the spade and to cancel the scheduled delivery of the hundreds of bags of salt he'd ordered from the local supermarket.

Mr van Z saved the Soutie days of hard labour and public humiliation, and not a little cash, but he also made a friend for life; one more friend in that close-knit little community.

Honiball St has a unique claim to fame: it is the scene of the first recorded sighting anywhere, at any time, of my Glesgie mother in a tender mood; a truly rare occurrence and one which definitely warrants a mention here. The incident in question occurred on what I've worked out must have been her 32nd birthday.

Apparently neither her husband nor any of her children, then aged 8, 7 and 5 (me), had marked the day on a calendar, so when she woke up in the morning there was no gift at her bedside, no card on the lounge table, no breakfast in bed.

There were no actual arguments nor bitter recriminations that morning, because my parents had a policy of never fighting in front of the kids, but I do remember a decidedly cold front sweeping in and settling directly over the Weir home. It lasted for hours and hours, and at some point I slipped out into the front garden for a bit of sunshine.

It must have been rubbish-collection day, because I could see dustbins lined up at the bottom of the driveways all the way along the street, ready for emptying into the lorry that would cruise by at some point. I wandered over to Archie G's bins for want of anything better to do, and because I could see something sticking out the top of one of them: a bouquet of faded plastic, red roses, I discovered.

I picked up the bouquet, brushing aside a potato peel. The fake blooms were mostly cracked or broken, but there was one that still looked to be in reasonable shape, so I snapped it off and dusted it down, and hurried back inside.

"Happy birthday mum!" I announced as I threw open the front door, pulling the flower from behind my back with a flourish.

She stared for a second, then she bent down and swept me up in a loving embrace and hugged me tight. That was something she didn't often do, and if I didn't know better I would have said her eyes may even have been just a little bit moist. And just for the briefest of moments, mind you. But, yeah, it was a happy moment.

CHAPTER FOUR

I've read books and seen movies down the years featuring brothers with an unbreakable bond; the older protecting the younger from a drunken Pa or a rabid dog, the younger providing a listening ear and a word of comfort when his brother has no one else to turn to; the two of them sharing the multiple little joys and miseries and wondrous adventures of childhood. Beautiful. I've always envied those boys. But there was none of that sentimental crap with me and Graham.

He was three years older than me, and although he wasn't the sort of big brother who passed the time beating seven shades of shite out of his shibling – sorry, sibling – he did have his own more devious ways of making my life a misery when he wasn't ignoring me.

When we were very small we used to have to bath together. An argument broke out on one such occasion and he shoved me backwards, under the stream of hot water gushing from the tap, leaving me with a line of freckles down my spine that is still faintly visible to this day.

When we were older, and if I decided to run myself a bath and step out for a moment to fetch a towel or whatever, he would nip into the bathroom and lock the door and enjoy that bath for himself. I'd make myself a cup of tea, and he would stroll by and dip his dirty, nicotine-stained fingers into it. If I was walking home from school alone, and he was far behind, he'd call to me to wait for him – and when he caught up, suddenly go running ahead; being three years older, he could easily outpace me. If he deigned to play a game of chess with me, and saw he was losing, he'd tip the board over.

I spent many long hours as a boy scheming and dreaming of how one day when I was a man, and he was a man, and a three-year gap didn't matter anymore, I would pick him up by his scrawny neck and shake him around like the dog he was and teach him a thing or two, or three or four. But the needling stopped abruptly after one climactic showdown between us when I was aged 13, and he was 16. I came close to beating HIM up that day, and may well have done if he hadn't managed to pick up a dining-room chair at a critical juncture in the fight and smash it over my head a few times. That was game-over for me.

He won that last-ever physical fight between us, but he never tried again, and it might even have felt like something of a victory for me if my parents hadn't decreed that all my pocket money for the next couple of months would be confiscated to pay for half of the broken chair; a gross miscarriage of justice that rankles to this day.

One of the earliest memories I have of Graham pops up when I was five years old. He is standing at the back door of the Honiball St house one sunny morning, flinging my favourite Dinky car as far into the overgrown garden as he can. I have no idea what we were fighting about, but I remember very clearly grabbing HIS favourite Dinky car at that point and rushing up to the back door and throwing it almost as far. At which point things degenerated into one of those Cold War scenarios of Mutually Assured Destruction, with the two of us running back and forward from our shared bedroom with handfuls of each other's toys and shirts and socks and even the odd pair of underpants and hurling them out into the long grass which my father rarely got around to cutting.

Many of the toys were never seen again or were found only a month later, when any metal bits were already beginning to rust. My little police car with the black-and-white checkerboard pattern down the side never rolled smoothly again.

Most of the low-level hostilities between the two of us went unnoticed by my parents, but that bonfire-of-the-toys incident may have been big enough to draw their attention; either that or money was getting tight in the Weir household, because Christmas that year was a bleak affair. Graham was up at the crack of dawn and he shook me awake, and Christine too, and the three of us hustled down the passage and into the lounge, elbowing each other aside and jockeying for position in anticipation of the mountain of presents that surely awaited us.

What we found was more of a molehill. Six small gifts lay beneath the sparsely decorated Christmas tree; two each. I honestly can't recall what Christine got, but I do remember me and Graham being bitterly, bitterly disappointed with our haul: each of us was given a Dinky car and a small Bible.

A frickin Bible? Like the ones they were always handing out free at Sunday School? For Christmas??? Suffice to say that if Jesus wanted me for a sunbeam on that particular morning, he was looking in the wrong place entirely.

Maybe the family budget really was under pressure, and we kids were aware of that on some level, because it was around that same time that I devised a get-rich-quick scheme. Did it work, you ask – did the Weirs get rich quick? Or even slow? Of course not, but it wasn't for want of me trying.

Someone had told me that a single diamond was so valuable you could use it to buy a thousand bowls of rice pudding – my favourite. Someone else had told me that a diamond was basically the same thing as the coal we used in the family fireplace, the only difference being it had been buried deep underground for a long time.

So one morning I rummaged through the coal scuttle we kept in the lounge next to the grate and I picked out the biggest lump I could find, then I fetched a spade from the garage and a bunch of bananas from the kitchen to keep me going until lunchtime, and I trekked out into the back yard with a steely glint in my eye.

I mentioned earlier that my father never cared much for lawn maintenance? Well, I may have underplayed that just a bit: our back yard was a vast, undulating African grassland, with the kakkiebos and the weeds taller than my head in places. I knew from harsh experience with my lost toys that if I chose some random place to bury the lump of coal I may never find it again, so I stayed close to civilisation, heading around to the back of the double garage and choosing a spot up against the wall that would be easy to remember. I ate all the bananas – I'd need my strength, I reasoned – then I started digging.

I'd planned to go down to maybe six feet, but I discovered there's a good reason that the victims of serial killers are usually found in shallow graves: digging a hole is a hell of a lot harder than it looks in the movies, especially when you're six years old and the spade is taller than you are. I stopped when I reached knee depth and carefully placed the lump of coal at the bottom, filled in all the soil and patted it down neatly. I scattered some dead leaves around to hide my treasure from prying eyes – though I was almost certainly the only human who'd set foot in that spot since the Weirs moved in – then I headed indoors again, feeling mightily pleased with myself.

I could hear my mother shouting from the lounge – something about someone having spilled black dust all over the carpet after knocking over the coal scuttle – but it sounded like Graham was getting the blame, so I hurried on by and left them to sort it out themselves, and I spent the rest of the morning dreaming about rice puddings. Lots and lots of them.

I had no clue how long it would take for the coal to turn into a diamond; I thought a few days might do it, but I waited a full week just to be sure before I dug the lump up and studied it closely. It looked exactly the same as when I had buried it, so I put it back and filled in the hole and patted down the soil again. I checked again a week later, and a week after that, but each time without success, and with dwindling enthusiasm.

I don't recall ever actually declaring the scheme a failure, but what I can say for sure is that there is nothing in the town records about a small boy with a big dream hitting the jackpot in the late Sixties; no reports in the *Benoni City Times* about a kid showing up at the local office of De Beers with a Cullinan-size sparkler in his pocket. I can only conclude that at some point I must have given up on the idea altogether and called a halt to the weekly exhumations.

But who knows what I'd find if I were to revisit 88 Honiball St today? I know from Streetview that the house is still there, and the double garage is too, and I can still pinpoint the exact spot where the lump of coal is buried.

It's been there for 54 years now, by my reckoning. I wonder if that's enough?

Times may have been hard for the Weir family but there was money enough to buy a piano, and time aplenty for my father to play it on those long winter evenings, in a land that had not yet been introduced to the all-consuming distractions of television (or much, much later, the internet). I have a copy of an old audio tape which features him tinkling the ivories while my mother, Graham, Christine and I take turns singing solo – all of us still boasting the broadest of broad Paisley accents. Me, I sang *Donald, whar's yer troosers!* and I didn't have to fake that accent at all; that was just how I spoke in those days. Man, I wish I still sounded like that – so much better than the mish-mash Scottish/South African accent I ended up with. Strangers sometimes ask me if I'm Australian. Or Dutch. Or just a bit, you know, slow.

I have fond memories of the New Year's Eve parties that started at midnight and carried on until breakfast, Hogmanay style, with my father accompanying the happily drunken crowd in many a ragged chorus of "*Ah belong ta Glasgow*" and other old favourites. Us kids were allowed to join in the fun, almost drunk too, but on too much Coca-Cola and crisps and sausage rolls and little cocktail sticks with bits of cheese and coloured pickled onions and vienna sausage – and the sheer excitement at being allowed to stay up all through the night. We'd all be hoarse by the time the sun rose, when the last guests would totter off home.

I had a good-enough singing voice, and Christine did too, but Graham was in another league: to borrow a line from that old Abba song, Mama said he could sing long before he could talk, and he was tipped from an early age for a career on the stage. My mother sought out a singing coach for him when he was seven or eight and he started winning all the local eisteddfods and even a national one. He joined the Benoni Boys Choir and soon after was given his first leading role, in a local production of the musical *Oliver*.

All was going well and there was talk of me joining the choir too as soon as I was old enough, but all of that came to an abrupt halt when the group was torn apart by allegations that the choirmaster, a suave guy by the name of Brian O who lived in a caravan with a boy called Claude – not his son – had molested a couple of the kids.

This being the late Sixties, polite society preferred not to talk about such things and the allegations might well have been swept under the carpet had my parents and a couple of other concerned individuals not confronted Brian O.

He was outraged. He demanded an apology. He threatened to quit the choir. He sent a lawyer's letter threatening to sue the Weirs personally for a crippling sum. But when it became apparent that no one was backing down he packed his bags and quietly left town, driving off into the night with his caravan and Claude, presumably to some new small town where the parents were more trusting and the boys less likely to report his wandering hands.

A dark shadow had lifted but the Benoni Boys Choir was never the same, and it broke apart maybe six months or a year later – and it was at that point that my parents decided to form their own group. They called it Protea Choral Society, and it would come to play a central role in the lives of the Weir family for the next couple of decades. We'll get to all that a bit later in the story, but there are a couple of other incidents I should probably mention first, before we drift too far from the timeline…

CHAPTER FIVE

L et's step back briefly to when I was four years old, and the day on which I had my first recorded brush with authority. The scene was Mrs Adams's nursery school and the year would have been 1966 – the same year, I believe, when Clint Eastwood delivered one of his most memorable lines ever, in one of his early cowboy movies: "There's two kinds of people in this world," he said. "Those who love Marmite, and those who hate it."

Actually, I'm re-reading that quote now and wondering if I've got it wrong: he may have been talking about something else entirely, because Marmite was only invented in 1902, according to Google, and the spaghetti westerns were set in the 1870s or so. Whatever, the line fits with this narrative, albeit with a minor tweak: there were two kinds of kids at Mrs Adams's nursery school; those who loved the Marmite sandwiches she handed out at lunchtime, and those who hated them.

Me, I was in the hate camp, and instead of eating them I buried them in the sandpit, day after day, week after week, month after month. That was only a short-term solution of course, because eventually there were almost as many mouldy bread crumbs in the pit as there were grains of sand, and when Mrs Adams realised what was happening, and who the culprit was, she locked me in her bathroom for the day as punishment.

Bad idea. I have a vague memory of being outraged by the injustice and retaliating by stomping a tube of toothpaste all over the floor and throwing wads of soggy toilet paper at the walls and ceiling and mirrors, and then systematically shredding a bathroom towel with my razor-sharp little teeth.

There was a furious showdown between Mrs Adams and my mother when she arrived to pick me up at the end of the day and the bathroom door swung open to reveal the devastation within, but I escaped between their legs and ran out to the car while they were shouting at each other, so I don't know what was said exactly. All I can say for sure is that I was no longer welcome in the Adams home from that day on. I was, in effect, expelled. From nursery school.

Who gets expelled from frickin nursery school? Doesn't bode well for the years ahead, does it?

I was determined to do better when I started at "big school", Rynfield Primary, a year or so later. My teacher was a dear old lady called Mrs Shaw, and I made a good first impression, I'm told, by showing off my cartwheeling skills a minute or so after meeting her, completing two full circuits of the classroom, head-over-heels, round and round in a near-perfect display of athleticism and grace, before my wrists started to tire and I veered off course and crashed into a wall.

Mrs Shaw made a fuss of me anyway and made me feel important by sitting me down in a desk at the front of the classroom, under her watchful eye. Which worked out well for me, because I was close enough to call out the answers to all the questions and still be understood, despite the broad Scottish accent that none of the other kids could quite grasp.

I went above and beyond for Mrs Shaw; positive adult attention was hard to find, after all, and she always made a show of being really impressed when I sidled up at the end of class and let her know, in case she was wondering, that 20 plus 20 equalled 40, and 30 plus 30 was 60. That sort of thing.

But I blew it, big time, barely a third of the way through Grade One when she asked all the children to go home one day and write an account of what we'd done during the Easter holidays.

I wracked my brains – what could I write about? Should I tell her about my home-made drum kit? I'd collected half a dozen used Frisco coffee tins, the ones with the resealable plastic lids, and I'd filled them with water to different levels to produce different tones; some nearly full for a dull bass thud, others nearly empty for a lighter "tink" sound. My drumsticks were two plastic chopsticks I'd borrowed from the local Chinese restaurant that we'd eaten at a couple of weeks earlier.

With hindsight, even Phil Collins would have struggled to wow the masses with that rudimentary kit, but at the time I was pleased as punch. Pretty innovative, I thought – but would it be enough to impress Mrs Shaw? What if she asked me to bring the drums in one day and play for the whole class? Graham loved nothing more than performing in front of a crowd, but for me that had always been a daunting prospect.

Also, the only time I had plucked up the nerve to showcase my drumming talents – just within the family, mind you – it hadn't gone so well. I'd drawn up my own publicity poster and sticky-taped it to our front door one day for my mother to see when she got home from work. It said:

"The GRATE GAVIANO
will parform in the lounge
AFTER SUPPER!"

But it just so happened that on that particular night my mother had invited her boss home for some reason or other, and she went all red in the face when she saw the poster and pulled it down before the boss could see it, and she hissed at me to get my blasted coffee cans out the lounge RIGHT NOW! If neither my mother nor her boss were interested in the Grate Gaviano, then Mrs Shaw wouldn't be either, I reasoned. I'd have to write about something else.

The Rand Easter Show maybe? The Weir family, like thousands of others in and around Johannesburg, had spent a day at the Show, a trade and agriculture fair that also had a bunch of rollercoasters and swings and fairground rides for the kids. I'd tasted my first-ever toffee apple that day, and yay verily, it was good, but that was hardly unusual and not worth writing about, surely.

The only other event of note was me getting separated from the family at one point, and then standing on the side of the road crying my eyes out until my father emerged from the crowd looking all irritated before leading me back to where the family was sitting. That didn't show me in a good light, I thought. Kind of irresponsible, and a bit babyish.

But ... but hey! Graham had a good story from the Rand Easter Show, didn't he? Yes! Certainly, the neighbours back home had laughed loudly when he'd told it! He and some other kid had taken a ride on the mini cable cars; open benches that went trundling along a stout wire maybe 30 feet above the main street. They'd seen some interesting stuff, and laughed a lot, he told the neighbours, but the highlight came when he and the other kid started spitting on the people below – who thought it had started raining!

Me, I'd certainly been impressed by that, and I was pretty sure Mrs Shaw was going to be too, so I wrote it down in graphic detail, with just one tweak: I said it was me doing the spitting. I was *that* clever and brave and adventurous.

Mrs Shaw was deeply, genuinely disappointed in me. She told me so the next day in class. I have a very vivid memory of me standing at my desk, staring down at my feet and feeling like the worst, most foul bastard on the face of the earth as she read back the line to the class boasting about how I had "sput" on the people below ("sput", not spat – no auto spellcheck in those days). Of course, I tried at that point to explain that it was my stupid big brother, not me, who had done the dirty deed, but she just shook her head and looked even sadder, and said I was only making things worse by lying.

I'd been her blue-eyed boy, she said. Now ... well, I wasn't anymore. I just wasn't and could never be again.

Damn, I feel like crying even now when I think about it. How often in life do you get to be someone's blue-eyed boy? Never often enough.

"Big school" dealt me another harsh lesson soon afterwards, and if the first had shaken my faith in my big brother, the second shook my faith in humanity as a whole. I was in the habit of taking a toy car to school every day, as were many of the other boys, and during the lunch break we'd go running over to a grove of trees in the far corner of the playground where we'd spend a happy half hour driving our pick-up trucks or Volksies around the network of tree roots that twisted over and under each other before plunging into the hard earth. Fun times. Until the day some little swine nicked my car during morning prayers.

We used to start the school day standing at our desks with heads bent and eyes closed while Mrs Shaw said a quick howdy to the Good Lord. I placed my car on the desk in front of me that day, as I always did, and I bent my head and closed my eyes dutifully ... but when I opened them the car was nowhere to be seen. Vanished. Kapoof. Gone in 60 Seconds, like in the Nic Cage movie.

I blinked, dumfounded. What? It was there – *right there*! Had I knocked it off the desk without realising it? Was it still in my pocket? Had I forgotten to bring it in that morning? I started patting down my pockets and rummaging through my school bag and tunnelling under my desk and under the desks around me. It had to be somewhere!

Mrs Shaw told me to sit down.

I started to explain. Mrs Shaw told me to sit down.

"But – "

Mrs Shaw told me to sit down.

A blue-eyed boy might have been given the latitude to disrupt the lesson further with tales of vanishing cars, but not me. I sat down.

I simply did not understand what had happened. Naïve, trusting, 6-year-old kid that I was, it didn't even occur to me that one of the boys sitting nearby – let's call him Damien, Spawn of Satan! – could have been so brazen as to steal the car while the rest of us were praying. Nobody was that evil, right?

Wrong. But it would be a few years yet before I wised up to the ways of the world and decided to adopt a few of those ways for myself.

Here's one last memory of my time at 88 Honiball St, and I mention it for no reason other than that it provides an accurate milestone along the timeline: I can remember very clearly lying flat on my tummy on the lounge floor one morning staring in shock and awe at the picture on the front page of the *Sunday Express* newspaper (the South African one, obviously, long since defunct). It showed Neil Armstrong bouncing across the surface of the moon, his spacesuit a brilliant white against the grey background, with another, tiny pic of the scene captured nicely in the reflection of his curved facemask; a truly iconic image, and one that we're all very familiar with.

The moon landing happened on July 20, 1969, and the newspaper would presumably have carried the picture the following Sunday – so that would have been July 27, 1969, making me seven years and a few months old.

Some time between then and the end of the school year we moved house again, this time to Morehill, another new suburb which was in the process of being carved out of the veld. A bunch of other families were moving into the area at the same time, and a few had the bad luck or poor judgment to settle near number 23 Barbara Avenue.

Our house. In the middle of the street. Where there would be madness aplenty.

CHAPTER SIX

Being a boy in Benoni in those years – just being a boy, before all the cares and dramas and bullshit of adolescence and adulthood kicked in – was to know happiness. The town had been born 80 or 90 years earlier in the gold-rush fever that drew speculators from around the world to a string of unremarkable Highveld farmsteads, and like frontier towns everywhere it had known its share of violence. By the 1960s and 70s, however, it had matured into a mostly respectable, typical apartheid-era town, with clean streets and manicured parks, shopping centres and public swimming pools but the evidence of those early mining days was still everywhere to be seen. The most prominent example of that was the huge mine dump that towered over the town centre; a local Everest of yellow-white processed sand that had sprouted bullrushes and even full-grown blue-gum trees on top and which, some said, was visible from Space.

They were lying, of course; it wasn't even visible from Springs, another former mining town a few miles to the southeast, but it was a much-loved local landmark nonetheless, and one that every Benoni boy knew was his solemn duty to climb at some point in his young life.

A number of lesser dumps surrounded the town, flatter but wider, and riven with caves and underground tunnels carved out over time by rainwater. Disused mine shafts were commonplace, most of them covered with concrete caps for safety but one or two still lying wide open; death traps for the unwary veld walker. There were dried-up pans and crumbling brick structures and dams filled with fish tough enough to live in water that, even several decades later, must still have had traces of the cyanide runoff used in those early gold-mining operations.

It was a truly wonderful world for a boy to explore. All of us had bicycles of course – me, just a three-speed Raleigh; a few of my friends the coveted ten-speed Peugeot or Carlton, which were lighter and faster – and by the age of ten we'd started cycling out to the mine dumps regularly, three or four of us together, sometimes a bigger group if it was during the school holidays. We'd secure our bikes to a tree or just in an unwieldy clump with our many bicycle locks, and then we'd go adventuring.

The Everest dump had soft sand perfect for sliding down on an old car bonnet, but if we climbed all the way to the top we could look out over the whole town and try to pick out our individual houses in the distance, or see how far we could throw a stone, or simply shout our names into the wind.

The surrounding dumps were nowhere near as high but they offered different delights; the compacted sand was as hard as stone, with literally dozens of caves and tunnels leading into the mysterious darkness within and ending ... well, who knew where? We'd follow those tunnels until they came to a dead end or until we simply didn't dare go any further, but there was one, I remember, that snaked underground for maybe a hundred feet before suddenly angling upwards and emerging on the top.

Sometimes we'd do it the other way round; we'd follow a tunnel that started on the top and work our way down, and one of those, we discovered, led to a huge cavern we'd visited a hundred times before from the outside and which we'd nicknamed The Cooler – because it was always refreshingly cool, no matter how hot the Highveld sun felt blazing down on us from above.

Of course, we'd heard tales of boys being killed by cave-ins, or falling into one of the mine shafts, or being bitten by a rinkhals or even a black widow spider, but we shrugged and laughed and carried on. The school holidays were too short to waste any time worrying about such things.

When we'd had enough of the dumps we'd cycle back to the house of whoever had a swimming pool – including me, by that stage – and sometimes dive in still fully clothed for a laugh, and then hit the kitchen and between us wolf down a loaf or two of bread with peanut butter and syrup, washed down with Oros orange squash. We'd be back in the pool soon after, playing Marco Polo for hours, or until a fight broke out because someone was found to be cheating by opening his eyes underwater.

One of the gang, Ilkka S, owned a vast Scalextric set and his parents were indulgent enough to allow him to take over the whole lounge with it. We'd build what felt like a mile of racing track across the room, allowing the miniature F1 cars to go snaking around the sofas and under the coffee table and over a couple of side tables, and we'd spend hours at a time running a mini-grand prix.

Me, I was hopeless at Scalextric and I usually came last; I just couldn't manage the control grip thingie with any kind of subtlety. No thumb-eye co-ordination. My car either sat on the track like a lump of old shite, dead and unmoving while the other guy's was racing around and clocking up the laps, or it would suddenly burst forward and become airborne at the first bend before smashing into the nearest wall and scattering little wheels and airfoils and things all around. At which point Ilkka used to get a bit upset and tell me that that was the last time I was ever touching his Scalextric set! Till the next time, of course.

Like most kids we'd often sleep over at each other's homes at weekends or during school holidays and, as was the South African way, a bunch of us boys would camp out in the back yard with a tent and sleeping bags, sometimes accompanied by the family dog. We'd build a campfire and burn some sausages and brew up a pot of Milo and listen to *Squad Cars* or *Destined*

Hour on Springbok Radio, talk about football and girls, tell dirty jokes.

One summer holiday a group of six or eight of us set up a permanent camp in Ilkka's back yard, alongside the swimming pool, and we cooked Ilkka's famous Bully Beef Stew for three nights running before we eventually admitted we'd had enough of the devilish concoction: tinned meat mashed up with fried onions, all of it swimming in tomato ketchup, with about a cup of salt. Tastes great when you're a boy. Not so much as an adult, I imagine.

I remember on another such occasion, at Richard V's house, waking up one morning at the crack of a bitterly cold Highveld dawn and poking my head outside the tent, then shuffling out, still hugging my sleeping bag around me, and trying to get the campfire going again by blowing on the coals. The other guys – Steve V, Reggie L, Bruce A, Craig T, Ilkka, a couple of others – also woke up and started shouting encouragement from the warmth of their own sleeping bags, but no one else ventured out into the chill until someone farted loud and long – and then they all came spilling out the tent together and in a hurry, laughing and cursing and tripping over the guy ropes in the rush for clean air.

If there's a soundtrack to these particular memories it has to be the old Terry Jack song *Seasons in the Sun*; whenever I hear it I'm transported back to those back-yard campfires. Magical times, man, and such good, clean, innocent fun.

Stephen King said it best (in *Stand By Me*, I think it was): you'll never find as good a bunch of friends in later life as you had as a boy. You just won't.

Documentary-makers from the US or Britain searching for the spirit of Africa often focus on the annual migration of the wildebeest, capturing spectacular images of millions of the beasts surging with single-minded determination across grassy plains and crocodile-infested rivers in search of new feeding and breeding grounds. Less well-known, perhaps, is an equally magnificent phenomenon that used to play out every December in apartheid-era South Africa: the annual migration of the Vaalies.

What's a Vaalie, the non-South Africans ask? These were white families, rich and poor, English and Afrikaans, mainly from the old Transvaal province, but also from the neighbouring Orange Free State and even Rhodesia who would descend in their thousands, their hundreds of thousands, upon the holiday mecca of Durban and the many small but beautiful towns dotted all the way up and down the adjoining coastline – Ballito, Umhlanga Rocks, Port Shepstone, Shelley Beach, Margate and Ramsgate (far classier than the bleak and rundown seaside dumps in England they were named after).

The beaches were the drawcard, of course, endless stretches of soft, golden sand lapped by the warm waters of the Indian Ocean, many of them boasting natural rock pools and gnarly surf breaks, protected by lifeguards and, crucially, shark nets – which meant the Vaalies could splash around in the clean sea for hours on end without fear of being ripped to shreds by a great white or a Zambezi, which always takes the shine off an otherwise enjoyable trip.

As schools closed for the Christmas holidays Vaalie fathers could be seen in their driveways loading up the family car with suitcases and strapping inflatable lilos to the roof and mothers could be heard shouting orders from the kitchen as they filled flasks with hot coffee and made huge piles of sandwiches for the road. The children would run back and forth between the two excitedly, packing a few favourite toys in the car and maybe an empty bottle to be filled with genuine sea water at the request of the black maid, who valued it for its healing properties.

The Weirs were no different. Almost every year we'd join the hordes heading south on the main road to Durban – not yet a highway, back then – and almost every year the holiday would start with a fight. The plan was always to leave at 4am, because it was an eight-hour drive and us kids wanted to get down to the beach as soon as possible, and because the traffic always got heavier the later you left. Instead, my father would still be snoring away at 5am despite my mother yelling at him to get up, and by the time we hit the road it would be 6am or later, with the sun already rising and everyone in a foul mood.

The frosty atmosphere in the car would prevail for the first couple of hours, broken only by the occasional flurry of blows between me and Graham, or a high-pitched keening from Christine when she was denied an early spell beside the window despite insisting she was feeling carsick and about to puke.

At some point we'd pull into a service station to top up the petrol tank and use the loos, and someone would crack a joke or ask how much further we had to go, and the mood would lighten. We'd always stop to take in the scenery from a viewpoint at Van Reenen's Pass, a narrow and tricky road that cut through the towering Drakensberg mountains and which marked the halfway spot. From that point on the excitement would build as we descended towards the sea, with everyone eager to win the one-rand prize awarded to whoever spotted it first.

By the time we reached the coast it would be early afternoon and we'd open all the car windows (no air con in those days) and stick our tongues out to taste the hot, humid salt air, marvelling at the distinctive hum of the cicadas in the dense, sub-tropical bush all around us. We'd arrive at our cottage or hotel later than expected – but very, very happy.

One of those trips stands out in my mind, to this day, as the best holiday I've ever had, anywhere, any time. I was 11 years old and I don't remember ever being as carefree again as I was for that one week. Everything was perfect.

We stayed at the trendy Claridges Hotel on the beachfront – following in the footsteps of luminaries such as Cliff Richard, and Pat Boone and Tommy Steele, I learnt later – located smack-bang in the middle of the action and directly across the road from the funfair. Our room was on the top floor, the corner one on the left, and it offered simply stupendous views. Look to the front and all you could see was deep blue ocean and the endless series of waves gliding in towards the land; look left and you could see all the way to Umhlanga; look right after dark and you'd see, near the end of the Marine Parade, the giant Coca-Cola sign tracing out a red neon circle all through the warm, humid night, something of a Durban landmark in those days.

We were there for Christmas and my main present that year was a chess set, packaged in a stylish wooden box that I still have to this very day up in the attic. Most of the pieces are intact, and that box also holds a few special coins and other childhood mementoes.

The Claridges had a lot going for it but, me being me, it was the quality of food on offer that was most memorable. It was top notch, man! Breakfast was informal but for dinner my father and all the other menfolk had to wear a tie or cravat, with the tables covered with crisp, white cloths and a bewildering complement of silverware set out for each diner, kids included.

We had a five-course meal every night, starting with a soup of the day served with freshly baked buns and a silver tray of delicately shaped butter balls, then a fish dish, then the main course, then dessert, and finally an extensive cheese board and fresh fruit, with coffee for the adults.

After dinner we'd go for a long stroll up the Marine Parade, or maybe see a movie at the Playhouse, which was styled like an old castle, with realistic-looking ramparts and tiny lights set in the high, black-painted ceiling to give the impression of a night sky. Later we'd have hot chocolate and biscuits back in the room, made all the tastier because it had arrived via room service, before turning in for the night, tired but content.

By day we'd go our separate ways; weird, I know, but that suited me just fine. My parents would find themselves a couple of deck chairs and disappear behind their books; Graham would go south and Christine would go north, doing whatever it was they did, while I headed straight for the beach, picking up one of the black rubber lilos available for hire and riding as many waves as I could before my hour was up and the attendant came wading out into the surf to reclaim his property.

I'd carry on splashing around for another hour or two, then maybe meet up with my family inside the Wimpy restaurant for lunch; usually a couple of toasted cheese sandwiches and chips, with a lime milkshake or Coke float – trying always to sit in one of the booths near the entrance to the adjoining aquarium so we could watch the sharks swimming around while we ate.

From there I'd hit the funfair with my daily allowance of two rand burning a hole in my pocket – the pocket of my swimming trunks, that is, because part of the joy of Durban holiday life was that I could spend the whole day in flipflops and cossie, my pale, freckled skin burning red and then turning a rich brown in the seemingly endless sunshine as the week wore on.

Two rand was more than enough for a couple of rides on the dodgem cars, situated in a cavernous underground bunker, and several go's on the hundreds of arcade games and pinball machines surrounding the dodgems, all the while boogieing along to the 70s tunes that were blasting out through the loudspeakers – *Crocodile Rock*, and *Angie*, and *Get Down*, and so on.

I always made sure to have enough money left to pay for one of those special soft-serve ice-cream cones back at the Wimpy which the guy would dip into a vat of melted chocolate, flipping it upright again and handing it over in a single polished move. Man-oh-man, I loved those cones!

When the money was gone I'd head back to the beach, bodysurfing the waves until twilight fell and the lifeguards announced they were going off duty. Every night, drifting off to sleep, I could feel the sway and rhythm of the ocean in my head. Simply magical.

Sadly, The Claridges is no more; it's been renamed and rebranded, and although the structure itself is still recognisable – I looked it up on Streetview recently – it looks like a bit of a dive these days, and the Tripadvisor reviews tell a bleak story of neglect and decay. Such a shame. I used to think that if I ever visited South Africa again I'd love to spend a night there, just for old times' sake, but that's looking less and less likely as the years go by.

As I'm writing this now I'm thinking about how, at some point in later life, many of us tend to look back and judge our parents. Mine, I think, did an awful lot wrong in the way they raised Graham, Christine and me, and the consequences of that would become apparent only years later. But it's fair to say those mistakes were made partly because parenting was done very differently a generation ago, and partly because they were obviously dealing with a lot of their own shit at the time, bequeathed to them by *their* parents.

They also did a lot right. They provided the setting for what was a truly wonderful childhood, and for that I'm eternally grateful.

CHAPTER SEVEN

For many, many years my parents poured every ounce of their energy, every last minute of their spare time, into the choir they had formed, the Protea Choral Society. It started in 1970 with just six boys – Graham and me, and four others. Television arrived late in South Africa, in 1975, which meant that Protea had a good five years or so to grow and prosper before its audiences were lured away, and it used that time well.

Rehearsals were held at our Barbara Avenue home initially, but when membership grew to 20 or 25 we had to relocate to a small church hall, and then a bigger church hall. A girls' choir was formed at some point too, with my sister Christine one of the founder members, along with the three Van Z girls, our former neighbours in Honiball Street, and it too grew quickly.

We had our own blazers (royal blue, with a badge showing a protea, South Africa's national flower) and we started out performing at school halls and old-age homes, where the sight of a bunch of fresh-faced cherubs with angelic voices invariably reduced the dear old ladies and gents to tears.

The first couple of choirmasters were enthusiastic if unexceptional, but things took a dramatic step forward when my parents signed up an especially talented pianist by name of Lydia van Rooyen as choirmistress, a young Afrikaans woman with sky-high standards and a relentless work ethic who grew to be loved and feared in equal measure by the kids.

Soon we were drawing crowds at the Benoni Small Town Hall and in surrounding towns on the East Rand. We cut an LP record (titled *On Wings of Song*), and we embarked on a national tour, performing in towns and cities around South Africa, travelling on a luxury coach and sleeping in dormitories or school halls at night, or in dozens of private homes offered by community organisations such as Rotary.

We appeared on national television on one occasion, but the high point of the choir's existence probably came on a memorable night, in 1975 I think it was, when we delivered a blockbuster performance of *The Hallelujah Chorus* alongside a full symphony orchestra at the Benoni Big Town Hall, an event that had been months in the planning.

At some point a year or two before that my mother had arranged for Protea to spend a weekend with the Drakensberg Boys' Choir, picking up tips, as it were, on how the pros did it. This was a big deal, because back then the Drakensberg choir was world famous; some said on a par with the Vienna Boys Choir.

It was also a thriving business; a boarding school for boys aged about 8 to 14, nestled among the majestic mountains of the Drakensberg range in KwaZulu-Natal. It had three or four different sub choirs, based on age, and they regularly toured the world, singing at some of the top venues in Europe and the United States and Asia. When they weren't off touring, the boys would have their daily school lessons, then choir practice, then head out into the wild to ride horses and play in mountain streams and so on – an idyllic existence, it seemed. We wanted to be like them. Very much so.

Both Graham and I auditioned for the Drakensberg choir during that weekend visit by Protea, as did another of our crew, a talented soprano by name of Rodney S. There was great excitement when all three of us were accepted, and in the months that followed my parents were busy scraping together the cash to pay the rather hefty fees when the school was engulfed by a nasty scandal that made national headlines: one or more of the adults had been caught sexually abusing the boys; an all-too-common trait among choirmasters of that era.

Of course, my parents called off the move immediately and I was bitterly disappointed to learn that I wouldn't be heading off to that mountain paradise after all, especially as they didn't explain why. It was a delicate subject to broach with a nine-year-old boy, admittedly … but they might have come up with a better explanation than the one they did, which was that Graham had decided he didn't want to go, and therefore it wasn't worth the effort to send just the one of us.

It was years before I learnt the truth; years in which I had one more thing to grudge my brother for (wrongly, in this instance. But this instance only; for all that other shit, I was quite right to grudge him!).

My parents turned their attention back to Protea but the emphasis began to shift more towards amateur theatrical productions rather than straightforward choral work, because it was becoming obvious that the age of the choir was drawing to an end.

That first show produced by Protea was called *The Bells of Bruges*, and it proved to be a lot of fun. Us kids had the chance to wear weird hats and plaster our faces with stage make-up, and dress up in exotic costumes which, in my case, included a pair of lime-green tights that showed off my matchstick legs to perfection. A real treat for the audience.

After rehearsals and between the two performances on a Saturday we'd descend on the local Wimpy restaurant en masse, 30 or 40 of us at a time, a huge, happy mob, and we'd munch on burgers and milkshakes. A bonus for all the boys involved in the show was that we'd get a letter to take to school asking permission to grow our hair longer than the regulation short-back-and-sides, to better fit whatever characters we were playing.

There was always a big cast party after the final performance, and countless romances blossomed among the hundreds of children who passed through the ranks of Protea as the years went by. Some of those romances persisted for years afterwards and even, in at least two cases that I know of, led to marriage.

The Bells of Bruges was followed by *The Wizard of Oz* in the second year, then *Whistle Down the Wind* the year after that, and then *A Christmas Carol*. Graham's star grew brighter with each one of those shows, as he always had the lead role, but it was his hip-grinding performance as Pharaoh in *Joseph and the Amazing Technicolour Dreamcoat* the following year that really wowed the crowds and won him legions of teenage girl fans all across Benoni.

Me, I'd long since given up on any chance of competing with him in this arena; he'd been blessed not just with that beautiful alto voice but also with an unshakable self-belief and an instinctive love of being in the public eye, neither of which came naturally to me.

Also, there had been a strange incident early on in that journey which had made it clear to me that a life under the spotlights was something best left to my brother. It happened at the auditions for the aforementioned production of *The Wizard of Oz*, and to this day I'm not sure what to make of it. I'll explain. Let's see what you think:

My parents had nominated a woman called Judy T, a leading light on the local amateur dramatics scene, as director of the show. Unfortunately, Judy and my mother had a falling out over something almost immediately afterwards, and there was talk of her pulling out, or simply being replaced – but with no time left to find somebody else to do the job, the decision was made to go ahead with the auditions anyway, despite the fact that the two of them had become bitter and implacable enemies.

Saturday dawned bright and full of promise for the 40 or so kids who showed up at the local church hall that day to try out for their favourite parts, Graham, Christine and me among them, of course. We took turns up on the stage reading out various lines from the script and singing a line or two from *Follow The Yellow Brick Road* and other songs. After a couple of hours Judy announced that she'd be retiring to the kitchen at the back to make her decision on who would play which role.

Breathless anticipation. Impatient rustling. Children laughed and were hushed by their equally excited parents as the minutes ticked by.

Eventually Judy emerged with her list in one hand. She sent all the kids to stand at the front of the hall and told them to step over to one side when their names were called. They did so, one by one, to a round of enthusiastic applause each time. "Mayor of Oz: John P ... Head Munchkin: Sally J ... Oz ... Richard M. ... and so on.

The pool of kids standing on the left shrank as the crowd on the right swelled, and the countdown continued until there were just five children remaining, the contenders for the lead roles. Judy called out: "Dorothy ... Anne W". There was a huge round of applause – Dorothy, of course, was the main character, the one played by Judy Garland in the movie.

"Scarecrow ... Rodney S." Applause.

"Tinman ... Graham W". Applause.

"Lion ... Bruce A". Applause.

And that left just one kid out of the 40 standing there on the floor, on his own, with no more roles to be handed out. Me.

At which point Judy thanked everyone for coming, said she'd see us all the following Saturday for the first rehearsal, and gathered up her papers and headed for the exit.

I was confused. Upset. Very, very embarrassed. Some mistake, surely? I'd auditioned for the role of Lion, and the audition had gone pretty well, I thought ... but there was Bruce looking over at me and laughing, because HE was going to play Lion. He was a friend from Rynfield Primary; a good singer and actor who, ironically, I'd urged to join the choir when he arrived as a new boy at school the year earlier. Yeah, it made sense for him to get a lead role ... but was there no part for me in the show? Nothing at all? Not even as one of the frickin munchkins?

I stood there, marooned, red in the face and fidgeting uncertainly, staring around me and then down at my feet, wondering if maybe there'd be some late reprieve, some last-gasp announcement – but no, the rest of the children were already stepping away and joining their parents, shaking hands and hugging each other. I melted away into the crowd and then slipped out the hall through a side door and went and sat under a tree for a bit on my own.

My mother was absolutely furious. She was convinced that Judy had worked out beforehand, very carefully, that she couldn't get away with denying Graham a lead role, because he was Protea's No 1 asset, but that his younger, less talented brother was an easy target who could be publicly humiliated – purely as a means of getting back at her.

Truth or paranoia? I honestly don't know. Looking back, it seems unlikely that any rational, normal adult could have planned such a diabolical revenge on a child – but it's also hard to believe that Judy couldn't see that there was still one lone, very self-conscious boy left standing out there on his own in the middle of no-man's land. I was directly in front of her, after all, no more than 20 feet away!

Surely, if it was an honest mistake, a simple miscount, she would have made some attempt to rectify the situation, rather than just walking off, smiling and nodding to various parents on her way out the door?

Whatever the case, that incident served to underline in my impressionable mind, once and for all, that I had no business being centre stage. I'd stick to the chorus from now on.

CHAPTER EIGHT

Our new house at 23 Barbara Avenue was perfectly placed to take advantage of all the delights Benoni had to offer a boy. Much of the surrounding area was still open veld, including the big chunk of land right across the road, bordered on four sides by Barbara, Jolin, Morris and Norman avenues. Call it up on Google Streetview and you can see the bit I'm referring to. Half of that chunk has since been lost to houses and new streets, but back in 1969 the town planners were still steering well clear of it because it was absolutely riddled with old mine shafts and sinkholes, some of them a hundred foot deep, with pools of mucky water at the bottom.

I loved that veld from the first time I set foot in it. Still do, in fact. Always will. Having lived in England now for more than two decades, I do occasionally miss Durban, with its sandy beaches and warm seas and humid summer evenings that are perfect for sitting out on a hotel balcony with an ice-cold beer in your hand – but the only time I feel any real sense of nostalgia, that genuine tug on the heartstrings, is when I close my eyes and picture myself running through the veld across the road from my house in Barbara Ave.

The grass was always lush and green in the summer from the scarily powerful electric storms and the drenching rains that hit like clockwork in the afternoons, but it was dry as straw in the winter, glinting with frost in the bright but freezing-cold mornings. Huge, delicately scented blue-gum trees, native to Australia, had been introduced to South Africa at some point in the previous century and they thrived in the Highveld climate. Khakibos and blackjack bushes were everywhere. Termite mounds dotted the landscape. There was even a peach tree still growing strong beside the ruins of an old house once used by the miners. In the centre of it all was a grove of tall pine trees.

I mentioned right at the start of this story that I burnt that veld to the ground every year to see how many times in a day I could get the fire department to come rushing out to the scene. That's the truth – but I also did it so I could watch the line of flame work its way across the land as night fell, filling the air with cinders and great clouds of black smoke, and that distinctive veld-fire smell that you'll find nowhere else on earth outside of the Highveld.

The sun would rise the following morning on a scorched and blackened wasteland, but by the time spring rolled around in September the first green shoots had appeared among the soot and the clumps of ash-covered roots; by Christmas the land was green and alive again with birdlife and insects; by Easter the grass was shoulder-high in places; by July the whole thing was parched again, and boys like me would find themselves climbing out of their beds one morning, answering some deep and irresistible primal call, and heading over to the supermarket to buy a box of Lion matches to set it all ablaze once again.

Cycle of life, right there.

Most of that big patch of land directly across the road had been declared off-limits to the public and encircled by a tall, sturdy wire fence topped with barbed wire and dotted with tin signs at regular intervals warning of the DANGER/GEVAAR that lurked within. The signs carried a skull-and-crossbones image and a stern warning that anyone dumb enough to trespass there would be percolated … persecuted … or it may have been prosecuted … whichever, it was enough to keep me out for a few years. Until the day I finally plucked up the courage to go and see for myself if I could find one of those skulls and maybe a few crossbones too.

It was the lure of the unknown, yes, but there was another pressing reason I wanted to breach that fence: the new Northmead Mall, filled with bakeries and toy shops and the likes, had opened on the far side, and it was a long walk to get there, but a much shorter walk if I could head across the forbidden zone. To do that, of course, I'd have to cut my way through.

I sneaked out of the house with my mother's good pair of scissors under my shirt one bright and sunny morning and I went to work on the fence. The scissors broke within ten seconds – cheap crap, obviously, and I had half a mind to tell my mother as much later, when she got home from work – but I decided I'd rather live to see my 10th birthday, so I tossed them out into the long grass and returned home in search of something tougher.

I homed in on my father's tool box in the garage. I use the term "tool box" loosely; my father was the most hopeless DIY practitioner on the continent and the box contained just one hammer and one pair of pliers, both in pristine, never-ever-used condition. On the plus side, he would almost certainly never notice if those pliers, like the scissors, ended up in two pieces somewhere in the long grass, so I slipped them under the same shirt and headed out into the veld again.

A sandy footpath had been worn all the way down the length of the fence by people taking the long walk around. I picked a spot where the grass was tall enough to hide me and I dropped to my knees – Crouching Boy, Hidden Pliers – and I looked left, looked right, looked left again and then I started cutting, one wire at a time.

Within a few minutes I'd carved out a Gavin-sized hole and I squeezed through and stood up on the other side, flushed with success and feeling what I imagine David Livingstone, the aforementioned Victorian adventurer (also a Scot!) must have felt when he gazed upon the Victoria Falls for the first time. There was a whole new land waiting to be explored!

That fence-cutting incident was my first recorded act of vandalism, but it wouldn't be the last. Not by a long shot.

CHAPTER NINE

I would have been about ten years old when the Great Chocolate Biscuit War with my father broke out. Every Saturday morning my parents would drive into town to run various errands and withdraw cash from the Standard Bank because there were no ATMs in those days; you either made it to the bank before it closed at 1pm, or you survived the weekend without any money. They would enjoy a cup of coffee at the Princess Café and then do the grocery shopping, and when they returned home us three kids would help to carry the bags from the car into the kitchen and unpack them.

On one very special Saturday I noticed something new in one of those bags: a box of Cadbury's shortcake chocolate biscuits, nestling innocently among the packets of soap powder and tins of soup.

Hmmm. Shortcake chocolate biscuits, you say?

I lifted the box and studied it closely. Some of the biscuits were visible through a diamond-shaped cut-out on the lid, each of them wrapped in a colourful foil, and of varying shapes and sizes. Almost like little Christmas presents. I weighed the box in my skilled hands. Sniffed at the cellophane outer wrapping. Was about to start peeling back that wrapping, bewitched, when my mother snatched the box from my hands. "Leave it," she said. "That's for Monday night."

"Monday? MONDAY? It's only Saturday!"

"And they're not for us anyway. They're for the choir committee meeting."

"But –"

"No."

"One! Just one!"

"No! Shut it!"

"The small one! Look – that little one in the corner!"

She swung around on me with one hand raised – nobody talked back in the Weir household – and I darted away and swivelled around and shot out the back door just in time. Years of practice. But I flicked a glance over my shoulder as I darted and swivelled, in time to see her hand the box to my father, who placed it in the top cupboard on the right.

Hmmm. Top cupboard on the right, you say?

I'll be back, I vowed. Arnold Schwarzenegger made that line famous many, many years later. But it was me who said it first.

I'm disappointed in myself that I cannot recall the exact name of this Cadbury's collection; this gift from God Himself, but I can picture the light cardboard box clearly enough: it was blue and silver in colour, flat and rectangular in shape, about 10 inches long by four inches wide and deep. Some of the biscuits were shortbread, some were wafers, some were part-shortbread, part-wafer; all were smothered in the finest, finest milk chocolate. I became addicted to those biscuits the way Renton was addicted to heroin; there's no other way no explain my obsession.

I woke early the following morning and crept into the kitchen while all the family slumbered. I climbed barefoot onto the countertop, lifted out the treasure from the cupboard where my father had stashed it, slowly-slowly peeled back the cellophane wrapping and lifted the little lid with the diamond-shaped cut-out. I studied the contents with an expert eye.

The biscuits were packed tight, side by side, row by row, but I was able to ease one out and kind of shuffle the others around a bit so that it wasn't immediately clear that one was missing. And if I'd taken just that one I may even have gotten away with it, but restraint was not my strong point.

I started with a little rat-nibble of that first biscuit, then a teeny, weensy little bite, then a bigger bite and … oh yeah, it was every bit as good as it looked. Better even. Mmmphfff-crunch-mmmphfff. Yeah, baby, yeah!

I watched, astonished, as my fingers picked out a second biscuit and directed it towards my mouth, and then a third. I shuffled the pack a bit more and tried to convince myself: "Okay, that still looks like a full box. Absolutely. No one will notice."

A rational voice somewhere inside me gave a hollow laugh and said "You're gonna get caught, man" … but I replied "Mmphff-crunch-ah-doan-fuggin-care-man!" and crammed a fourth biscuit into my mouth, and then a fifth. At which point I knew there was no point in trying to cover up my crime, and that I might as well be hanged for a sheep as for a lamb, so I finished off the rest of the packet and went back to bed. Uuuurp!

Strangely, I have no recollection of the consequences of my actions that morning. I would almost certainly have gotten a hiding and probably had my pocket money confiscated too, but I can only conclude that the reward must have been worth the punishment, because exactly the same thing happened the following month when my parents bought another packet of Cadbury's shortcake chocolate biscuits for the next choir committee meeting.

The month after that I went hunting-and-gathering again, but the top cupboard was bare. I'd seen the biscuits being unloaded on the Saturday morning, of course, and I knew they were somewhere in the house, so I went looking for them. It didn't take me long to find them: my father, exhibiting a marked lack of creativity, had hidden them in the top cupboard of his bedroom. Mmphff-crunch-gone-in-60-seconds.

The next month he got a bit more creative, hiding them not behind nor above nor under the lounge sofa, but within it, between the springs and the cushions. I found them. He tried the broom cupboard next, inside an old box full of clothes pegs and things. I found them. He left them in the car overnight one time and they melted, but I found them anyway.

The battle of wits lasted at least six months and I wish I could remember the final outcome, but I have to be honest and tell you that I can't. Did my father finally concede defeat, and simply stop handing out biscuits at the choir committee meetings each month? Did I eventually decide that a monthly hiding was too high a price to pay for so fleeting a reward, however heavenly it might be? Who knows? Not me.

But what I can say is that it was around this time I started spending all my pocket money on my own packets of biscuits – Choc-Kits, Romany Creams, Nutticrusts, you name it – all of them devoured while lying flat on my tummy on my bed reading *Archie* comic books. More magical times.

CHAPTER TEN

This seems as good a spot as any to fill out the picture with a bit of background on my parents, to give a bit more context to the incidents I've mentioned, and those still to come. We'll start with my mother Mary, by far the more straightforward of the two and therefore easier to understand. She was born in 1935 in a deprived part of Glasgow, and some of her earliest childhood memories involved cramming into a stuffy air-raid shelter along with dozens of other people as the Nazis carpet-bombed the streets above them during the Second World War. Times were hard, and they didn't get any easier in the austere post-war years, which meant she quickly developed a steely outer skin to get by in what was an often-ugly world.

She had a grandmother, she told me, who'd been a leading suffragette before developing a drinking problem. She had a grandfather who started out baking bread in his kitchen and selling it from barrows he trundled around town before setting up his own thriving bakery, but the business was stolen from his side of the family by a scheming brother on the day he died. She had an Uncle George who was a feared gangster in the Glasgow underworld until the day he found Jesus and devoted the rest of his life to service in the Salvation Army.

She'd grown up as the poorest kid in her school, with holes in her shoes and a hunger in her belly. Her family were the "scruff" of the street and her own mother was a slob, she confided to me at one point – but, despite all of that, she had risen above her circumstances to excel at school and then find a husband from a better part of town, and later still make a career for herself as an architectural draughtswoman, without the benefit of any higher education.

My mother was determined to give her children a better start in life than she had had, but I think it's fair to say she was driven by a fierce sense of duty rather than any maternal, softer instinct; that sort of thing had been squeezed out of her a long time before. She valued hard work, but she had zero compassion for the struggles of others – her children included – and weakness, in any form, simply wasn't tolerated.

I saw her cry just once throughout my childhood, presumably after a behind-closed-doors argument with my father (as I mentioned earlier, they never argued in front of the children – which, let's face it, is probably not such a great policy). Disobedience was a direct challenge to her authority and likely to be met with a swift snotklap; that was something all three of us kids learnt at an early age.

In short, you always knew where you stood with my mother: at least 6ft away, in case you had to make a run for it.

My father, Andrew, was six years older than her and … well, he was a far, far more complex individual; something of an enigma to me, in fact, because he never, ever spoke about himself, or his youth, or his own parents, his hopes and dreams, his successes and failures, his likes and dislikes, his childhood adventures, what exactly he did at work five days a week, his friends, his enemies. Nothing like that. Keep the conversation light and he was an amiable companion, and good company; try to talk about anything personal, to him or yourself, and the shutters came crashing down.

He was a self-taught pianist and without doubt an intelligent man, with an extensive general knowledge and a good grasp of world affairs, but he lived out his working days as a lower-level draughtsman in various mining companies in Johannesburg. It was a respectable job, certainly, and one which paid the bills and put food on the table and which, with my mother's earnings, covered the countless expenses incurred by three growing children ... but it was also something he could have done with his eyes closed. I believe he could have made a whole lot more of himself if he'd had any interest in doing so.

I've searched my memory banks for any early recollections of him, good or bad, and, strangely, I can find just two. In the first I can see him arriving home from work one day when I was about five with a new toy car each for Graham and me; in the second, about a year later, he is swinging me around the room like an aeroplane, holding one arm and one leg tight – and that is the only spontaneous, joyful physical interaction I can remember sharing with him, ever. And the older I got, the further into his shell he withdrew.

In a sense it's easier to list the things my father didn't do than the things he did. He didn't do hugs and he didn't offer solace when things were going badly, probably because he hadn't actually noticed. He never kicked a ball around the yard nor played in the surf with us kids on our family holidays, and he gave not a word of fatherly advice on how fight off a bully, or talk to girls, or build a campfire, or repair a flat bicycle tyre or solve a maths homework puzzle.

He didn't bother to attend the annual parent-teacher meetings at school (though, in fairness, neither did my mother, until the day both were summoned to meet the principal – more on that later!). He never showed any interest in my day-to-day activities or in my badminton or soccer games, preferring to spend his evenings either dozing in his lounge chair or away from the house at rehearsals for an endless series of Gilbert and Sullivan shows staged by a local amateur dramatic society. In later years there was no guidance regarding the career path I might want to choose, or what pitfalls in life I should beware of.

I hasten to add, before this pity party goes too far, that I'm very well aware that the world is absolutely full of shit fathers – drunks, wife-beaters, sexual abusers, men who simply abandon their families – and, in his defence, he did none of that stuff either. Yes, it fell to him to administer the many hidings I was given as a boy but he did it reluctantly, at my mother's urging, and he did it without any real force – and many of those hidings, to be fair, were richly deserved. I saw at least two of my friends given *real* hidings by their fathers, one of them with a military-style cane, and that was after he had shaved his son's head just because he fell asleep during a church service!

There was none of that viciousness from my father. He was a steady provider; essentially a good man at heart, and a gentle soul, but completely detached from me and everybody else around him, including his wife. He was remote and repressed, wary of any display of emotion, an active participant in my brother's burgeoning singing career, but simply not interested in any parental activity beyond that … however baffling that seems to me today, as a father myself.

It's a harsh truth, but my mother was in many ways a single parent to her three children, because her husband was ever present but strangely absent at the same time.

CHAPTER 11

My father had several bad habits but there was one in particular that used to drive my mother absolutely nuts: there was a period of two or maybe even three years in which he used to lie in bed until at least 2pm every Sunday, simply refusing to budge, no matter how many times she screeched at him to get up because this or that had to be done. At some point, in desperation, she enlisted the help of Graham and me, authorising us to creep silently into the room while he snored before suddenly tipping up the side of the mattress, or shouting at the top of our voices, or simply switching on the radio, full volume, before running out again.

He'd jump up, enraged, and chase us down the passageway in his pyjamas, but if we could make it to the back door we were safe, because he couldn't follow us out into the yard in his bare feet. He'd turn around and go straight back to bed – and we'd wait half an hour and do it again.

Tranquil, lazy Sundays? Not in the Weir household.

He must have gone through some kind of mid-life crisis at about that time because, with no warning at all, he suddenly threw himself into the world of home DIY, with sadly predictable consequences.

Our house was one of the first to be built in Barbara Avenue, along with that of our immediate neighbours to the right, Derek C and his wife Liz. Derek was a bit of a handyman, and he continued improving upon his property long after the builders had left – and it may have been his efforts, easily visible from our lounge window, that inspired my father to attempt to follow suit.

He would have been in his early forties then and, to the best of my knowledge, had never so much as attached a picture frame to a wall before announcing one day that he would be laying a concrete driveway from the road to the carport at the front of the house. By himself.

"What? WHAT?" my mother asked, incredulous.

"A driveway. Concrete."

"You don't know the first thing about it!" she hooted.

He shrugged. "You mix the concrete and the stones with a bit of water. You pour it between the wooden planks and you let it dry. I saw Derek doing it."

Derek had indeed been a busy man. He'd added a swimming pool in his front garden and several rows of peach and plum trees in the back. He'd also built a rather impressive brick wall all the way along the front boundary of his property and had even allowed me to help him out for a time – although that particular phase of the project had ended badly, with me being fired after just two days. Why, you ask? Well, it was an entirely innocent mistake on my part. I'll explain:

My job was to load the loose bricks onto a wheelbarrow and ferry them across to Derek, who was placing them with expert precision, lathering on the mortar and checking that each was level and perfectly aligned, humming a little tune to himself all the while. His eye was true and his hand was steady and we had built the wall up to maybe eight or nine bricks high before I decided that things were taking longer than they should.

Why not load the wheelbarrow with twice as many bricks as Derek had suggested, I asked myself? That way I could make exactly half the number of trips and get them across the yard in exactly half the time – which would free me up for an early lunch break. Excellent idea!

I struggled to get the wheelbarrow moving that time, because it was obviously a lot heavier than it had been before, but once I managed to get a bit of momentum behind me I was able to pick up the pace very nicely. So nicely, in fact, that by the time I drew alongside Derek I was flying along at a hundred miles an hour and was completely unable to slow the bastard thing down: it smashed into the wall like a runaway freight train, and because the mortar hadn't had time to set properly the whole structure came tumbling down along almost half the length of the boundary.

Derek leapt to his feet shouting: "No-no-noooo!"

I stammered out an apology and scrambled forward and began trying to put a couple of the bricks back together again, but he pushed me aside. "Yaargghh!! Leave it! Just bloody leave it!"

"But – "

"Get out! Piss off! Just … Ffff! Fff! Fffffffff!!" Controlling himself, but only just.

"This one fits here! And this one too. Look, I can – "

His cheeks turned purple and he grabbed at his hair and screamed at me in a surprising falsetto: "GO! GO! GO! GO! JUST … GO!!!"

I went.

Dumbass probably didn't mix the mortar right, I told myself as I marched off in a huff. Stupid place to put a wall anyway.

I had another brush with Derek a few months later when he complained to my parents about me stealing the peaches off his prize trees; he knew it was me, he told them, because I'd left a perfect set of bare footprints in the soft soil when I clambered over the 6ft-high boundary between our properties.

He wasn't wrong, of course, but I felt aggrieved enough to convince Graham and a couple of other kids to join me in paying him a visit in the early hours of the morning during that year's Hogmanay party. We crept into his garden, hushing each other and giggling all the way, and sidled up to the main bedroom window. It was open, and we could hear both Derek and his wife snoring gently within as Graham gave a silent countdown: three, two, one … at which point I let rip with a toy trumpet somebody had brought to the Hogmanay party: "PAAARRRRPPPP!" and the others shouted at the top of their voices "HAPPY NEW YEAR DEREK!!!"

He leapt out of bed screaming in that same falsetto and charged into the nearest wall then bounced back and fell over his wife's slippers or something, while we scampered back to the party.

Derek came banging on our front door at an indecent hour the next morning and demanded that me and Graham follow him back to his house to apologise to his wife, which we did. He made us promise to never do anything like that again, and so we never did.

Not to him, at least.

My father chose not to ask for my help on the driveway project but that may have been the only good decision he made in the entirety of his short-lived DIY phase. I don't recall the step-by-step construction process, or how long he laboured on the project, but I can say with confidence that the end result was a miserable, abject failure; that driveway was a lopsided trapezoid riven with a long crack all the way from the carport to the road.

Worse, he had apparently mixed in too many stones and not enough cement, because within a few days of completion it was fraying and collapsing at the sides. Within a few weeks the top layer was crumbling away and sharp stones were sticking out here and there. Within a few months the whole thing had degenerated into a tyre-shredding, bone-jarring, ever-shifting pile of shit and rubble straight outta Pompeii, and he finally had to call in the professionals to clear it all away and do the job properly.

More bad news: he had a packet of cement left over, and Derek had a few excess bricks from his wall project that he was happy to donate, so he put two and two together and came up with a five-star plan: he would build a braai, or barbecue stand, for the back yard.

My mother rolled her eyes but didn't object – until she saw where he'd placed it: barely six feet from the back door. "You've got the whole yard to chose from! Why there?" she demanded.

"You need to be close to the kitchen," he explained. "So you don't have to walk too far with the sausages and things."

"But the smoke's going to blow right inside the house!"

"Not really. Okay, maybe some days. If it's a southwesterly. Maybe."

She had an excellent point, of course, but he had made up his mind and would not be dissuaded – though she needn't have worried because, as it turned out, the barbecue stand lasted no longer than the driveway. It turned out to be far smaller and less grandiose than he'd probably envisaged, a simple structure just five single bricks high, joined to another five bricks on the other side by a flimsy wire grid that would hold, at most, a single spiral of boerewors and maybe one malnourished chicken drumstick.

A sixth brick on top, on either side, held the wire grid down and in place … for perhaps an hour before somebody bumped it and one of the top bricks fell off. Apparently, my father hadn't yet got the hang of mixing cement and sand in the right quantities.

Declared not fit for purpose, the barbecue stand was dismantled and disposed of just a few months after its completion – but, undeterred, my father announced soon after, as we were eating dinner one night, that he would be building a patio in the back garden.

My mother sprayed out a mouthful of mince and tatties and choked and coughed for a few minutes before asking weakly: "Why? For the love of God: why?"

"Eh? Well, now I know what I did wrong with the driveway.

And the barbecue. Might as well use that knowledge."

He picked a spot a bit farther from the house and measured out a rectangle perhaps 16 feet wide by 20 feet long. A fresh batch of cement and gravel was delivered to 23 Barbara Avenue, along with a few dozen of slabs of slasto, large slate paving stones that, in the right hands, could be laid alongside each other in a pleasing jigsaw puzzle to form a stylish base.

These, of course, were the wrong hands entirely; also, my father had apparently never heard of a spirit level, because not a single one of the slasto slabs that he plopped down into the wet concrete ended up level with its neighbour. Some were left sticking out a full inch higher than the next, an open invitation to the unwary to stub a toe or twist an ankle; others tilted drunkenly to one side, forming puddles on rainy days that dried to slimy, hazardous patches that could send you sprawling on your bum if you didn't watch your every step. What a mess!

Sadly, the only thing he had gotten right, at last, was the concrete mix … which meant that those slasto slabs were stuck very firmly in all the wrong places and couldn't be budged. They stayed where they were for at least a decade longer, daring the reckless to try their luck in crossing that Plain of Broken Toes until the day we finally left the house and bequeathed them to the unsuspecting family that moved in.

My father had taken three solid blows to his self-esteem but, like the guy in that old Arlo Guthrie song, he wasn't tired, or proud. Time passed, but not a lot, before he declared on another night, defiantly almost, that he'd always wanted a garden pond, with goldfish and water lilies and things. "Maybe a couple of stone gnomes standing at the side," he added. "You know, with little fishing poles. And hats."

My mother, generally not a spiritual woman, closed her eyes and appeared to offer up a silent prayer. Then she sighed: "Can we ... hire someone?"

"Eh? D'you have any idea how much those people charge? No, this is really simple. See, you just dig out a big hole in the garden and you use the same soil to build up a rockery around it. Then you buy the base and drop it in the hole and turn on the garden tap. It's as easy as that. You get your lilies from the garden centre, and the goldfish from the pet shop, and ..."

By early summer the hole was dug and the fibreglass base of the pond, kidney-shaped and about 8ft long and 4ft wide was in situ. The decorative stones for the rockery hadn't yet been delivered but the stone gnomes had, so they were wedged into temporary positions among the piles of soil that were still piled high around the edges. The four of them looked on, expressionlessly, as the rain came pouring down on the very first night, washing about a ton of that soil into the pond and staining the freshly poured water a delicate shade of Sewage Brown.

My father waved away any concerns: the lilies would filter it clean in no time, he promised; that was what lilies did, after all, and the main reason they could be found in garden ponds all around the world. Also, there was no time to replace the water because he'd already ordered a dozen goldfish from the pet shop.

They arrived in peak physical condition a day later but were dead within the week; something to do with the PH levels in that muddy water, or possibly the bloated, rotting corpses of the hundreds of caterpillars that marched into the pond each night to drown themselves. We found a mouse floating face-down one morning, piling an unreasonably heavy workload on those poor lilies, which had themselves been attacked by some kind of malevolent beetle and munched to near-extinction.

By mid-summer the stagnant, scum-covered water was attracting all manner of stinging, biting insects, along with a small army of frogs that yodelled long into the night; a deafening chorus of amphibian Pavarottis vying for the attentions of the opposite sex.

My mother had had enough. After one especially difficult late-summer night when it was too warm to sleep with the windows closed, but impossible to sleep with them open because of the frogs and the squadrons of mosquitoes circling overhead, just waiting for the chance to whine and dine on sweet Scottish blood, she laid down an ultimatum: either the pond had to go or she would.

My father admitted defeat, finally. He backfilled the pond with the surrounding soil, an old tyre and the four stone gnomes, then he chucked a bit of grass seed on the top to cover the scene of the crime before heading back indoors, picking up his newspaper, and slumping into his favourite armchair, never again to wield a shovel nor any other DIY implement for all the days of his life.

Google Streetview is a wonderful thing. You can go online and type in "Barbara Avenue, Benoni" and you can see for yourself, today, the tall, white-painted brick wall at the front of Derek's property (which he successfully rebuilt from the ground up, without my help). It still stands proud after 50 years.

Slide the cursor to the right, to number 23, and all looks pretty normal too, at first glance. The rebuilt driveway looks like any other driveway along the street. The spot outside the back door where the barbecue rose and fell has been built over at some point by a subsequent homeowner, and the slasto abomination in the back yard is long gone.

But ... but is that a patch of slightly discoloured grass you can see from above, right there in the middle of the front lawn? Almost as if, buried just a few inches below the ground, there lies some pond-shaped mass of radioactive matter that is still festering away to this very day? A cursed spot on God's good earth, a corner of a foreign field that is forever fubared? A place where no grass will ever be able to sink its roots deeply enough to attain the healthy shade of green you might expect in a suburban Highveld summer garden?

Hmmm. Hard to say for sure. Could be just the shadow from a nearby tree ... or it could be that my father has indeed left his mark on the land; an indelible tribute to DIY no-hopers everywhere; a legacy of ineptitude that will endure for a thousand years to come.

CHAPTER 12

I re-acquired Blue-Eyed Boy status in my Standard Three year at Rynfield Primary but again, sadly, I could not hold on to it for very long. The teacher this time was Mrs Staley, a kindly, rotund woman who was about 50 or 100 years old – you can't really tell the difference when you're ten – and she, like Mrs Shaw, had a knack for making kids like me feel special.

I was good with numbers, so she nominated me to mark the other children's arithmetic homework, and for a time I was also one of the privileged few encouraged to show up at her house before school started each morning to help her carry her books across the road. This was a bit like being president of the European Union, in that it was an honour that was rotated regularly between different candidates, none of whom were given a permanent position, but I was happy to do it anyway. Positive adult attention, as I may have mentioned before, was hard to come by.

There was no traumatic fall from grace this time, no single incident that I remember, but at some point relations with Mrs Staley cooled. I know this because midway through the school year my grades suddenly took a disastrous downward spiral and I started playing up in class and finding myself in the principal's office once or twice a week as a result.

It started with me bringing a football into music class. The teacher, a Miss Francis if I remember right, told me to leave it outside next time, so of course I brought it along again the very next day and began bouncing it surreptitiously every time she turned her back.

She told me to stop. I feigned innocence, then gave it another quick "boing" as she turned away. Annoying, right?

"Stop it!"

"Miss?"

"Right, class – let's turn to …"

Boinng!

"Gavin!"

"Miss?"

"I'm warning you!"

"Me? Sheesh!"

"Okay class, let's – "

Boing! Boing! Boing!

"That's it! Out! Get to Mr Ablett's office right this second!"

I stomped out the room, but with no intention of continuing on to Mr Ablett's office; that would have meant an instant caning – two or maybe three cuts. The music room was in the main admin building, at the end of a long corridor, and Mr Ablett's private office was worryingly close, just three doors down.

I couldn't simply stroll by, mid-lesson, without being seen, because he had a window that looked out into the corridor. I couldn't stay where I was either, because one of the school secretaries could chance along at any moment and start asking pointed questions about why a freckled boy with a guilty look on his face was hanging around outside the music room, almost as if he'd just been booted out.

There was, however, a third option: a number of filing cabinets had been lined up all along one side of the corridor, with a gap between the two that were closest to the music room. It was a thin gap – but I was a thin boy, and I was able to slide into that tight spot and out of sight, albeit with my head twisted uncomfortably to one side. Moments later one of the office doors opened and I heard a pair of high heels go clip-clopping down the corridor. One of the secretaries, presumably; Mr Ablett was a chunky guy, and high heels didn't seem his style.

The footsteps returned soon after, now heading up the corridor in my direction, and I held my breath and sent up a quick prayer to the Patron Saint of Little Shits – I'm not even Catholic – and whoever it was turned back into the same room they'd come out of, and the corridor fell silent again. Whew!

I stayed in that spot for a full 15 minutes, shifting my weight from one foot to the other every now and then, my face still twisted to one side, until the bell finally rang to signal the end of the lesson. The door to the music room burst open and my classmates filed out, and I slipped in among them and walked past Mr Ablett's office boldly and with a spring in my step. Success! Freedom!

I used the same trick at least half a dozen times more before my luck ran out and Mr Ablett himself came lumbering up towards the music room one day and stopped and stared in amazement at the sight of me squashed in between the filing cabinets.

"What exactly are you doing there, boy?" he demanded.

"Was just on my way to see you, sir," I replied with my brightest smile.

"And … you took a wrong turn? Got wedged between the cabinets? Couldn't get out again?"

I tried to give a nonchalant shrug but there wasn't enough space to move my shoulders.

"Follow me," Mr Ablett said, and headed back towards his office.

Three cuts, I think it was on that occasion; three of the best, and man they were painful. Mr Ablett, as I said, was a chunky guy.

I continued getting thrown out of music class, and a few others besides, in the months that followed. Various teachers broke a wide variety of educational supplements over my bended arse – big blackboard rulers, small blackboard dusters, and even, one time, a blackboard compass – but it appeared to make no difference. My grades, never spectacular but usually somewhere in the 70s, took a dive, in part because I quit doing any homework at all.

Eventually my parents were called in to the school one evening to be told that unless I shaped up, and quickly, they would ship me out.

You'd think that would have worked but you'd be wrong, and things came to a head very soon afterwards.

CHAPTER 13

Today, looking back as an adult (with a psychologist for a wife), it's not too hard to work out what was going on in my head at that time. My brother Graham was the absolute focus of the Weir household and always had been. He was the first-born, the boy with the huge talent, the star of the future. My parents had started up the Protea Choral Society and they built it largely around him. He was the key soloist, with me and my sister Christine mere backing singers.

Protea staged its first amateur dramatic production that year, *The Bells of Bruges*, and Graham had the lead role. I had a bit part and Christine did too.

I had by then discovered that I was reasonably good at a reasonable number of things apart from singing – the sporty stuff like football and badminton, schoolwork in general – but not especially great at anything. Graham was the exact opposite; he was rubbish at just about everything except singing and acting, but he did those two things exceedingly well, and that meant I lived in his shadow for many, many years.

He was hogging the limelight, and I desperately wanted a piece of it. Positive adult attention was what I was craving – but if that was not forthcoming then negative adult attention was the next best thing. Anything was better than being ignored.

That was presumably my thinking one fine afternoon when

I opted not to head home at the end of the school day as usual, but to check out the small farm plot where a new friend lived instead. Greg R was his name and he was definitely one of the cool kids. He had arrived at Rynfield Primary a few months earlier and fitted in right away.

Easy-going and funny and a good footballer too, he spoke often about how his afternoons were filled with fun stuff like horse-riding or swimming in the family reservoir; there was no time for boring homework. Intrigued, I joined him at the bus stop after school one day and climbed aboard with a handful of other kids lucky enough to live on smallholdings in Putfontein, a few miles out of town.

Putfontein, by the way, is the part of Benoni where the Oscar-winning movie star Charlize Theron grew up – and, who knows, she may even have been neighbours with Greg R and his family? Entirely possible. Imagine her disappointment when she reads this and realises that, if she'd just been a few years older, and if she'd only known to go and hang around at her neighbour's fence on the right day, and at the right time, she might have caught a fleeting glimpse of Mr One Hundred Billion in his youth! What a story to tell her Hollywood friends!

Anyway, I had a great time at Greg's house that day. I had never ridden a horse before, and I didn't that day either – have you seen how big those things look up close? When you're ten years old? – but I did get to swim in the reservoir, and run around with the family dogs, and explore the smallholding, and when night fell I joined the family at a delicious farm-style dinner. Terrific. The only thing I didn't do was to call home at any point and let my parents know where I was.

Turned out they'd been searching for me for hours, phoning my usual set of friends and asking if they'd seen me. They'd called the local hospital, and the police, and the fire brigade. They'd scoured the veld around our house, peering down into the mine shafts and sinkholes and shouting out my name, heading back to the house to fetch flashlights when it got too dark to see. Eventually one of my friends told his mother about the new boy at school, and his mother phoned my mother with the tip – but of course nobody had a telephone number for Greg because, well, he was new.

They finally got hold of a teacher who was able to go into school and find a phone number for Greg's parents, and when it was established that that was where I'd spent the day, my father drove out to Putfontein to pick me up.

He walked me back to the car in silence – the stony type, not the companionable type. There was more stony silence on the way home, and as we pulled into the driveway, and as we walked to the front door. When I stepped inside I saw my mother standing at the fireplace with fury in her eyes and her jaw clenched so tight she could barely speak. "You're … getting … the hiding of your life!" she rasped and pointed to the bedroom with a shaky hand. My father closed the front door behind me and then threw the car keys on the coffee table. He started taking off his belt.

I was beginning to wonder at that point if there was maybe an easier, less painful way to get a bit of attention, but then my mother added, very grudgingly, almost spitting out the words: "We do … *love you*, you know!"

I stared at her, dumbfounded, because that was the first time I'd ever heard those words. That sounds melodramatic, I know, but it's the truth. There are obviously many bits of this story where I've had to flesh out the conversations and fill in the blanks because, after 50 years, some of the finer details have been lost. I've put words into the mouths of various characters based on what I believe they would have said and how they would have said it, but this particular quote I can remember verbatim, word for word. It was, after all, what I had been waiting to hear all my short life.

As Samuel L Jackson put it so eloquently years later in *Pulp Fiction*: "Shit, Negro – that's all you had to SAY!"

❖ ❖ ❖

If this was a Hollywood movie then that incident would have represented a huge turning point; the moment at which the troubled young protagonist realises his self-worth and recants his sins, becomes a star pupil and a model citizen. Not the case, I'm afraid.

Yes, I stopped misbehaving in class and I started doing my homework again, and my grades shot up almost overnight – proving that the Love vaccine was immediately effective in preventing the symptoms of Juvenile Delinquency. But, as AstraZeneca would discover half a century later, in the war on Covid, the vaccine had to be administered more than once to have a long-lasting effect. You needed a second dose, and maybe a third, and a couple of booster jabs too, and the Weir household simply did not have the resources for that. My mother had let herself down by using the L word in front of the kids, but it was a moment of weakness and she never did it again.

The focus turned firmly back in Graham's direction soon afterwards when Protea staged its next production, *The Wizard of Oz*, with him starring as the Tinman, and my short spell in the limelight came to an end.

I would have to try a little harder, it seemed, to hold my parents' attention ...

CHAPTER 14

O ne of those things I mentioned that I was reasonably good at, but not great at, was sprinting. Every single year, from Standard One through Standard Five, I was fast enough to be one of the eight boys in my age group who lined up for the 100m flat race at the annual Rynfield Primary School sports day, and every single year, without fail, I came either second or third. Never first.

The pupils were divided into three houses, named after Victorian-era explorers: Rhodes (red), Stanley (white) and Livingstone (grey). A handful of the older pupils would dress up in various colourful outfits and lead the masses of pupils crammed onto the Willowmoore Park grandstand in tribal chants and wild cheering and foot-stomping every time one of their athletes won a race. A hot sun always seemed to blaze down, and at the end of the day all the kids would go home exhausted and sunburnt and hoarse from all the shouting, but happy.

I looked forward to sports day as much as all the rest, thinking that maybe *this* year I would finally finish first, but it never happened. Not once did I get to be the kid whose name was called out at the prizegiving ceremony at the close of the day, who sprang to his feet and picked his way through the other athletes sitting cross-legged on the field, climbing the podium to receive a handshake and a certificate amid a deafening chorus of cheers.

And it wasn't even the same kid who beat me each year; it was always someone different, someone new, some other bastard who'd just joined the school and who was also, apparently, distantly related to Usain Frickin Bolt. Despite the fact we were all white! Soooo frustrating!

It was a similar story with the badminton: I managed to earn a place in the Eastern Transvaal provincial squad, but in the B team, not the A team. One year me and a friend called Shaun F paired up to win the boys' under-15 doubles title, and I beat Shaun in the semi-final of the boys' under-15 singles – only to lose to a chubby but surprisingly agile lad called Craig L in the final. My ever-tactful mother added salt to the wound when she commented, on the one time she showed up to watch an inter-provincial tournament, that, wow, those kids in the A team were so much better than us guys in the B team!

Same thing with football: I was good enough to be in the school's A team, but not all of the time. Occasionally I'd have a bad game and be dropped to the B squad the following week.

It didn't help that Rynfield Primary seemed to be comprised almost exclusively of right-footed boys, which meant we didn't have a natural left-winger and so I was nominated to fill the gap, despite not being able to kick the ball with any power or accuracy with my left foot. I'd go sprinting down the wing – at a reasonably good pace, of course – but I'd have to screech to a stop, every time, and transfer the ball to my right foot before centring it, giving the defender who was chasing me more than enough time to catch up. Not ideal.

The absolute highlight of my footballing career came on a Saturday morning in Standard Four when we travelled to a neighbouring school and thrashed our opponents 8-0, with me scoring no fewer than six of the goals. At least two were flukes, and at least two were credited to me because I just happened to be in the right place at the right time, with the ball landing at my feet in front of an open goal. But, hey, they all counted – it was a double hat-trick!

I was wearing a brand new pair of Adidas football boots that day, jet black, with three orange stripes on each side, and my team-mates were cheering me on with each new goal and joking about how those boots must have had some kind of magical properties to them. I kind of half-believed them; I hadn't ever scored more than two goals in a game before.

The team bus dropped us back at Rynfield Primary afterwards and I jogged home on a wave of euphoria, taking a short cut through the veld as always, bursting to share my good news. I found my father washing the family car in the driveway, bent over the rear bumper with a soapy sponge in one hand. "Dad!" I shouted as I got within earshot." Dad, I scored six goals!"

He straightened up. "Eh?"

"We won 8-0. And I scored six of the goals!"

He stared for a second and said: "Awa'," then went back to soaping the car bumper. Awa' being the equivalent of "bullshit!"

"It's true! I'm not lying!" I told him, outraged and a bit wounded, because I would never lie. Well, not unless I was in trouble. And, yes, I was in trouble quite a lot by then so I was probably lying all the time. But not THAT time! Sheesh!

He refused to believe me, but my story must at least have piqued his curiosity because a bit later he said he would come along to the game the following Saturday to watch me play for the first time. He was true to his word: he did come along the following Saturday, but he showed up late, as was his way, just as the ref was blowing the final whistle. Traffic was bad, he told me.

I couldn't say it out loud, of course, but in my head I was thinking: "Awa'".

A couple of months later he finally did get to see me play, on a midweek night. Our team had won the Benoni primary schools league and we faced off against Selcourt Primary, from Springs, the neighbouring town, in the cup final. I tried my damnedest to produce another six-goal thriller that night but whatever magical qualities my boots may have had had long since worn off.

We went 1-0 down early in the game and I did, at least, set up the equalising goal by – you guessed it – sprinting down the left wing at a reasonably good pace and then fumbling the ball past two defenders before crossing it to Johnny F, who thumped it past their goalkeeper. Oh, and I also broke the leg of the boy who was marking me, which may have affected our opponents' morale.

Wait – what?

It was an accident, I hasten to add, and I didn't exactly get off scot-free myself. About 20 minutes into the game our goalkeeper, my good friend Richard V, booted the ball high into the air, in my direction, and I began running backwards, my head titled upwards, tracking it as it arced overhead. Travelling in the exact opposite direction, also looking up and watching the ball and nothing else, was the defender in question.

We clattered into each other at full speed and I went flying, banging my head on the ground as I landed. I lay there stunned and unmoving for a bit but I was eventually able to sit up and stare around me groggily. The other boy was rolling around on the floor screaming, and not like one of our modern-day Premier League wimps who've perfected the art for dramatic effect; this poor kid was in genuine pain and had to be carted off the field with what we learnt later was a broken leg.

The game ended 1-1 and the teams shared the honours, which was enough to get our coach, Mr van Papendorp, drunk and happy. I celebrated along with the rest of the squad, toasted by my team-mates for my part in our only goal, but I followed it up in the weeks thereafter with a string of dismal performances and before I knew it I was back in the B team. My father never came along to watch me play again.

Another thing I was reasonably good at, but not great at, was fighting. I'd expressed an interest in judo when I was five and had even won a silver medal at a tournament at one point (bloody second place again!) but, like 99 per cent of kids I dropped out within a few months. Later I also tried my hand at jiu-jitsu and then karate but lost interest when it became apparent that becoming the next Bruce Lee would involve rather a lot of hard work. I did finally get a black belt in karate but only many, many years later, as a young, single man living in Durban – but that's a story for another day. Back to Benoni.

I was mostly able to hold my own against various schoolboy bullies, but that was thanks to my mother having shoved me into the garage with Archie G that day, rather than the teachings of any sensei. In Standard Three, however, the challenges seemed to come thicker and faster than ever before.

Perhaps that's the age at which boys naturally seek to assert their dominance, or it may just have been that unidentified something in the Highveld water I mentioned earlier, bringing out the Inner Savage in all of us. Whatever the cause, I'd already won two playground punch-ups by the middle of that year (neither of them instigated by me, I hasten to add). The third one, though, was the biggie.

I had a classmate at the time by name of Richard M, a fellow Protea Choir member and a good friend, but more of an academic than the sporty type. Some kid grabbed him on the playground one day during lunch break and tried to goad him into a decidedly one-sided fight, and within minutes a crowd of pupils had gathered in a tight circle around them and the chanting began: "Barnie! Barnie! Barnie!" – which, loosely translated, means "fight, you chickenshits, we wanna see some blood!"

I stepped in front of Richard and told the kid he'd be fighting me instead, and for a moment it looked like that would be the end of it – until the crowd parted and Mark V stepped forward and demanded to know why I was picking a fight with HIS friend.

This was a very worrying development. Mark V was the toughest kid in our year group, an Afrikaner with a close-shaven head and a pitbull physique, and probably the last guy in the school I would have chosen to tangle with. But I couldn't have backed out at that point even if I'd wanted to, because the crowd was already four or five deep and the chanting had reached fever pitch – and Mark suddenly came charging forward, two big, meaty fists flailing in my direction.

I often wish I had access to God's video records of life on Earth. I'd love to see the continents forming and drifting apart again; the dinosaurs having their day in the sun; the first early humans venturing out of Africa; the various empires rising and falling. I'd also love to see that fight with Mark V, because I remember almost nothing about it other than being punched really, really hard at one point and then reeling backwards in slow motion, wondering if I'd just been shot in the head by a Sherman tank.

I was told afterwards by my friends that it was epic; that the two of us punched and wrassled and kicked the crap out of each other until a teacher finally came running across the playground to break it up. Popular consensus was that the fight had ended in a draw – which meant I emerged bloodied and bruised, but with a reputation as the joint-toughest kid in our year group. Also, Richard M's mother phoned my mother that night and gushed about how I'd saved her son and what a brave young chap I must be, so I was a hero in my own home for a day or two. Wonderful!

The downside, I discovered later, was that having a tough-guy reputation pretty much guarantees that you're going to get into more fights, not all of which you'll win, because any boy willing to challenge you is obviously pretty tough himself.

One such incident involved a tall, stick-thin, bespectacled boy called Bob H who I barely knew and who, for no good reason at all, walked up to me between classes one day and told me he could probably beat the shit out of me if he felt like it. I blinked and sized him up for a second or two and decided it was safe to reply: "We'll see about that. Second break. In the playground."

"Sure," he said, and wandered off, leaving me scratching my head.

The bell rang for second break and I marched out onto the playground surrounded by my homies, feeling reasonably confident. Bob H? He was a dweeb, we all agreed. With a death wish, apparently. He was in the B class; me and my crew were all A-stream kids, and a sizeable crowd from both sides had already gathered on the playground in anticipation of the class war – but there was no sign of Bob.

Someone said he'd seen him heading for the library to catch up on some homework he'd forgotten about, and my friends jeered. One of them ran off to fetch him, and a couple of minutes later he returned with Bob in tow.

I half-expected him to apologise, maybe try to wheedle out of the showdown, but he seemed genuinely eager to get started. Apparently he really did have some homework that he'd had to finish off, but now … now he was raring to go. The first nagging doubts surfaced in my mind as he pulled off his school tie with relish and turfed his spectacles carelessly towards one of his friends and started flexing his scrawny but very, very long arms … but, as with the Mark V fight, there was no turning back because the mob had encircled us and the chanting had begun: "Barnie! Barnie! Barnie!"

I darted forward and he eased aside like a matador. I swung a punch and it whistled through thin air. I went in with a full-power haymaker but again he stepped back neatly and watched me almost overbalance – before nipping forward himself and raising his fist and spiralling one of those unnaturally long arms in my general direction and … BOOOOM! A flash of red light! A momentary loss of vision! A taste of blood – my blood!

I was stunned for a second, quite literally, and if he'd pressed his advantage he could have easily landed a second or third or fourth blow, and I'd have woken up in the school sick room. But very fortunately for me, whoever it was who taught Bob H to box – because that, I worked out later, was what was going on here; he was a trained boxer, not just another schoolboy brawler – hadn't taught him how to finish the job.

My vision cleared in time to see him soft-shoe-shuffling forward again, his fists raised in classic style, and I backed up hastily – which got the crowd booing and jeering. He landed another blow to my head, but not quite as hard as the first. He reset his fighting stance and bobbed and weaved a bit more, planning his next assault – and I rushed him, not trying to do any punching myself but determined to simply get to grips, to nullify his obvious advantage.

I grappled his featherweight arse to the ground easily and got him in a headlock I'd practised a hundred times before in my jiu-jitsu class, and immediately wondered why the hell I hadn't just done that in the first place! I held him down until he conceded defeat, which meant that, technically, I'd won the fight. But somehow it didn't feel that way. After all, it was me who sported a black eye for a week afterwards, not scrawny Bob!

There were a couple of other clashes that went my way over the next few months but also a couple that didn't, and by the end of Standard Five my reputation had tarnished and faded considerably. I was no longer the joint-toughest boy in my year group; not even close.

I had learnt that it's better to be a blue-eyed boy than a black-eyed boy; also, although it sucks coming second in a 100m sprint, it sucks a whole helluva lot more coming second in a fight.

CHAPTER 15

Probably my best friend in my primary school days was one of the boys whose name has cropped up here already, but who I'm not going to identify any further from this point on, not even with just a first name, because he still lives in Benoni and might suffer some damage to his reputation even after all these years. He is, today, a highly placed company executive, a loving husband, father and grandfather; a good man and a successful one, a respectable pillar of society. Which, let me tell you, is nothing short of a miracle when you consider what fiendish little bastards me and him were in those early years.

Let's just call him X – unoriginal, I know, but it does the job.

Our friendship was built on trust: every school day, from about Standard Two through to the end of Standard Five, I trusted him to give me the chocolate-sprinkle sandwiches that his mother packed into his school lunch, and he did so without fail, because he wasn't that keen on them anyway.

Why didn't I have my own sandwiches? Well, I used to have a big, big breakfast before setting off in the morning and I'd have a big, big cooked lunch when I got back in the afternoon, and for the average boy that would have been enough. But Hungry Haggis was always able to squeeze in a couple of chocolate-sprinkle sandwiches for elevenses, and X was happy to oblige.

From the age of about 11 onwards we used to sleep over at each other's houses from time to time – mine in Morehill, his in Rynfield, the adjoining suburb – and we'd often camp out in the back yard. One of the advantages of that was that it was easy to slip out into the night as soon as the lights in the house went out and we knew our parents were safely asleep.

Remember my neighbour Derek? The guy with the brick wall? Well, he must have been the Nostradamus of the Highveld; a man who could see half a century into the future, to a time when Benoni would be blighted by crime and all of the houses would be protected by walls like his, and topped with razor wire or electric cables, with CCTV systems and video entry phones above every front door.

There was none of that stuff in the early Seventies. Many of the homes in the suburbs lay completely open and unprotected, with no boundary fence at all, or maybe just a half-height decorative wall that a couple of mischievous boys could leap over with ease.

Dressed all in black and wearing balaclavas like the Navy Seals we felt we were, we prowled the streets in the early hours of the morning, diving into hedgerows at the first hint of a car's headlights and communicating in stage whispers that were probably louder than if we'd just spoken normally – but it felt right!

We started with the basic stuff, a bit of Tok-Tokkie, just knocking on doors and then running off and laughing from the shadows as the befuddled homeowner came out onto his porch in his jim-jams, squinting into the darkness or occasionally shaking a fist and swearing. But that soon lost its novelty. We upped our game.

Many households used to have bottles of fresh milk delivered to the doorstep overnight and we'd help ourselves to a few of those as we passed down the street, usually sipping off the top layer of cream and then discarding the rest. At some point we began carrying a few eggs with us to lob at any especially clean and attractive home exteriors, or a couple of potatoes to ram into car exhaust pipes so they would struggle to start in the morning.

Occasionally we brought along an old tin can that we would pee into, filling it to the top before leaning it up very carefully against someone's front door and then knocking loudly and running off, turning back and watching from a safe distance as the can spilled its contents into the victim's entrance hall when he yanked his door open.

X knew a guy who had apparently taken this stunt to the next level: he'd find a moist dog turd and wrap it in newspaper before placing it on someone's doorstep and setting the paper alight; the thinking being that the homeowner would rush out and start stomping out the flames, with disgusting consequences. We talked about adding this trick to our repertoire but decided against it, because neither of us fancied the idea of carrying a moist dog turd around in our pockets for any length of time.

Also, it wasn't like we were short of other ideas. If a homeowner was still awake, with the lights on, we'd creep into his garden and locate the electrical fuse box on the exterior wall and flick the main switch off, imagining the confusion within as he was plunged into darkness. If the homeowner was already asleep we'd prowl around the garden at leisure, seeking out garden chairs and sun loungers and little marble statues and things and then gently, quietly, lifting them over the fence and placing them in strategic spots in the neighbour's garden. Anything we deemed to be of value, like a good-quality football, we'd carry off with us, stashing it under a nearby hedge so we could collect it and take it home at the end of the night's festivities.

A block of flats near my house called Morehill Gardens was one of our favourite haunts, with long corridors offering multiple easy targets. If we got there early enough, before the milkman had done his rounds, we'd help ourselves to the coins the various residents had left out in their empty bottles as payment for the next delivery; if we were too late, we'd collect as many of the freshly delivered bottles as we could carry and stack them all outside one particular door.

Some nights we'd take along an old piece of rope and tie the handles of two adjoining front doors together, leaving maybe

10 or 12 inches of play in the rope. We'd knock on both doors and then stand back and watch as one of them was pulled open by the occupant within – only to be slammed shut a moment later by the second flatowner tugging *his* door open. The scheme actually worked that way only one time in five, at most, but the anticipation and the planning of it was a lot of fun.

Most of the houses with the half-height decorative front walls also had wrought-iron gates at the top of the driveways. These could easily be lifted free and swapped with a similar set of gates next-door, to create a little confusion the following morning. Most also had a postbox mounted on the wall somewhere, some shaped like miniature houses, or little animals, and these too could be pulled free and repositioned somewhere farther up the road.

Some still had letters inside them that the homeowner hadn't gotten around to collecting that day, so we did the job for him, carrying them off to a safe spot and ripping them open in the hope of finding a bit of money inside that someone had sent as a birthday gift. We flipped through literally hundreds of electricity bills, and traffic fines, and lawyer's letters and one time even the Benoni mayor's new passport – which presumably the poor guy was waiting on to allow him to make an important trip overseas somewhere – but I don't recall ever actually finding any hard cash. Didn't stop us trying though.

One of the back gardens we crept into one dark night had a trampoline, and I remember the two of us bouncing up and down on it for several minutes, doing somersaults and back flips while trying to stifle our laughter, until suddenly the house lights came on and a door flew open and a big guy came charging out with what looked like a rifle in his hands. We ran like the wind. I was, after all, a reasonably good sprinter. X was too.

On another night we found half a dozen kayaks lined up alongside a family swimming pool, so we eased a couple of them into the pool and paddled around silently for a bit. At one point X manoeuvred back to the side and climbed out, and I was about to do the same when he gave my kayak a shove, back out into the middle of the pool— and then started whacking the water with his paddle, loudly, snorting with laughter all the while, which of course woke the homeowner. I paddled frantically back to the side of the pool just as the lights in the house came on and someone gave an angry shout from an upstairs window. Again, we ran like the wind.

Camping out in the back yard requires a campfire, of course, and at X's house it was sometimes a bit of a problem finding enough firewood. Not so when we slept over at my house: within the forbidden zone of the veld across the road, among the sinkholes and concrete-capped mineshafts, was that grove of huge pine trees which I mentioned earlier, and which every year produced hundreds of freakishly large cones, some the size of a rugby ball.

We'd slip through the hole in the fence I'd made – which, by the way, had to be maintained and re-cut every couple of months whenever the Council sent someone around to repair it – and we'd load up a couple dozen of the cones at a time into plastic shopping bags and carry them home. They burnt well, better than any shop-bought charcoal, but the day came eventually when we'd collected them all, along with every last dry branch or twig we'd been able to find as we foraged across the veld. With the campfire burning perilously low one night, we were forced to consider other options.

We didn't have to look too far: the Council had planted healthy young saplings all along the verges of Barbara Avenue, and the surrounding streets too, doubtless imagining a future in which the residents of Morehill would one day amble along under shady, tree-lined boulevards. The saplings themselves, still green and tender, were obviously no good as firewood but each one was held in place by a sturdy, 6ft stake that had been soaked in creosote to fend off pests ... which would have done an excellent job under normal circumstances, but the Council obviously hadn't considered the impact of human pests such as me and X.

We started with the one planted directly outside my house. Sapling and stake were bound together with nothing more than a thin, coarse rope, we discovered, so we trotted back indoors and fetched the good breadknife from the kitchen, and a small gardening trowel in case we needed to do any digging.

It proved to be a ridiculously easy operation. We sawed through the rope within a few seconds, and the soil, not yet compacted, gave up the stake after just a few hard tugs – no trowel necessary, it turned out – and we carried it around the side of the house and fed it directly into the struggling campfire.

Instant success. In fact, I'd go so far as to say that it burned like a bastard! The creosote gave off an unnaturally bright flame, along with a deeply satisfying aroma that, decades later, I believe I would recognise in a heartbeat! Over the course of a few short months we systematically uprooted every stake we could find along the surrounding streets, giving us a whole series of unnaturally bright campfires that lit up the entire back yard, with that heady scent infusing the air on many a night, all across the suburb.

Again, I direct your attention to Google Streetview. Call it up on your computer and zero in on Morehill, Benoni. Take a virtual drive down Barbara Avenue and stop when you get to the grey driveway leading into Number 23. Take a look at that first tree we targeted, on the verge directly outside my old house, and you'll see that it appears to have started out very promisingly, the trunk growing straight and true for the first three feet or so ... before suddenly taking a definite, drunken tilt to one side. Almost as if, 50-odd years ago, the stake that was holding it upright was cruelly ripped away, leaving the sapling to grow at any old angle it wanted to from that point on.

I like to think that, like my father before me, I've left my mark on Morehill in some small way...

From time to time X and I were hotly pursued by angry homeowners and we came close to getting caught more than once, but somehow we always managed to give them the slip, either by diving out of sight under a nearby bush or running directly into the veld and into the forbidden zone, where no sane adult would follow after dark. Eventually, though, our luck ran out and we did get caught – and through an embarrassing, rookie-level error too.

We were camping out in X's back yard on the night in question and his little brother, two years younger than us, had decided to join us in the tent. We followed the usual routines, waiting till his parents were asleep, shushing the family dog as we tip-toed around the side of the house and then emerging on to the silent street and looking around to make sure the coast was clear. I can't recall the exact route we took that night, or which houses we targeted along the way, but at some point we found ourselves up at the corner of Davidson Street and Pretoria Road. By day this was a busy intersection, with a constant stream of traffic in both directions, but by 1am it was absolutely quiet, with not a vehicle in sight.

There was a public telephone on the corner – a tickey box, as it was known, because in the early days you used a tickey coin to make a call – and the three of us crowded into the cubicle, jockeying for position to see who would get to make the first prank call.

I picked up the handset and dialled a couple of numbers at random. X produced a piece of wire from somewhere and began threading it into the coin slot, hoping to dislodge a couple of 5 cent pieces that might somehow have gotten stuck up there. His little brother began trying to grab the wire; X told him to wait his turn; I began spinning some unlikely tale to whoever had just picked up the phone at the other end of the line ... all of which meant that we were so distracted that we didn't notice a van pulling up on the side of the road, just a couple of yards away. A police van.

The officer jumped out and shouted at us to stay right where we were, to not even think about running – which is exactly what we would have done if it had been just me and X on our own, but with his little brother in tow there was no chance of escape. The cop lined us up in front of the tickey box and stared at us for a moment, trying to assess what exactly he was dealing with.

"What are you doing?" he demanded.

"Calling home," I said confidently. "To get my dad to pick us up."

"At one in the morning? Where you coming from?"

"Ah! Well! Um ..."

X was standing with his hands in his jacket pockets, and one side had a bit of a bulge to it, almost as if he was holding some kind of concealed weapon in there. The officer, suddenly wary, backed up a step and pointed. "What's that in your pocket boy?" he barked, his hand straying towards his holstered gun.

X paused a second, then he withdrew his hand reluctantly and showed him. "Egg," he said with a faltering smile. "Just an egg, sir."

At which point the officer grabbed the two of us by the scruff of the neck and frogmarched us around to the back of the van and flung open the door. "Get in," he ordered. "You too," he said, pointing to X's little brother, who already appeared to be on the point of tears. "What's your address? Where do you live?"

X told him. It wasn't like he had a choice.

It should have been a five-minute ride back home, but the cop had obviously decided to teach us a lesson, because he took the long way around. For 10 minutes or more he raced that yellow police van up and down the streets of Rynfield, accelerating and then suddenly braking hard, throwing the three of us up against the cold and unyielding metal sides, then spinning into a left turn, and a right, flinging us from one side to the other, causing us to bang our heads and our knees and our elbows painfully.

We finally slowed down and came to a stop and I pressed my face up against the metal grille that passed for a window. We were in the driveway. The officer left the engine running and the van's headlights on bright, pointing into what I knew to be X's parents' bedroom. He banged on the front door, and it was yanked open a minute later.

X's father was a big guy, I remember, and a forbidding one at the best of times. The sight of him standing there in his bare feet, wearing just a pair of baggy, white Y-fronts as he squinted into the light and tried to flick the hair out of his eyes should have been a comical one ... but, believe me, it wasn't. I was scared, and I could tell X was too.

The officer explained the situation, then he returned to the van and opened the back door. "Out!" he said. We complied – though, judging from the thunderous expression on X's father's face, I was wondering if it might be the safer option just staying in the back of that police van for the rest of the night.

Little brother was sent straight to his bedroom but me and X were shoved down in a couple of chairs in the lounge. His father never laid a finger on me but he laid into X, verbally and physically, lashing out with his big hands and even a foot at one point as he stalked him around and around that chair for what seemed an eternity. X, pale in the face, his eyes fixed firmly on a spot somewhere on the carpet and his hands clenched in his lap, endured it all without a sound. Brave kid.

His mother phoned my mother first thing in the morning to tell her what had happened, and to say I'd be arriving home a little ahead of schedule and in disgrace.

I made the long walk back to my house in a state of

mounting trepidation, dragging my feet as I turned the last corner into Barbara Ave. Dead Man Walking. When I reached the house I slipped around the side to Christine's bedroom window and tapped on it lightly, thinking she could give me the lay of the land; let me know just how pissed off my parents were and what kind of punishment awaited me – but it was my mother's voice that rang out from within: "The back door's open, *Gavin!*" she said in chilly tones. I let myself in, braced for the worst.

This being a Saturday morning my parents were getting ready for the usual trip to the bank and the shopping centre and so on. They said not a word to me, and neither did Christine or Graham. I retreated to my room and sat on the bed, miserable and apprehensive.

When they were ready to leave, about ten minutes later, my mother popped her head around the door and said: "Get in the car. You're coming with us."

I blinked. "Shopping? But -"

"Dad and I are going shopping. You're going to the police station. We have to drop you off on the way. You're being charged."

My blood turned to ice. "What? Charged? But – but…"

She refused to elaborate. I climbed into the back seat of the car, my stomach churning. We made the journey in complete silence, my father driving in his usual slow and methodical manner. We reached the town centre and the intersection where he should have made a left turn, but he carried on going, steering straight ahead.

"Isn't that …" I began, pointing towards the police station sliding by – at which point my mother threw her head back and burst out guffawing and hee-hawing. It had all been a hoax! Turned out she wasn't angry at all; quite the opposite, in fact, she thought the whole thing was a bit of a hoot!

I joined in with a shaky laugh of my own, and we carried on towards the bank, and on to the shopping centre after that – and the police matter was never mentioned again.

I was massively relieved, of course, but looking back today I have to wonder about the blurred lines that were being drawn in the Weir household. Dare to speak your mind and you get a slap in the face; get arrested at 1am for trying to break into a phone box and you're A-OK. How's a boy to know right from wrong?

That's my excuse, anyway, and I'm sticking to it …

CHAPTER 16

Which brings us rather neatly to the next topic: shoplifting. Graham started the trend, surprising the whole family with a veritable bounty of presents one Christmas Day, all of them suspiciously expensive and well outside the reach of a teenager on a pocket-money budget. He would have been 15 at the time; I was 12.

I remember tearing off the wrapping paper on the crudely wrapped gift with my name on it and pulling out … a shirt? A colourful, striped T-shirt? Puzzled, I tried it on, and it proved to be a couple of sizes too small for me, but I was very grateful nonetheless, because that was the first time he'd ever bought me a present, and I certainly hadn't bought one for him.

I don't recall what exactly it was he gave the rest of the family, but I do remember a general air of wonderment around the Christmas tree as the gifts were opened. Such generosity! How long had he been saving his pennies for this? Wow!

Except he hadn't been saving any pennies at all; he'd shoplifted each and every one of those presents, and he showed me his technique on a breezy autumn morning a few months later. We walked over to the Northmead Mall, taking the shortcut through the forbidden zone, of course – which gave me the chance to show off *my* technique; how to re-cut a hole in a wire fence that had been repaired by some amateur down at the Council – and then he led the way into the CNA store.

Like any good newsagent, the back wall was lined with hundreds of books and magazines and newspapers. He ambled over in that direction and I followed. He scanned the racks of music magazines and selected one that had a picture on the front of Marc Bolan, the T-Rex singer, his idol at the time. I lined up alongside him and found one with an image of Slade, my favourite band.

Graham flipped through a couple of pages before appearing to lose interest, then he started scanning the other magazines on the rack, but without replacing the Marc Bolan one. After a casual look around him, he rolled it into a tight tube and eased it up the sleeve of his duffel coat, then he looked at me. "You too," he said.

I felt the blood pounding in my gut and my breathing grow very shallow as I followed suit. I rolled up my Slade magazine and slid it out of sight. A moment later we headed for the exit.

We must have looked sooo suspicious; two boys wearing duffel coats on the mildest of autumn days, the younger one with his face flushed red and his eyes darting nervously around him, the older one whistling nonchalantly as if he had not a care in the world … but somehow, astonishingly, nobody noticed us. There were no security cameras in the stores back then, and no security guards either.

We walked right past the lady at the till while she was busy serving a customer and out into the mall itself, and when we reached the absolute safety of the forbidden zone I began laughing and shouting with relief and exhilaration. What a rush of adrenaline – I was hooked! Graham looked pretty pleased with himself too, and we compared our magazines and chatted excitedly all the way home.

It was probably the best bonding experience we ever shared as brothers.

I visited that CNA store several times a week in the months that followed, surely becoming its most frequent but probably not its best customer, on account of I never actually bought anything. Graham and I shared a bedroom in those days, and I plastered the walls on my side with dozens of stolen centrefold images of Slade and Leo Sayer and Suzi Quatro, all harvested from the many music magazines that populated the shelves. Graham did the same on his side of the room, covering every square inch with the face of Marc Bolan and Ian Anderson of Jethro Tull. Our parents never asked how exactly we were able to afford to buy so many magazines.

When the walls were full we papered over the entire ceiling, and then the back of the door and even the cupboard doors, inside and out – but as satisfying as all that was, food was still my most powerful motivator in those days, and it wasn't long before I turned my newfound talents in that direction.

Walk into a supermarket these days and pick up a packet of jelly, and you'll get a slab of gel-like cubes that you dissolve in hot water and which you then pour into a mould to set. Boring! Back in the Seventies they were still selling it in powder form; little cardboard boxes filled with artificially coloured and flavoured sugar that could be eaten raw, spoonful by delicious spoonful – or, if you were a dopamine-starved little animal like me, you could simply tear off a corner with your teeth and chug it directly into your mouth, a box at a time. Absolute heaven! All hail Moir's! Praise be to Trotter's!

The boxes were maybe an inch thick, three inches wide and five inches long, which made them a bit awkward to slide up your sleeve. You couldn't fit more than one at a time in your pocket either, not without creating a suspicious bulge ... but like those ancient tribes who were committed to using every part of any animal they hunted, I was willing to use every part of my duffel coat on my foraging expeditions, and that included the gaps between the silky inner lining and the rough outer material.

With that in mind, I visited my parents' en suite bathroom one day and removed the blade from my father's shaving razor, and I used it to part the lining from the outer material along the top right-hand side, stitch by stitch, for perhaps four inches. Just wide enough to get a box of jelly in there.

I did a couple of dummy runs at home using a packet of my father's Ransom cigarettes, and the system worked perfectly. The packet fell directly to the bottom of the duffel coat and stayed there between the layers of fabric, completely invisible to the casual observer. I stuffed a few other items down the slit as well to gauge how much I could carry on any single trip and the answer was: quite a lot, but not too much, because there came a point at which the bottom of the coat developed an unnatural swaying motion which I could see clearly as I practised my casual walk back and forward in front of my parents' big bedroom mirror.

So no more than four packets of jelly on a single trip to the Checkers supermarket at the Northmead Mall, I decided.

I would launch Mission Imperceptible first thing in the morning.

I awoke the next day to agitated sounds coming from my parent's bathroom: my father had gotten halfway through his usual morning shave before he noticed that there was no blade in his razor holder, and that all he had been doing for a couple of minutes was to lather up a faceful of foam and then wipe it away again with the blunt edge of the holder. Not terribly effective.

"What the …?" I heard him say, and then: "Eh? Where's the blade?", and then, after the briefest of pauses: "Gavin! Wee swine! GAVIN!"

He came stomping into my bedroom, pointing an accusing finger at me as I propped myself up sleepily on one elbow. "Where's my bloody razor?" he demanded, then he spotted it on the bedside table where I'd left it the day before, fully intending to return it until I'd been distracted by the smell of dinner. "There!" He snatched it up, giving himself a little nick on the thumb in his haste. "Why's it here? What were you doing with it?"

I opened my mouth to reply but he said: "Wait! I don't want to know!" and turned on his heel and stomped out again. Tetchy guy!

I felt a thrill of anticipation as I pulled on my duffel coat that morning; a rather pleasant, butterflies-in-the-stomach sensation. As I crossed the forbidden zone, chewing on a piece of grass, I was already envisaging that sweet, sweet taste of jelly powder on my tongue. Raspberry or lime, I wondered? Greengage or lemon? Blackcurrent or strawberry? So many flavours, so little time.

I walked boldly into Checkers and headed straight for the aisle where they kept the good stuff. Staff members appeared to be few and far between, and the couple I did encounter showed no interest at all in the skinny boy in the big coat ghosting past them. I'd intended to take just one box of jelly powder on this, my first run, but I picked up a second on the spur of the moment, and both disappeared without trace into the slit in the coat lining, then I turned and headed back the way I'd come.

Just a few minutes later I was reclining against one of the giant pine trees in the middle of the forbidden zone, my head tipped back to the skies and my eyes closed in reverential bliss as I emptied the contents of a Moir's greengage box directly into my yawning maw. Yeah baby yeah!

Mission Imperceptible had been an absolute, unqualified, smash-hit success, and I was eager to spread the gospel to X and my other friends, to win them over to the Way of The Duffel Coat. I don't recall if X ever invested in his own slit-lining coat, but the truth is he didn't need one, because he operated more on the principle that if you looked confident enough in what you were doing, no one would challenge you, no matter how nefarious your purpose – and it always seemed to work.

Example: I remember us walking through the Northmead Mall one day, doubtless planning to commit some fresh atrocity, when we drew alongside that same Checkers store and X paused in mid-conversation and said: "Hang on Gav, just going to grab a Coke – you want one?" He strode over to the fridges lined up along the wall, maybe 20 feet inside the store, helped himself to a couple of cans, and walked out again without even bothering to look around him to see if anyone was watching.

He handed me one and cracked open the other and drank deep, then he went straight back to talking about whatever it was we'd been talking about a moment earlier, and we carried on along our way. Brazen, man!

I did, however, have two very willing apprentices in the dark art of shoplifting: Stephen and Graeme J, a pair of brothers who had moved into a house down the road from mine a few months earlier. Like so many of the families in the area they were recent immigrants, from England, in their case.

Stephen was a year younger than me and Graeme was two years younger than him, and it helped that each of them already had a duffel coat and a set of morals every bit as questionable as my own. Graeme, in fact, would go on to star in his very own episode of *Police File* several years later – South African television's equivalent of *Crimewatch* – with the presenter warning the public not to approach so dangerous a character, who was wanted on a bunch of outstanding warrants.

I remember staring open-mouthed and shocked at the TV screen that night: was I responsible, I wondered? Had I put him on that path? Was this where the Way of the Duffel Coat led, if followed with blind allegiance? I really hope not.

In my defence, there were quite a few other factors that were already propelling young Graeme towards a life of crime, not least of which was the fact that his older brother Stephen was one of those natural-born psychos I described right at the start of this story, and he made life very, very difficult for him.

Also, it was Graeme, not me, who suggested one day as we joined a long queue of boys waiting outside the local barber shop for the usual end-of-school-holidays haircut that we do the job ourselves, and instead spend the cash our mothers had given us on a couple of sausage rolls from the bakery around the corner. That plan ended badly, of course, because although the sausage rolls were perfection itself, the haircuts we gave each other were not, featuring misaligned sideburns, multiple rat-bites and hopelessly skew fringes – partly because we used an old and blunt pair of scissors; my mother's good pair having vanished mysteriously a few weeks earlier. Something to do with somebody cutting a hole in the forbidden-zone fence.

Stephen had a vicious temper and he believed that Graeme should be struck regularly, like a gong (to misquote Noel Coward) – and their father, weirdly, did nothing at all to discourage him. Quite the opposite. I remember one time the brothers were playing over at my house when they started arguing about something. Stephen, who would have been 11 at the time, got Graeme, 9, down on the ground and began punching him in the head.

I dragged him off, but that savage light was still in his eyes and I could see him weighing up the situation for a split second, coldly assessing, calculating, wondering briefly if he could take me on – and then deciding against it, because he'd lost the fight the last time he tried that. The savage light dimmed and sanity was restored, for the moment at least, and he marched off instead back to his house – but not before warning Graeme that he'd be picking up later where he'd left off.

Graeme was too scared to go home that day. He hung around for hours afterwards until eventually I said I'd walk back with him and deliver him safely to his front door. "Tha won't stop im, Gav," he said shakily. The J brothers hailed from Newcastle, and both of them still had the broadest of Geordie accents. "Ee's mad as ell."

"You'll be fine," I said. But he wasn't, not at all. When I knocked on that front door it opened to reveal Stephen, still white in the face with suppressed rage all those hours later, with his father alongside him, looking equally pissed off.

"Hello Mr J ... " I started saying, but he ignored me, turning instead to his elder son and giving him a nod – at which point Stephen flew forward, fists windmilling, and began beating the shit out of Graeme all over again. I tried to intervene but Mr J shouted at me to leave it, to back off, to get off his property.

I was appalled. Aspiring juvenile delinquent that I was, I had never seen anything like that before – an adult goading one son on to batter the other!

And that wasn't the last such incident: a few months later the three of us were playing together again, this time in their back garden, when another ruckus developed. Graeme managed to break free and run back inside the house and lock himself in his bedroom, but Stephen fetched a golf club from the garage and smashed out the big picture window and climbed through into the room and laid into his little brother with the same club, stopping only when his mother appeared from somewhere to drag him off. Savage.

Some time after that me and my badminton buddy Shaun were over at Stephen's house when things turned nasty yet again. He got into a lot of fights, Stephen did. I can't remember how this particular one started, but I do remember how it ended: with Stephen fetching his father's gun and pointing it directly at Shaun's forehead from a distance of maybe four feet. His hand was rock steady.

Shaun gave a mocking laugh and said: "You wouldn't dare."

Stephen cocked the gun and that savage light dawned in his

eyes and I knew with absolute certainty that Shaun had maybe two seconds to live if he didn't back down. I grabbed him by the shoulder and pulled him away urgently and we hurried off up the street. Crazy bastardo would have pulled that trigger, of that I have no doubt.

Both Stephen and Graeme were fascinated by the idea of an endless supply of jelly powder and were impatient to see how the duffel coat thing worked, so I took them along to the Checkers store one morning for a quick crash course. I went through the usual routine, picking up four different boxes as if trying to decide which ones to buy, but replacing only two of them, with the two others going into the slit in the lining.

Graeme began giggling uncontrollably at one point, which may have been what attracted the attention of one of the shop workers – who swooped on us as we rounded the last aisle on the way to the exit. "Stop! I've been watching you boys!" she announced in a loud voice, grabbing Stephen by the arm. "What've you got in your pockets? Turn them out – right now!"

She patted down Stephen, then Graeme, then me – but of course none of us had anything at all in our pockets that we shouldn't have had, and it simply didn't occur to her to check down near the hems of my duffel coat. With the three of us protesting our innocence she had no choice but to finally admit defeat and send us on our way: another success for Mission Imperceptible.

The brothers J cut slits into their own duffel coats the very same day, and profits at Checkers, from that day on, were just that tiny, tiny bit lower, for years to come.

CHAPTER 17

I'm not sure I believe in the concept of karma but I can tell you that I too suffered the effects of petty crime, albeit on a low level. Quite a few of my toys went missing over the years after visits from various childhood friends, the most highly prized of which was probably my collection of marbles. I kept them in an old Wilson's butterscotch sweets tin and they brought me joy even on rainy days when I couldn't venture outdoors, when I'd lovingly sort them into piles of matching colours and pop-eyes and goons and irons, sometimes playing them off as teams against each other or running convoluted experiments to see which ones ran fastest across the bedroom carpet.

I built that collection up over several months, shoplifting one small bag at a time from the Northmead Mall or earning them the old-fashioned way by playing against other boys on the Rynfield Primary playground during lunch breaks. When I came up against a superior player and lost my marbles, so to speak, I'd simply don my duffel coat the next afternoon and head over to the Northmead Mall for a top-up.

Some days I'd join the many boys setting up a "shya" in the hard and dusty soil against the side of one of the classrooms. This was a small pyramid of four marbles, or ten, or even 20, which the customer would try to knock down by tossing a single marble from a set distance: four paces away for a shya four; ten for a shya ten, and so on. If he succeeded he'd win all the marbles in the shya, if he missed he'd lose the one he'd thrown.

We'd compete for business like street hawkers, trying to lure the kids who were milling around, all of them carrying a sock bulging with marbles. I'd yell "Shya four, easy four!"; the kid next to me would shout "Shya ten, easy ten!". Every other week there'd be a fight when some kid scored a direct hit on a shya but, miraculously, it failed to break apart – because, it turned out, it had been glued together illegally, and with so much Bostik that it could only be separated with a stick of dynamite!

I remember one enterprising kid setting up a shya 100 one day, and he did a roaring trade because just about every last boy on the playground was determined to win that jackpot. Of course, the rules dictated that we had to stand so far away that we could barely see the kid, never mind his little pyramid, which meant that nobody got within ten feet of it.

I joined the line anyway and I gave it my best shot, but I aimed too high and my marble went whizzing through the air and clean through one of the classroom windows, not shattering it but leaving a perfect, bullet-shaped hole in the glass. My parents had to pay for a new windowpane (and sadly that wasn't the sort of thing they sold down at the Mall, and even if they did, it wouldn't have fitted down the lining of my coat).

Anyway, one day I went to look for my precious tin of marbles and discovered that it had vanished without trace. Stephen had come calling the day before, which made him the prime suspect, but I could never prove him culpable. The other suspect was Shaun F but, again, there was no proof.

Shaun, by the way, was a cunning lad with a real talent for thievery and I daren't leave any money lying around the house if he was coming over to play, because he didn't mind who he stole from. Many, many times I watched him open his father's wallet when no one was around and lift out a crisp ten rand note, and we would head over to the Northmead Mall and buy great quantities of Fizzerbars and Curliwurlies and Simba crisps and bottles of Coke and carry it all back to the forbidden zone. If it was the right time of year we'd buy dozens of packets of firecrackers and stage our own Guy Fawkes celebration, or set ourselves up in rival forts among the old mine shafts and lob lit thunder crackers at each other with a reckless disregard for safety.

Ten rand went an awfully long way in those days and we'd usually have a bit of cash left over. Neither of us could take it home obviously so we buried it in little plastic baggies at strategic spots among the pine trees or alongside the sinkholes ... and as often as not I'd slip back out there a day or two later and dig those baggies up again and either spend the money myself or re-bury it somewhere else. No honour among thieves.

I made one feeble attempt to compete with the light-fingered Shaun in this arena, starting small by taking a 20-cent coin from my mother's purse one day but, being Scottish, she noticed the shortfall immediately and crushed my soul by telling me, scathingly: "If you're going to be a thief, Gavin, be a clever one!" I never stole from her again.

Psycho Stephen didn't do much better. He showed up at my house one morning with a bunch of cash, and when he heard that it would be my birthday in a couple of days' time he insisted on buying me a present. We walked over to the family supermarket near the mall – the same one we'd been thrown out of a couple of months earlier for letting off a stinkbomb in the meat aisle – and he picked out a giant, rooster-shaped chocolate Easter egg for me. "Appy berthday Gav!" he said, handing it over with a flourish.

We took it back to my house and were munching away happily when his dear old grandmother arrived in a bit of a state: someone had been into her purse and taken all the money she had there, and that someone was, you guessed it, Stephen.

He adopted his usual tactic of outraged denial, but she was

wise to his ways and took him by the ear and led him out the house ... at which point he broke free and ran off down the road, after giving her a violent shove which sent her crashing to the ground, banging her head on the concrete pathway.

Problem kid. The only real surprise is that it was Graeme, not him, who ended up with his mugshot on *Police File*.

Sticking with the karma theme: anyone looking to prove that there is indeed such a thing might want to point to a disturbing incident that occurred sometime around my 12th birthday, again during the school holidays. X and I were out and about, cycling around Morehill somewhere, when I discovered that my front tyre had begun to deflate and that we would have to head back to my house to make an emergency repair.

We got the wheel off the frame and used a few spoons to lift up the side of the tyre and pull out the inner tube, then, as was customary, we plugged the family bathtub and turned on both taps – the thinking being that, if you held the tube under the water, you would be able to spot any tiny air bubbles appearing, thereby identifying the exact location of the puncture. Great idea – but when I fetched my puncture-repair kit from the garage I discovered that I'd used up the last of the rubber patches at some point, so we wouldn't be able to finish the job.

X said that wouldn't be a problem, because he had some at his house, so the two of us jumped aboard his bicycle, me balancing awkwardly on the frame, him pedalling bow-legged, and we headed off to Rynfield ... somehow, unfathomably, forgetting all about the two taps still gushing full-force into the bathtub!

Sadly, we didn't go straight to his house and back again directly afterwards; the situation might still have been salvageable if we had. Instead, we took time out for a bite to eat, then a swim in his pool, then we played a bit of chess – he usually won – and then finally, maybe three hours later, we saddled up and cycled back to my house.

I remember pausing at the back door, key in hand, and staring down at my feet. It was wet down there. Very wet. In fact, the whole courtyard area around the door was wet. Puzzled, I turned the key and opened the door – and a frickin tsunami came spilling out onto my shoes. X shouted: "The taps! We forgot the taps!", and the two of us ran inside, splashing through maybe two inches of water all the way, slipping and sliding as we raced for the bathroom to shut them off.

That was way too little, too late obviously. The whole house, a big three-bedroom, with ensuites and a sprawling lounge and dining-room and kitchen, was completely flooded. Both my parents were at work, as usual – but where the hell was Graham when you wanted him? Or Christine? Or the maid? Like just about every white South African family in those days we had a fulltime black maid but, for whatever reason, not even she had been at home that day to see what was happening and to stop it.

The result was that me and X spent the next couple of hours frantically sweeping as much of the water out the back door as we could, mopping it up with towels and wringing them out in the garden, opening all the windows to take advantage of whatever breeze might develop. I was down on my hands and knees using the iron to try to dry out the lounge carpets – the brand-new lounge carpets, I should add, which had been fitted barely a month earlier – when my mother arrived home from work and the screaming began. X made a hasty retreat.

The beds and most of the furniture survived the flood but the carpets were ruined, not just in the lounge but in all the bedrooms too, and all of them had to be ripped out. Worse still, the wooden parquet flooring underneath, swollen with moisture, expanded dramatically and heaved upwards in the days that followed, creating a series of wooden-block waves at least three feet high that undulated gracefully all the way across the lounge and dining-room and into the hallway.

My punishment was to spend the next three weekends picking those waves apart, one wooden block at a time, and carting the rubble out to a growing pile in the back yard. Miserable times, man.

I'd just about finished the job when a family friend by name of Eddie C, the father of Deon, one of the Protea Choir boys, dropped by one evening for a visit. He expressed surprise when he heard the cause of the disaster: the overflow outlet on the bathtub, he told my parents, should have been able to handle the water produced by the taps, even if both were running at full volume.

"Lemme take a look," he said, standing up and heading for the bathroom. He inspected the tub, removing the little metal grille that covered the overflow outlet, then he used a torch handed to him by my father to peer inside. "Ah! There's your problem," he said. "Stompies!"

"Eh?" said my father.

"Stompies. Cigarette butts. Someone's been shoving their cigarette butts down the overflow pipe. It's completely blocked. That's why the water spilled over the bathtub. That's why the house was flooded."

Bloody Graham!!! He'd taken up smoking at some point in the year before and had developed the habit of slipping into the bathroom to sneak a fag from time to time, pushing the stompies through the little metal grille of the overflow outlet rather than just flicking them out the bathroom window where they might be spotted by somebody.

He got a lengthy lecture from my parents, who were none too happy to learn that their talented son was risking his singing voice by smoking, and he got one from me too: I'd worked my fingers to the bone picking apart those stinking parquet blocks for three weekends, and by rights he should have been right there alongside me the whole time, doing penance too! Bastaaardooooo!

CHAPTER 18

There comes a point in any coming-of-age story when the author shares his treasured memories of that most exciting of times in a boy's life: young love. He writes of stolen kisses under a starry sky, passionate fumblings in a darkened cinema, love letters and secret meetings and so on. With this author, and for this story, it's going to be a tragically short chapter, I'm afraid, because young love was *not* one of the things that I was reasonably good at. Quite the opposite, in fact: I was reasonably shit at it, because to be a hit with attractive girls you need to believe you're an attractive boy, and I most definitely never felt that to be the case.

I can't say when exactly that all-pervading self-doubt set down its roots in my psyche, I only know that it's always been there, ever present, a constant but very unwelcome companion. Did it have its beginnings as far back as my first days on this earth, I wonder? When passing strangers might have smiled at my mother and peered down into the pram for a look at the new baby – skew-faced, remember, and bruised all over – and gotten a bit of a shock?

Did they rear back in horror at the sight of the little bastard grinning back up at them from the side of his head? Did they maybe make the Sign of the Cross and exclaim "Mother of God!" or "Abomination!" and wonder aloud if it might have been kinder to have just, you know, left little Gav out in the snow somewhere? Am I being a bit melodramatic?

Whatever the case, I grew up with an idea – nay, a firm belief, a deep-seated conviction – that I was a particularly ugly boy, and the first time I became aware that a girl was interested in me I had absolutely no clue why that might be the case, nor what I was expected do about it.

It happened in my Standard Five year at Rynfield Primary. I would have been 12 at the time. One of the teachers had come up with the idea of showing movies on a Friday afternoon in the school hall, rigging up a giant screen on the stage and renting a projector and titles such as *Smokey and the Bandit*, and *The Good, the Bad and the Ugly*, from a nearby outlet.

The scheme was a smash hit with the kids. We'd buy Cokes and crisps and Tex bars from the school tuck shop and settle in for a fantastic afternoon's entertainment, the girls shrieking during the scary bits, the boys laughing louder than necessary and making farting sounds during the sensitive moments. Good times, as long as that old hag Mrs Vosloo didn't show up halfway through and drag you back to the afternoon detention session that you'd skipped out on.

On one particular Friday I was standing at the back of the darkened hall with a bunch of my friends, enjoying the show, when a girl in my class stood up mid-movie and came walking across towards us with a weird smile on her face. Towards me, in fact.

"Hey Gavin," she said as she drew level. "Margie wants to know if you'd like to come over and sit with her."

Eh? What?

"Do you want to sit next to Margie? For the movie?" she repeated.

It felt like every eye in the hall was suddenly on me. Certainly, my friends were all staring, and grinning, and so too were Margie's friends over on the other side. She herself was looking fixedly at the movie screen, apparently oblivious to what was going on. Margie S, I should add, was without doubt the prettiest girl in the school – long blonde hair, slim and stylish, one of the cool kids – and, yes, I already had a huge crush on her ... but, jeez, I'd never contemplated actually doing anything about it! Nor had I dreamt she would make any kind of move herself – on me! That was the stuff of dreams, not reality.

I gulped. The girl raised an eyebrow. Reggie L gave me a dig in the ribs. "Go!" he said. But one of my other buddies, Bruce A, barked out a laugh at that point – and the thought crossed my mind that this was a joke. A cruel hoax. Margie *obviously* wasn't interested in me. Couldn't be. No way, Jose.

"Well?" the girl asked. "Are you –"

"No," I said.

She looked a bit surprised but she had her answer, so she turned and headed back across the hall.

Reggie whispered urgently: "Gav! Call her back. Go on – quick!" A couple of the other guys said similar things. Bruce laughed again.

Someone gave me a shove, and I took a half step forward but then stopped, because the moment had passed. The friend was already sitting down again next to Margie and whispering in her ear. Margie glanced back at me briefly then tilted her chin up a little and looked back at the screen again, probably hurt and more than a little embarrassed, and wondering how'd she'd misread all those surreptitious glances she must have caught me casting her way in the weeks and months beforehand.

And just like that I'd messed up the biggest break of my life to that point. Caught off guard. Hopelessly unprepared. Chicken-shit, man, frickin-chicken-shit!

Many long and miserable nights followed thereafter with me lying in bed staring up at the ceiling, reliving that moment in my mind, over and over again, wondering how things might have played out if I'd been just a little more confident, a little less concerned with what everyone was thinking, a little less inclined to doubt myself.

We had a school trip planned a couple of weeks later to a nearby pleasure resort called The Rocks, and I decided I would use that outing to try to redeem myself. We'd been on one of those trips every year since Standard Two, and they were usually a lot of fun. The pupils would each pack a bag with enough T-shirts and toiletries for a weekend and we'd spend the days swimming and playing organised games and competitions, or splashing around in a nearby stream and searching for iguanas (which thankfully we never found). At night we'd cluster around the braaivleis fires and tell tall tales or swim some more, and then head back to our sleeping bags on bunk beds in a couple of dormitories. Inevitably, a bunch of guys would sneak out again after lights-out and get up to no good, knocking on the windows of the girls' dorms or gumming up the eyelids of the younger boys with lines of toothpaste while they slept, that sort of thing.

By Standard Five most of the girls and boys were pairing up in advance of the trip, innocent romances that were mostly short-lived but no less exciting for all that. I plucked up the courage to send Bruce along to ask Margie if she'd like to sit alongside me on the school bus on the way to The Rocks ... but it turned out she didn't. She and Michael V were now a thing, apparently.

That last trip to The Rocks wasn't fun at all because I had to watch Margie and Michael snuggling up to each other around the fire on the Saturday night. All my buddies seemed to have found dates too, and I was the only one standing at the braai holding a Coke rather than a girl's hand.

At some point I trudged back to the communal hall where the younger kids were watching a movie and I found a seat by myself at the back. Halfway through, one of the girls from my class appeared and asked me if I wanted to join Jennifer B at the side of the fire. I shrugged and said okay and followed her back to the campfire.

Jennifer B was a nice enough girl, and I held her hand for a bit, but my heart wasn't in it. She wasn't Margie S.

I spent a couple of months just moping around, building

solitary campfires in my back yard at night and staring moodily into the flames, listening to radio shows that had once brought me joy but which now seemed a bit dull. Some days after school I'd walk the mile or so to Margie's house, passing back and forward in front of it and pretending to look for something I'd lost on the pavement, hoping that she'd glance out the window maybe, and come outside and ask if she could help me find whatever it was. Something like that. Anything like that.

Margie and Michael broke up at some point – he was a momma's boy, she said, which filled me with renewed hope, because I was most certainly not a momma's boy! – but sadly that didn't mean her interest in me was rekindled in any way.

I moped some more. And then a bit more too. Eventually, however, I roused myself from my depression and I started looking around at the other girls in Standard Five, and I noticed Wendy L for the first time. She was reasonably pretty – not in Margie's league, of course – but with a mop of curly dark hair that she used to toss around in a certain way that caught my eye. Not literally. I don't mean that she flicked her hair one day and I was standing close by and it went in my eye. No.

What I'm saying is that I became aware again that there were actually quite a few pretty girls at Rynfield Primary, and that there might indeed be life after Margie … but any slim notion I had that I might be able to make an impact on any one of them was nipped in the bud right away, and in a spectacularly cruel fashion. How? I'll explain – and let's see if you can make any sense of it. I still can't, all these years later.

Me and my classmates had filed into Mr van Papendorp's room after lunch break one day and were busy finding our seats when a girl called Caroline B suddenly stepped up to me and said, right into my face: "Do you like Wendy?"

"Yes!" I answered instantly, remembering all too well how I'd messed things up before, and determined never to repeat that mistake, never to show any kind of hesitancy, not ever again. "Yes, I do!"

"Well, she hates your guts," Caroline replied with a triumphant smile, spinning on her heel and marching away.

Eh? What? What the hell was that all about, I wondered? I opened my mouth to ask the question but Caroline was already halfway back to her desk. I stared around me, absolutely stunned.

To this day, I'm not quite sure what to make of that incident; why Wendy L would want to do such a thing, or why Caroline agreed to do it for her. I had no history with either of them, good or bad, so ... why? All I know for sure is that that sentence, delivered with such vicious delight, snuffed out completely any teeny-tiny, flickering flame of inner self-belief that might have been breathed into life by Margie's overture on that Friday afternoon in the school hall. *Of course* Wendy hated my guts, I reasoned later – she had eyes, right? She wasn't stupid. She could *see* what an ugly boy I was.

How dumb I had been to dare to think otherwise. What an idiot. What a thick, ugly idiot.

CHAPTER 19

My academic record at Rynfield Primary was, as I said earlier, a chequered one, and with increasingly more black squares than white ones as the years went by. There was one area of schoolwork though in which I was uniformly crap right from the very start, in every way and in every manifestation of the subject, without any exception at all, and that was Arts and Crafts. The first example I can remember dates all the way back to Grade Two, when I was seven years old, with the teacher revealing to the class one day that we'd be learning to knit. She told us all to bring in a couple of knitting needles and a ball of wool the next day, and she showed us how to knit, purl, loop, repeat – something like that – with the idea being that we'd create some lovely scarves for our mothers. Sounded wonderful, and some of the children's creations proved to be genuine little marvels; six-foot long and cuddly, some even with coloured stripes and woolly bobbles on the ends.

Mine was a dismal flop because I'd gotten the instructions wrong. I was beavering away as earnestly as anyone else but was somehow adding a knit or a loop or a purl or something to each row I completed – meaning that my scarf slowly but surely grew into a weird pyramid shape. By the time it was a foot long it was also two foot wide; by the two-foot mark it was almost four-foot wide and I'd used up six times as much wool as everyone else, despite the multiple gaping holes and missed stitches that were visible all along the way. Hopeless. It went in the bin.

◆ ◆ ◆

Fast forward to Standard Three, when we were shown an ingenious and inexpensive way to make a light shade. Each of us had to bring an inflatable beach ball into class, along with several balls of thick string, a bottle of fabric glue, and a bit of paint for the finishing touches. The plan was to wrap the string around the ball, over and over again, leaving a round hole at the bottom for easy access later, before coating the whole thing with the glue and putting it aside to harden before painting. We would then deflate the beach ball and extract it carefully, leaving behind a slightly bohemian, perfectly spherical light shade. Voila!

Which worked fine for all the kids except me, because when my mother had given me the money to go and buy all that stuff I'd opted for a plastic football rather than an inflatable beach ball; the thinking being that me and my friends could have a bit of a kick-around in the playground before I started work on the project.

Of course, a football is a hell of a lot smaller than an inflatable beach ball, which meant that my light shade turned out to be barely half the size of everyone else's; a dwarf, a minimus, a bead, to quote that Shakespeare chappie, even after I'd triple-wrapped it in string.

More importantly, I discovered on the final day, when we had to present our masterpieces to the teacher for marking, that I was unable to extract the football from within because it simply refused to deflate to anything like the tiny circumference required to squeeze it out the bottom, no matter how vehemently and frantically I stabbed it with a pin, and then with a pen, and then with a pair of scissors.

I'd created western civilisation's most perfectly useless object: a football that couldn't be kicked, within a light shade that couldn't hold a light. Nul points. Hopeless. It went in the bin.

Next up was the sugar scoop. It was a simple structure, just an old tin can with half of one side cut away to create a hollow within, and a little handle soldered onto the back. Unfortunately, I was a day behind all the other kids in the class on this project because I'd forgotten to bring in a can on the first day, as instructed, and the nitpicky teacher was of the opinion that the old Coke tin I'd found in the trash outside the classroom moments earlier was too lightweight to be suitable. Such a pessimist.

I did remember to bring in a proper can on the second day but of course I was playing catch-up from that point on and I can only assume that I missed an important step towards the end somewhere, the bit where we painted our newly forged sugar scoops. Mine somehow, miraculously, ended up looking pretty much like anybody else's, but it had a hidden flaw that revealed itself only in the weeks and months that followed: the alluring metallic blue paint I'd used began peeling off, depositing ever-larger shards of alluring metallic blue paint in the family sugar bowl that really didn't taste so great when they ended up in a cup of tea. Hopeless. It went in the bin.

Next came the breakfast tray, and this was a big success in my book, if not the teacher's, because although the handles on mine had somehow been screwed on upside-down, and the wooden frame had been left un-sanded – meaning you'd get a splinter in your right-hand pinkie if you didn't pick it up very carefully – it did at least provide a couple of weeks' service in the Weir household before the bottom fell out unexpectedly one morning and it too ended in the bin.

The teacher was Mr Kruger, a muscled but miserable man who used to manoeuvre himself around the classroom on a pair of crutches while chain-smoking Rothmans cigarettes from the start to the end of every lesson. The story was that he'd been a talented trampolinist in his youth with dreams of earning his Springbok colours, until the day he mistimed his triple-loop-de-loop jump and landed on his head, not on the trampoline but on the floor alongside it. The door swung closed on a career in athletics and he found himself instead serving out a life sentence of demonstrating to bored schoolboys how to wield handsaws and drills and sanding blocks; tools that were, to me at least, the son of Andrew Weir, completely alien technology. He was a bit bitter, and no wonder.

He despised me personally. Couldn't hide it. Didn't even try. I can still remember the contempt in his voice as he attempted one day to explain the difference between a drill bit and a drill chuck, and looked up to see me staring at him uncomprehendingly.

"Clear as mud, Weir?" he asked.

"Sir?" It was the first time I'd ever heard that expression.

"Ja. Clear as blerry mud," he confirmed to himself. He shook his head. Bitterly. His eyes narrowed. Bitterly. He set his mouth in a tight line. Bitterly. He took another drag on his Rothmans and tilted his head back and expelled the smoke towards the ceiling. So very bitterly.

The only surprise, really, was that I got a "D" for my tray on marking day, which was a step up from my usual "E" or outright fail. That was, in fact, the zenith of my Arts and Crafts career to that point.

Moving on to Standard Five: about halfway through the year we had the chance to express our creativity by building a matchstick fort, and some of the boys really went to town on this one, crafting intricate motte-and-bailey castles on a big hardboard base, with the palisades made up of hundreds of used matchsticks, the tips burnt and blackened to sharp points. A few of the kids went still further, adding blue-painted plasticine moats and even working drawbridges, and flagpoles and toy soldiers.

Remember my friend X? Well, he was actually a top pupil when he wasn't terrorising the local community in the wee hours of the night, and he'd tackled the project with relish, going so far as to add a double-storey structure in the centre of his fort and a separate stables block with little oxcarts and straw. I was genuinely impressed, and I told him so, and he very kindly gifted it to me at the end of the day, after the teacher had given him yet another A-plus.

Did I not have my own fort, I hear you ask? Why did X give me his? Well, funny you should ask: yes, I did build my own fort, but it had died a horrible death just a couple of hours earlier and I can only assume X was feeling sorry for me. I'll explain:

Most of the boys had spent a month or more creating their masterpieces; me, I'd started on the project the night before it was due. I'd bought all the basic equipment at the same time they had – a baseboard, a tube of Bostick, and a dozen boxes of matches – but somehow I hadn't quite gotten around to putting it all together. Snowed under with all my other schoolwork, I imagine.

If X's fort represented the best of medieval technology – sturdy and proud, the sort of stronghold that King Edward, say, would have hesitated to try to conquer as he headed north to sort out that troublesome William Wallace chappie – then mine was more a homage to the neolithic age in Britain; a far simpler time in the nation's history, when the average villagers did nothing more than sink a few poles into the ground that they could huddle behind and hope for the best. Which is a fancy way of saying that it took me all of ten minutes to build, from start to finish.

I unscrewed the lid on the tube of Bostick and squeezed out a thick line of the stuff around the outside of the baseboard, then I planted a double row of matchsticks, upright, all the way along that square ... and voila, job done! True, the wall wasn't perfectly straight and, yes, it appeared to buckle here and there, swaying precariously outwards on the nor-nor-westerly rim especially. And, no, there wasn't any kind of door or gate on any of the four sides, which was something even the most humble of neolithic Britons would probably have insisted upon ... but, hey, it would have kept the attackers *out*, right? And that was the whole point of a fort. Right?

Wrong, Mr Kruger decreed. He gave me an E minus, just one notch above an outright fail.

Later that same day we had a bit of time to kill as we sat in Mr van Papendorp's class, just counting down the minutes until the final bell rang and we could head home. We'd collected our forts earlier from Mr Kruger's class and they were laid out on the desks in front of us. Some of the boys were whispering among themselves, trading off toy soldiers for flags, or surreptitiously throwing marbles at each other's forts to see if they could breach the walls, that sort of thing, all of which was being done very, very quietly, because Mr van Papendorp had his head down at his desk, busy with some kind of admin work, and he generally didn't take kindly to being disturbed.

Somebody noticed that I was the only guy in the class who hadn't bothered to burn off the sulphur heads on his matchsticks to create the appearance of sharpened stakes. Somebody else produced a box of matches that they'd brought along for any last-minute repairs. A third somebody suggested that I borrow that box of matches and light one and apply the flame to that double line of fresh matchstick heads that topped the walls of my fort, just to see what would happen ... and me being the impressionable type, and easily led astray, I did exactly that.

I watched with glee and then growing alarm as the first matchsticks burst into flame and fire went racing down the line, pausing only momentarily at the corner before shooting along the second wall, and then the third and fourth.

Did I mention earlier that, in a lame, last-minute bid for authenticity, I'd garnished my fort with a few handfuls of dry grass that I'd pulled from the veld on the way into school that morning? No? Well, I had, and I'd glued that grass to the baseboard with liberal dollops of the inflammable glue – which meant that within half a minute the whole lot of it was ablaze; a Bostick-bright fireball with flames leaping 20 inches up into the air.

There were no fire alarms or sprinkler systems back in those days, of course, but Mr van Papendorp was alerted to the danger by the shouts of sheer joy and terror from my classmates, and the clatter of a couple of chairs crashing to the floor as panicky boys and girls all around me scrambled backwards for safety.

"Who? What? Weir! *WEIRRRRR!!!*" he bellowed, leaping to his feet and clutching his head. He grabbed the jug of water that he kept on his desk and rushed forward and emptied the contents all over my desk, dousing both me and the flames. In one smooth motion, he used the other hand to lift me bodily from my seat by one arm and drag me to the front of the classroom. He snatched up the first weapon he could see – another of those big blackboard compasses I'd become so familiar with during my Standard Three Troubles – and he battered my arse with it until it broke into two pieces, at which point he tossed the smaller piece aside and resumed the battering until his arm grew too tired to carry on.

I hobbled home in some discomfort that day but I wasn't unhappy. I had my schoolbag in one hand and X's fantastic medieval fort balanced in the other, and I was already imagining the many pleasurable hours I'd spend playing with it ... when a little bastard who lived a couple of streets away from me came cycling up from behind, also on his way home from school, and reached out a hand and flipped up one edge of the fort as he whizzed past. The fort went tumbling to the ground, spewing oxcarts and flags and things on the way down, and the double-storey keep shattered into a dozen pieces as it hit the tarmac. Ruined! Reduced to rubble! Never the same again!

I roared curses at the kid as he accelerated away into the distance, laughing at the top of his voice and giving me a cheery wave. Man, I was furious.

I was up early the next day and I waited for him at the traffic lights on Malherbe St near the school, determined to beat the living shit out of him before he ever got to the safety of the classroom. I caught him without any bother at all – but he didn't try to put up any kind of a fight. He just stood there gripping the handlebars of his bicycle, shaking and pale in the face, a tear already in his eye, waiting to be punched ... but as much as I wanted to, I couldn't bring myself to do it in cold blood, because he was quite a bit smaller than me.

I spat out a few curses and threats, and he promised never, ever to do it again – which was pretty meaningless, really, because the odds of me ever walking home with another matchstick fort balanced in one hand were not good. I had to leave it at that.

Soooo frustrating – but it did at least give me a sudden insight into what my good neighbour Derek C must have been feeling that day when I destroyed his wall; when he had so clearly, dearly wanted to rip my obnoxious head off my skinny shoulders and drop-kick it into the veld across the road but couldn't allow himself to lose control.

The second-from-last Arts and Crafts project involved mallard ducks. We were told to bring in a wire coat-hanger along with a bunch of old newspapers and a bag of flour, the idea being that we'd twist the wire into a basic frame, use the paper and flour to mix up a batch of papier mache, and plaster it around the wire skeleton to form a model of our little feathered friend. We'd then paint it in appropriate colours and add a couple of beads for eyes.

I have to be honest and admit that I don't have any clear recollection of how exactly things went wrong on this one. All I can say for sure is that my duck's head fell off shortly before it was due to be marked, and that I have a vague memory me and my friends spending an entertaining ten minutes afterwards kicking the decapitated torso around the playground during lunch break until it disintegrated entirely, taking care all the while to avoid being gored by the wire hook that had been left sticking out of what should have been the poor bird's neck.

Nul points again? Probably. Hopeless? Yup. Did it go in the bin after the impromptu football session? You gottit.

And so we come to the wicker basket, the last in a long line of abominations and outright foul-ups that peppered my Arts and Crafts classes during my years at Rynfield Primary. The records show that, miraculously, I achieved a B for this one, and if you're immediately thinking to yourself: "Hmmm … a B for Gav? At Arts and Crafts? That can't be right", well, you'll have hit the nail on the head (which, as we've established, is something I myself could never have done back then – ha!).

Again, my recollection of how exactly things played out is a bit hazy; all I know for sure is that, on the final day, all the kids in the class had a wicker basket to present to Mr Kruger except me. If I had to guess, I'd say I probably bought a month's supply of Cadbury's shortcake biscuits with whatever money my mother would have given me to buy the raw materials; either that, or I'd messed things up by weaving when I should have been wickering, or vice versa, and that the end product was a piece of premium-grade shite that I'd given up on altogether and tossed into the bin.

Whatever the case, I found myself sitting at my desk sweating bullets on that last day and trying to think of a plausible excuse as Mr Kruger worked his way down the class list, calling on one kid at a time to carry their baskets up to the front for marking. My surname being Weir – W – I was always last on that list.

He reached S ... then T ... and with just one pupil left before my name came up, I turned in desperation to the boy sitting alongside me, David C; not a close friend, as such, but I had at least helped him out a couple of times in the past when he'd been bullied about his abnormally large feet. Size 12 on a 12-year-old boy, if you can believe that!

"Dave! Buddy! Can I borrow your basket" I whispered.

"What? Why?"

"Just for a minute."

"Ooh ... I dunno. Kruger will know."

"C'mon man! He's seen 30 of these things in a row. Yours is nothing special. He'll have forgotten it by now."

"Eh? What's wrong with my basket?"

"No! Nothing at all! That's not what I meant."

"I think it's a pretty good basket. I worked really, really hard on it."

"It is! It's a very, very good basket. I just want to borrow it for 60 seconds. Please!"

"Ooh ... I dunno."

Mr Kruger's voice rang out from the front of the classroom. "Weir! Let's see yours."

I gave David C an imploring look. He hesitated, then shoved it across the desk to me. I snatched it up and rose to my feet and walked confidently to the front of the room. I presented it to Mr Kruger with a flourish and held my breath for 10 seconds ... 15 seconds ... 20 seconds.

He hefted it in one strong hand. Turned it over a couple of times and examined the joints and the weaving and the patterns and things. Lifted a surprised eyebrow. Gave an impressed grunt. This was of a far higher quality than the usual burnt offerings from his least-favourite pupil.

"B," he said and handed it back to me.

I walked back to my desk on shaky legs, but with my heart singing the *Hallelujah Chorus*. As I sat down David leaned over and retrieved his basket.

"He didn't guess?" he whispered.

"Nope!" I whispered back excitedly. "And I got a B!"

David's eyes bulged. "WHAT???"

"Shhh! He'll hear you! What's the problem?"

"You got a B! He gave me a f***ing C-minus! And it's MY basket!"

He stood up, filled with righteous indignation, determined to lodge a stewards' inquiry there and then, but at that very moment the bell rang to signal the end of class and I was able to hustle him quickly towards the door amid the confusion and the end-of-day babble from the 25 or 30 other kids in the class. David kept looking back over his shoulder and complaining loud and long as he went, but Mr Kruger was already packing up his things, as keen as any of the kids were to get out of there, and I got him out into the hallway without further incident.

Saved by the bell. Literally.

CHAPTER 20

My classmates and I were all very well aware, as that Standard Five year drew to a close at the end of 1974, that our lives would change forever when we started high school in January the following year. I remember us joking among ourselves about how we were kings now but would be pawns later; how we'd go from being the biggest kids on the playground to the smallest. We understood all that on a theoretical level, but I doubt any of us realised just how fundamental, how dramatic, that change would be. I certainly didn't.

With perhaps a month to go, myself and half a dozen of my friends bunked off school for a day and headed over to Karen Y's house. She opened a bottle of her father's peppermint liqueur, drank about half of it herself and threw up all over the lounge carpet while everyone else had a swallow or two and decided it tasted horrible. We weren't quite ready, just yet, to make the leap to teenagehood, it seemed.

With the clock running down and maybe just a couple more weeks to go to the end of our primary school days the teachers threw us a farewell party at the school's new swimming pool which, if I remember right, had been completed just six or nine months beforehand. Again, you can check it out on Google maps: the school is located on Malherbe Road, Rynfield.

It was a summer evening and the air was heavy, as they say, with the scent of jasmine and braaivleis. Somebody had brought along a record player and a pile of seven-singles, and the PA system blared out *The Night Chicago died*, and *Butterly* and various other hits of the day. One of the teachers strung up a row of coloured bulbs along the perimeter. Mr van Papendorp was in charge of the braai and the boys helped him cook the meat while the girls joined his wife, Mrs van Papendorp, in preparing the bread rolls and the potato salad and the melktert in a nearby classroom.

We splashed around in the pool as night fell, diving into the deep end to stare up close at the underwater light or racing each other from one end to the other. Some of the kids danced to the music or slipped around behind the classrooms to play spin-the-bottle. Later we stood by the side of the braai fire, poking the embers with sticks while munching our third or fourth boerewors roll (okay, that was me; most of the others stopped after two) while we debated the merits of the various high schools we would be heading off to, a little excited, a little scared.

It was a wonderful night, and one I have very fond memories of.

My final day at Rynfield Primary was bitter-sweet indeed. I said a relieved goodbye to a couple of teachers I'd hated for years, chief among them old Mrs Vosloo, with her nagging questions about various homework assignments I'd somehow overlooked, and her ever-present tube of Wilson's XXX Mints at her side (which always left globs of white gunk at the corners of her twisted, wrinkled mouth – yuck!). But I also bade farewell to friends I'd known for seven years, some of whom I would, quite literally, never see again.

Many of the kids brought in presents for their favourite teachers. Mrs van Papendorp's desk, in particular, was piled high with gifts; she was the cool chick who'd taught us English for the past couple of years, always trying to find innovative ways to deliver her lessons, even going so far as to write out her own short version of *Macbeth* for us to perform in the school hall. I had one line to deliver, which I still remember to this day:

Macbeth (played by Bruce) strides to centre stage and says: *"How goes the night, boy?"*

Me: *"The moon is down. There are no stars."*

Anyway, I remember signing my name on my classmates' white school shirts, and all of them doing the same for me, some of them adding a farewell message or drawing faces or little stick figures ... and I wonder whatever happened to that shirt? I'd dearly love to see it now, almost 50 years later, and read those messages again ... conjure up those faces in my mind ... try to recapture that innocence of youth. Cliched, I know, but that doesn't make it any less true.

Many, many years later, when South Africa's crime rate was soaring and I was looking for somewhere safe to raise a family, I took my young bride to Vancouver, Canada. That didn't work out so good, in part because my young bride didn't like the fact that you only get to see the sun for six weeks a year over there ... but that's a story for another day. The point I'm trying to make is this: Vancouver lies on the western side of a vast chain of high mountains, and the rest of Canada lies on the eastern side. The difference between the two is absolute in terms of climate and even the kind of people who live there. It's almost like two completely different countries, joined by name and a constitution but nothing else, forever separated by a towering wall of granite.

That's how I see those first two distinct phases of my life: a mostly joyful childhood, followed by an unrelentingly miserable adolescence, with that last day at Rynfield Primary the clear and indelible dividing line.

A storm was coming my way and it was a big one, because the teenage years are difficult for even the most well-adjusted boy – and, as you'll have gathered by now, I was a million miles from being well adjusted. I was wholly unprepared. Naïve in the extreme, despite my delinquent tendencies. There was not a soul in the universe I would be able to share my fears and questions with.

Like the guy in the Bob Dylan song *Hurricane*, I had no idea what kinda shit was about to go down ...

End of Part One

PART TWO

Prologue

It's time to 'fess up: I may have implied at the start of Part One that a certain Professor JJJ Madoff working at the Office for National Statistics sent me an email saying I was Mr One Hundred Billion. He didn't. I'm not. That was a blatant fabrication; a crude attempt, dear reader, to grasp your attention and hold it, because I'm reasonably certain that if I'd started with *this* intro you'd never have bothered reading to the bottom of Page One:

Still no exciting news. Sigh. The only emails that drop into my inbox these days are from my orthopaedic clinic asking about my arthritic big toe, or from the Milton Keynes Funeral Home telling me that there's still time, just, to reserve a corner plot at the local graveyard. Call me Mr Nobody. Everyone else does.

Depressing, right? No one's going to read that and shout out: "Holy Cow, this is going to be a rip-roaring, rollicking ride; I just hope I can get my hands on a copy of this ballsy blockbuster before it sells out!"

No, the truth is that I've got too much time on my hands these days because, like Tom Waits, everyone I used to know is either dead or in prison. So I decided to jot down a few thoughts about my journey in case my descendants ever get to wondering, as I often do, about the day-to-day lives of the countless generations that came before them. This story will offer a bit of info on at least one of those lives. Assuming, of course, that I actually have some descendants – and that's not going to happen until my son decides to get his laconic arse into gear and heads on down to London and starts sowing a few reckless wild oats around.

Anyway, if you've stuck with me this far hopefully you'll stay to the end, so let's continue where we left off ...

CHAPTER ONE

Benoni High School had served the white, English-speaking half of the town with distinction for half a century, but by the Seventies it was no longer able to cope with the sheer number of pupils being funnelled towards it each year from the new suburbs springing up across the area. A new school was built in Northmead and one morning, late in the whole process, an urban planner down at the Council spread out a thematic map of the town on his desk and stared at it for a long time, trying to decide which pupils should be enrolled where.

Still a bit drunk, apparently, from a six-day booze, babes and boogie binge, he fumbled out a red marker pen from his top pocket and drew a completely random line that zig-zagged across the map from the top to the bottom, and he declared that all the teenagers living on the left would attend the new school and all the teenagers on the right would stick with the old one.

Good job, he told himself. Great job. But what name should he give to the new school? He hiccupped and took a furtive sip from the quarter-jack of brandy concealed in his blazer pocket. He screwed up his eyes in concentration and knuckled his brow. Nothing came to him. He dozed off for a bit. But then his eyes shot open again suddenly and he jumped up and said out loud: "Yesh! We'll call the NEW school Benoni High! And we'll call the old one … … shumthing like … agh, it can find shum other blerry name! Nobody ish ekshpekking that!"

And, no, nobody was. Not remotely. There were protests, of course, because the grand old institution in the centre of town had carved out a reputation for academic excellence and sporting achievement over five decades, and many of its old boys and old girls complained that it just didn't feel right to rob it of its heritage. But the decision had been made. There was no going back.

Parents across town were confused and angry, mine among them, because our house in Morehill was a whole lot closer to the new school than it was to the old one but we'd been zoned for the latter. The complaints were not just about the distances involved and available school bus routes and so on: it was rumoured that the new Benoni High would be granted substantial funding and all the best resources and would attract the best and brightest young teachers. The old one, by contrast, would be left to slowly moulder away into oblivion, starved of the budget it would need to compete at any level, and forced to start building a reputation from the ground up, all over again.

They called it Willowmoore High, and any misgivings that the parents of that first cohort of pupils might have had were confirmed when the hideous uniforms were unveiled: mud-brown blazers for the boys matched with faded beige trousers; a sickly green blouse for the girls, complemented by a mud-brown crimplene skirt and cardigan-thing that made even the prettiest among them look like a warden from one of Stalin's Siberian gulags.

Willowmoore opened for business in 1974. I was then in my final year at Rynfield Primary but Graham and Christine, three years and two years ahead of me, respectively, were among the few hundred kids that lined up for the first assembly in the school hall.

It was all a bit of a shambles, that first year. There were not enough teachers and too many kids per class, too little consultation with the parents and not nearly enough money to pay for the multiple unexpected expenses that cropped up. Also, there were simply too many problem kids from the rough part of town and no established procedures for how to deal with them. Within a couple of months a turf war was being fought out on the playgrounds each day; "skinheads" on one side, "poros" on the other – poros being the derogatory term for Portuguese. Police were called in more than once to break things up. A few of the kids were even found to be carrying knives, although thankfully they were never used, as far as I know.

The whole student body went out on strike at one point, hundreds of surly teenagers sitting down on the rugby field one lunchtime and refusing to return to class until their grievances had been addressed and doing the same thing for several days thereafter. Graham was one of the ringleaders, and I remember listening in awe as he told my parents each night how he and his buddies had parleyed with the principal, Mr Vos, negotiating various point and refusing to budge on key issues.

There was a rumour that Mr Vos, aged somewhere in his sixties, had suffered some kind of injury or trauma during the Second World War and was still suffering the effects of shellshock decades later. True or not, he was certainly given to unpredictable and emotional outbursts, and he did his street cred no good at all when he marched out onto the rugby field on one of those strike days and began hollering at the massed ranks of teenagers sitting there, telling them how much easier life was for them than it had been for his generation.

He and his friends had gone off to fight a war, he said; they'd had to shoot people and get shot at themselves; they'd had to dive for cover when the enemy planes appeared overhead – and he suddenly flung himself violently to the ground to illustrate his point, landing face-down on the grass. The kids craned forward to see if he was okay, but he bounced upright again a second later – holding handfuls of cigarette stompies, because that was the exact spot where all the teenage smokers used to hang out during lunchbreaks. "Yaaahhh!!!" he roared incoherently, and the titters of laugher from the pupils turned to outright guffaws. "YAAAAAAAAAAH!!!"

Poor guy resigned before the end of the first year.

The strike was finally resolved but the chaos and disorder at Willowmoore continued throughout that first school year. With no sign that things would improve any time soon, and no chance that the Council would reconsider its zoning policies regarding Benoni High, my parents decided that they had no choice other than to send all three of us to private schools the following year, at huge cost.

Fortunately, the Weir family budget was looking pretty healthy by then. I know that because, although I can't give you a monthly tally of parental salaries, and debits and credits, etc, I do remember that my mother took a job at about that time with a local housebuilding company called Goede, who were apparently willing to pay top dollar for a hard-working architectural draughtswoman. Also, I remember that the freezer was always stocked with multiple tubs of ice-cream in those days – a sure sign of prosperity – and there were few things I loved more than a bowl of Coco-Pops with two large scoops of vanilla bobbing around in the middle. I had that for breakfast, and lunch too, on many a day. Along with the usual breakfast and lunch, of course.

There were no private high schools in Benoni but quite a few to choose from in Johannesburg; some of the best in the country, in fact, and after some deliberation they settled on Jeppe Boys' High for me and Graham, and Waverley Girls' High for Christine.

My father was still working for one of the big mining houses in central Joburg at the time, Anglo-American, I think it was, and he used to commute in by train every day. That, though, wasn't deemed a realistic option for the three of us; either that, or my parents were looking forward to a bit of quiet time at home, because they decided we'd be better off boarding at the schools from Monday to Friday every week.

So far, so good. In fact, it was an exciting period, that December of 1974, filled with promise and a sense of new adventure just beyond the horizon. I can remember taking a couple of drives into Joburg with my mother and brother to get fitted for our new kit: grey shorts (four), grey longs (four), khaki shorts (two), black sports shorts (two), black socks (ten pairs), khaki socks (ten pairs), Bata Toughee black shoes (two pairs), hideous khaki shoes (one pair), white, long-sleeved collar shirts (ten), khaki, short-sleeved shirts (ten), white vests (ten), school tie (two), black school jersey (two), black Speedo swimming costume (two), school towels (six), flannel dressing gown (one), pyjama suits (four), leather slippers (one pair), white Jockey underpants (ten) and of course the school blazer, with its distinctive white vertical stripes (several). Whew!

The crowning glory was a straw boater hat with the school's badge on the front; stylish, if completely pointless (and it hurt like hell, we would learn soon enough, when some bigger kid walked by and whacked you on the top of the head, causing the rigid brim to smash down onto the bridge of your nose). Oh, and every single one of those items, down to the very last sock, had to have a name tag sewn or ironed on.

All of this stuff, and a bunch of other things like pencil sets and toiletries bags, had to be delivered to the boarding house in a giant steel trunk the size of a coffin, and that trunk had to have your name stencilled onto it so that it could be stacked up in a storeroom somewhere along with dozens of others just like it. Christine went through a similarly convoluted process for her enrolment at Waverley.

It must have cost my parents an absolute fortune. The school fees alone would have been substantial, never mind the cost of boarding the three of us, but they never said a word about it, then or in later years.

My mother drove me and Graham to Jeppe on the Sunday before the first day of the school year, our old Ford 17M car wheezing along under the weight of the two giant trunks. I was in the back seat, and I noticed a letter resting on the console between the front seats. I leaned forward and picked it up.

It was from the school, addressed to Mr and Mrs Weir, presumably containing information on where to go and what to do on the first day, that sort of thing. The school badge was printed on the envelope and I studied it closely for the first time: a shield, decorated with a thick yellow band across the middle, and wavy black-and-white lines above and below, underpinned with a banner bearing the school motto, in Latin. It read: *Forti nihil difficilius.*

"Mum – what's that mean?" I asked.

"What's what mean?"

"This badge thing – forty kneel diff … diff…"

"BUGGER!" she shouted and shook her fist – but not at me; a big truck was trying to crab sideways into her lane, and she was letting the driver know that there was no way on God's good earth that that was going to happen, not today, not on her watch. NNN-nnnh!

"Mum?"

"WHAT!"

"What's it mean? The badge?"

She hit the accelerator and pulled ahead of the truck and gave the driver a furious glare from her rearview mirror – which, let's be honest, he probably couldn't see – and then she returned her attention to the matter at hand.

"Forti nihil difficilius. I looked it up," she replied. "It means Nothing is too Difficult for the Brave."

"Ah. OK. Hmmm."

We drove on in silence. Nothing is too Difficult for the Brave? Was that just a bit … ominous? I gave a shrug and thought to myself, hey, this was one of the top schools in the country, with a reputation for excellence in all things, and top-notch boarding facilities. Nobody, surely, was suggesting that life at Jeppe Boys' High would be *difficilius*, were they? Right?

My mother flicked on the indicator and we turned into Marshall Street, Jeppestown, and I got my first glimpse of the grand old double-storey mansion that would become my new midweek home.

The interior, I saw moments later, was equally impressive, with high ceilings and a sweeping central staircase and ornate wood panelling throughout; an elegant, sprawling property that presumably had been built for a wealthy mining boss at the turn of the century, and much later repurposed and divided up into half a dozen dormitories, with communal bathrooms and dining areas.

It was a three-minute trek from the boarding house to the school itself, on the other side of a small, wooded hill.

CHAPTER TWO

Dinner that first night was a cottage pie, eaten at a crowded table along with seven or eight other new boys while my mother sat at another table with the other parents. Graham was in a separate dining hall somewhere with the older boys. I remember tucking into that cottage pie with gusto and thinking that it was simply delicious – though I hasten to add that my standards back then were unusually low, because my mother was and always had been a terrible cook. Have I mentioned that before? No? Well, I'm mentioning it now, because food, or the lack thereof, is going to be a central theme of this particular chapter, and I need to set things in context.

Our maid's name, in our home back in Benoni, was Anna and she had been with us for many years, an amiable, overweight and reassuring presence who did all the cleaning and some of the cooking, allowing both my parents to work fulltime. The dishes she presented were nothing fancy, just your basic hamburger patties and chips, or scrambled eggs on toast, but they were always tasty.

By contrast, the dishes my mother prepared on those nights when she did the cooking were most definitely not. Her idea of a tasty and nutritious meal for the family was a macaroni-and-glue bake, or greasy mince and tatties, or just a couple of pies from the local bakery with lots of chips. Some Sunday nights she would cook a beef roast and it was always exceptionally well done – and by that I mean overcooked, not expertly prepared – and on the Monday she'd slice off pieces of the leftover joint and deep-fry them to the consistency of 2,000-year-old biltong, then slap them down onto a plate with a bit of lumpy mash. Eeish!

All of that, admittedly, was standard fare in post-war Scotland, but she dropped things down to a whole new low with her Sausage Stew – and believe me when I say that it tasted every bit as foul as it sounds. The recipe was simple: she would throw a packet of sausages into a big pot of bubbling water, along with a few onions and carrots and any other vegetables that had been forgotten at the bottom of the fridge, and simply boil the whole lot to extinction. It would be served with a side of boiled potatoes. Spices? Condiments? Gravy? Nae time fir that!

The onions and carrots would bob around for as long as they could before becoming waterlogged and sinking to the bottom, where they could, at least, escape the layer of scum collecting at the top. A gawd-awful smell would permeate the house. Flies would gather, rubbing their little forelegs in anticipation. Neighbours unlucky enough to have a window open would catch a whiff and decide to go visit somebody somewhere for the day.

The sausages themselves were the worst aspect of that meal. When has it ever been a good idea to boil sausages? Never! Because they swell up horribly inside their casings; they grow obese and deathly pale, like a Liverpool girl on Grand National day who's squashed her lumpy arse into a translucent catsuit two sizes too small for her. Stab one of those sausages with a fork and it would send a spray of molten fat clear across the table, or up into your eyes if you got the angle wrong. Disgusting. Simply vile. Downright obscene. My stomach turns even now when I think about that Sausage Stew.

To be fair, there were two things that my mother did cook nicely: her rice pudding, which was my childhood favourite, and her homemade soup, which, again, involved boiling a bunch of stuff in a big pot – lamb bones and leeks and other vegetables, mostly – but which somehow tasted a whole helluva lot better than her Sausage Stew. Sadly, though, she only made the pudding or the soup a few times a year.

Anyway, when I sat down at the boarding house dinner table that first night and I saw those big platters of wholesome, tasty food being passed around, I was more than a little excited. We were urged to take as much as we wanted, and the cottage pie was followed by a tart of some kind, with warm custard, for pudding. Yeah, baby, yeah! I was thinking that I could definitely get used to this. Life at Jeppe Boys' High was going to be absolutely fine. Nothing *difficilius* at all to worry about.

I had a rude awakening, literally, at 6 o'clock the next morning when the school bell rang – very, very loudly – and one of the house prefects marched into the spartan dormitory I was sharing with those same seven or eight boys I'd met at my dinner table the night before and started yelling at us to get up and hit the showers. I stumbled out of my narrow, uncomfortable bed and stripped off my pyjamas like all the other boys were doing, grabbed my towel from a hook on the wall nearby and wrapped it around me.

We were herded through a couple of adjoining rooms and then down a corridor and into the large communal bathroom where we joined a queue of kids from the other dorms, all of them rubbing the sleep from their eyes and grumbling and holding onto their towels until the last possible moment before exposing their bare arses to the world.

The good news was that the queue moved quickly. There were three or four open-bay showers running at the same time and the rule was you had to stand under one of them for 30 seconds, giving yourself a quick once-over with a (shared) bar of soap and then moving along. The bad news was that this was a *cold* shower, at 6 in the frickin morning! Which was bad enough in January, mid-summer on the Highveld; the winter months were going to be absolute torture.

We had to repeat the process again at 5pm, and conversely, perversely, this was a scalding-hot shower, at the warmest time of the afternoon. The whole room was baking, steamed up like a Turkish bath, meaning that by the time you finished … well, you were hot and sweaty, and in need of a cold shower. No o'er bright, as my mother used to say.

The boarding house breakfast was OK-ish; a bowl of porridge, with maybe a boiled egg and a couple of sausages or bacon, and lots of toast – nothing remarkable, but adequate. It was over by 8am, however, and it was a long, long stretch from then until lunchtime at 1pm, and that was a problem for me from the very first day. By mid-morning I was feeling the first pangs of hunger; by noon I was ravenous and struggling to concentrate on whatever the teacher was saying in class.

When the bell rang for lunch break at 1pm I'd hurry back over the hill to the boarding house on trembling legs, a bit light-headed, and I'd be the first kid sitting at the table when the servers brought out the food – but there were no giant platters of cottage pie anymore; no tart and custard, not after that first night when all the parents had been present. This was a pauper's lunch, maybe one piece of battered fish with four or five chips, or one sausage with a miserly dollop of mash. Each boy was allocated half a bottle of milk, and although I'd never been a big milk fan I gulped mine down quickly and then tried to fill the great void in my belly with slice after slice after slice of buttered bread, because there was, at least, no shortage of that.

At 2pm we were back on the other side of the hill for another hour of school lessons. From 3pm to showers at 5pm we were free to do what we wanted – which, for me, meant trying to find something, anything, to do to keep my mind off the fact that dinner was still a long way off.

When the bell finally rang at 6pm I was, again, the first kid at my table, and I'd wolf down whatever stingy rations the cook had prepared and then get stuck into the buttered bread. Many slices. I was fortunate, at least, in that I was at a small table with just three other Standard Six boys, and we were left to eat in peace. The bigger tables, with eight or ten boys each, all had a Standard Ten prefect sitting with them, and they would often lean across and steal a chip here and a sausage there off the plates of the smaller kids. One of those boys tried to protest one day but paid a high price: he was made to hold out his hands in front of him while the prefect whacked him hard on all ten knuckles with a spoon, and he kept going until the kid cried.

From 7pm we sat in absolute silence in that same dining hall after the plates had been cleared away, doing whatever homework had been set out for us in class that day – and there was a lot of it, especially for a pupil like me who'd always had more of a take-it-or-leave-it approach to that sort of thing. Usually erring on the side of leave-it.

At 9pm we were sent to change into our pyjamas and dressing gowns, and brush our teeth, and at 9.30pm we climbed into bed and the lights were switched off and we were ordered to sleep. No talking allowed. No late-night trips to the bathroom. You stayed in your el-cheapo bed until the bell rang again at 6am to summon you to another day in paradise.

There were multiple other sources of misery at that boarding house besides the starvation rations. On the very first night after the parents had eaten that tasty, one-off cottage pie dinner and said goodbye to their kids us Standard Six boys were summoned to a communal hall adjoining the boarding house and told we were to undergo an initiation ceremony. This involved us taking turns to stand on a table in the middle of the room while all the older boys, ranging from Standard Seven up to Standard Ten, called out insults and flicked spitballs and aimed balls of crumpled tin foil and things at our heads, before the prefects agreed on a derogatory nickname for each of us.

Remember my old friend Shaun F, he of the light fingers? Well, he had also been packed off to Jeppe, and to the same boarding house as me (there were at least two other houses on the other side of the school). I remember him taking his turn up on that table and being roundly mocked for his English accent and his chubby knees, and coming away with the nickname Jack the Kipper. Quite witty actually, but not so witty that I was looking forward to my turn up there, and when nobody was watching I managed to slip away from the pack and out a side door.

An hour or so later, when the ceremony was over, one of the prefects grabbed me by one shoulder as I walked by and said: "Hey! I don't remember seeing you at initiation! Where were you?"

"I was there! Up on the table," I protested, my years of experience in evading awkward questions from teachers and shop assistants kicking in smoothly.

"Really? What nickname were you given?"

"Haggis," I replied promptly – and it had the ring of truth, because that had, in fact, been my nickname among my Rynfield Primary buddies, and I had the part-Scottish accent to back it up. He stared for a moment but then gave a shrug – and the side of my head a smack, for good measure – and then walked off, and I breathed a sigh of relief.

Us new boys were the lowest rung on the hierarchy, and we weren't allowed to forget it for a moment. The rule was that any time a Standard Ten kid needed something fetching or carrying he would shout out the magic words: "NEW BOY!" and we'd all have to drop whatever we were doing and sprint over and line up in front of him and await our orders. Whoever got there last got a hard punch on the shoulder.

Each of the Standard Tens had also assigned themselves a personal skivvy, with various duties to be carried out on a daily basis. I don't remember the name of my new lord and master but I do remember having to polish his school shoes every afternoon and leave them alongside his bed, and lay out his blazer and tie, and take his schoolbooks up from the study hall to his dorm at the end of the night, and various other menial tasks. I messed up a couple of times, forgetting to do this or that, and he gave me a few solemn warnings but left it at that, because he wasn't the worst of the bunch.

Some of the other new boys had it really bad, especially the kid who was skivvy to that same bastard at the dinner table next to mine, the one who liked hitting knuckles with a spoon – Mark Somebody, I think. I don't remember his whole name. Lots of freckles. Pug ugly. He made that poor kid's life a living hell, to the point that he finally ran off one afternoon after lessons and never came back.

About a week into my life sentence at Jeppe I was accosted by one of the prefects one morning as I shambled towards the bathroom for my 6am shower, bleary-eyed and still half asleep. I had to pass through the bedroom where this guy slept, and he was pissed off with me, he told me, because I was thumping my feet too loudly on the wooden floorboards as I went by.

He was trying to catch another ten minutes of sleep! I was waking him up every morning! He punched me on the shoulder, paralysing that arm for half an hour afterwards, and told me that if it happened again he would ****ing kill me. I kind of believed him. Hitchcock, his name was. Bastard.

That wasn't a great start to the day, especially as he'd held me back long enough to mean I was late getting to the showers, which earned me an automatic demerit. Three demerits in a week meant you were hauled before the housemaster on Sunday night and given a lecture on the values of discipline, followed by a caning that was far more painful than anything I'd suffered at primary school. Mr Ablett and Mr van Papendorp, it turned out, had been amateurs; this was a big-boy caning, the type that left purple stripes across your arse for a couple of weeks.

Routine was king at the boarding house. We woke, ate and slept by the bell, we showered and brushed our teeth by the bell, we changed from grey longs to khaki shorts to pyjamas by the bell, we studied, studied and studied some more by the bell, and throughout it all, 24 hours a day, we were subjected to the tyranny of the bullying, older boys.

On Friday afternoons we'd flee to our various homes and enjoy a two-day respite – but on Sunday evenings we'd be dragged back kicking and screaming. By Saturday night I was already dreading it, all the more so if I knew I'd accumulated three or more demerits the week before, meaning the first thing I'd be doing after I got back and changed into those hateful khaki shorts was report to the housemaster. Not the sort of thing to inspire a love of alma mater.

In truth, I might have been able to endure all of that and maybe even emerge stronger as a result, if not for one crucial factor. Certainly, my school marks were soaring under that harsh regime and I was scoring in the 80s and 90s in every subject, even German. I was eine kleine wunderkind, Achtung! (or in my case Ochtung!).

But the thing that ground me down was the ever-constant hunger, the ache in my empty belly that never went away and which left me thoroughly miserable from the moment I opened my eyes in the morning till the time the lights went out at night. I was Hungry Haggis, after all. Locust Boy. Dances with Sandwich. Born to eat.

I complained bitterly to my mother and when she dropped me back at the school on the following Sunday she gave me a few extra rand to keep in my pocket. There was a tuckshop at the school, she said, and I could use the cash to buy myself a meat pie every day to bridge the great void between breakfast and lunch. That helped a bit.

She also gave me a big packet of Sparkles sweeties to sneak into my dorm. That same night, when the lights went out at 9.30pm, I waited in the darkness for 10 or 15 minutes until I heard the first gentle snores from the beds around mine, and then I eased the bag out from under my pillow. Carefully, painstakingly, I tore an opening in the top and reached in and pulled out one of the sweets. Carefully, painstakingly, I peeled back the cellophane wrapper – but just as I opened my mouth to pop it in a voice rang out from the darkness: "Weir! What've you got there!"

It was Mark Somebody. My bed was up against a window that had once looked out on to a balcony. That balcony had been enclosed at some point, and another three or four beds had been squashed in there – one of which was his; close enough to mine, apparently, that he could hear the crinkling of a cellophane sweetie wrapper being slowly twisted open. Sigh.

I handed over the bag of sweets, fully expecting him to report me the following morning, earning me another demerit, but that never happened. Instead, he kept the bag for himself, and every night for the next couple of weeks I had to listen to him unwrapping my sweets, two or three at a time it sounded like, and then sucking noisily on them until he drifted off to sleep. Bastard.

Things came to a head on the Monday four weeks after the start of term. I'd had my breakfast and I'd wolfed down my meat pie at the 11am break but I was still starving when lunchtime finally rolled around. I jogged over the hill and took my spot at the table and was waiting, knife and fork in hand, when the servers carried out that day's lunch.

It was another miserly offering, and I can still picture this particular lunch very clearly in my mind's eye: a thin hamburger patty with a sliver of tomato on the side. No bun, no cheese, no lettuce. This wasn't a burger, it was just a patty.

It was gone in two bites, and so was the slice of tomato. I was reaching over for the first of what would be multiple slices of buttered bread when Mark Somebody appeared at my side and whacked the back of my outstretched hand with his blasted spoon. "Leave it," he said. "Don't touch the bread."

"What? Why?"

"We're on strike, that's why. A bread strike. Cos every day they put the same pieces back on the plate that weren't eaten the day before, and we don't like that."

"I do! I like that!"

"They're stale!"

"That's okay! I'll eat them!"

"Nobody's eating them!" he shouted. "And we're not eating any of the bread at all, the old stuff or the new stuff, until they agree to stop doing that!"

"But – "

"You arguing with me?"

"No. But … but I'm hungry."

He stared at me, dumbstruck by the insolence. It was a scene right out of *Oliver Twist* – with sadly predictable consequences. He leaned forward and whispered in my face: "Prefects' room after school. Three o-clock. And God help you if you're even a second late."

I was on time, not even a second late, but I had the feeling that wasn't going to help me much as I stepped inside the prefects' room, just off the big communal hall where the initiation ceremony had been held. They were waiting for me – Hitchcock, Mark Somebody, and three others whose names I've since forgotten. One of them was a very tall and skinny guy; so tall, in fact, that although he was sitting at a writing desk his head was still a good few inches higher than mine. "Hungry, eh?" he demanded as I stood there uncertainly, mute. He punched me suddenly, in the chest, hard enough to lift me right off my feet and send me flying clear across the room.

I landed in a heap and one of the others immediately screamed down into my face: "Get off our floor! Get up!" I tried, but he shoved me down again. I rolled onto my hands and knees and started to push myself upright but a third prefect, Mark Somebody I think it was, booted me hard in the arse, sending me flying back across the room in the other direction.

This went on for maybe three minutes – shout-kick-shout-punch-shout-shove – over and over again. None of the blows were to my face, because they were being careful not to leave any obvious bruises, but my shoulders and thighs and chest took an absolute battering, and by the time it finished I could barely stand upright. Eventually they opened the door and booted me back out into the communal hall, with the threats of what would happen if I dared to challenge them ever again ringing loud in my ears. Bastards, all of them.

I'd held it together up until that point, but as I hobbled away the tears finally came. A couple of the other Standard Six boys were standing nearby and had heard the commotion, but they weren't my friends and they didn't come over and offer any kind of comfort.

Feeling just about as low as I'd ever felt in all my life, I headed for the wooded hill between the boarding house and the school. There were a few quiet, shady areas there, away from prying eyes. Private. The sort of place where a 12-year-old aspiring juvenile delinquent who'd kind of fancied himself as a street-smart tough guy, way, way back in his primary school days, could sit and simply sob his eyes out like a little boy. Until, that was, his stomach sent out a familiar distress cry: "Gav!" it said. "I'm still empty! You're still starving hungry!"

I wiped my eyes and looked at my Timex wristwatch.

The stomach knows, man. It never lies. I was indeed still starving hungry, and it was more than two hours until dinnertime. Plenty of time to cry some more before I headed back down the hill and rejoined the other inmates.

CHAPTER THREE

I t's a measure of just how distant Graham and I were, how tenuous a bond existed between us brothers, that I never even considered taking my troubles to him at that point. We lived in that same boarding house five days a week, albeit in different dorms, but I have not a single recollection of even bumping into him in the hallways at any point, never mind actually talking to him about any of the stuff that was happening. My old buddy Shaun commiserated with me over the bread strike and the beating, and even gave me a bit of money – doubtless stolen from one of the other kids in his dorm – to buy a second meat pie the next day, and that helped enormously.

Two more of the Standard Six boys had had enough by that stage and had quit the school, heading for their homes rather than the boarding house one afternoon when classes ended, never to be seen again. As I sat on the wooded hill that afternoon, drying my eyes and wiping my snot-stained hands on those stinking khaki shorts, I had seriously contemplated doing the same thing; walking the short distance to the George Goch station and catching a train back to Benoni, as I did every Friday. I was reasonably certain, however, that my parents would simply turn me around and put me on the next train back, so I'd decided I had no choice but to stay where I was.

There were no mobile phones in those days, and no email or social media, and the single communal telephone at the entrance to the boarding house was strictly for emergencies, so I had to wait until the weekend before I could tell my parents that I'd been beaten up by five teenagers.

My father was raging mad when he heard the details. Well, he was angry. Okay, annoyed. Maybe a bit miffed, on the inside. Really deep down. He said: "Oh? Sorry to hear that, son," and returned to his newspaper.

On another day my mother might have been relied upon to show a bit more interest, but she was focused on other news: it would be me and me alone who would be heading back to Jeppe on the Sunday, she told me – because Graham was pulling out.

What? Why? And why just him?

Inexplicably, astonishingly, nobody had thought to check the list of school subjects on offer when my parents had signed him up, apparently. He needed to be doing biology and science, or maybe it was geography and maths – some such thing – but once lessons commenced he'd discovered that that particular combination was not available to him after all. So he'd be going back to Willowmoore High on the Monday while I reported for duty as usual at Jeppe.

Looking back today, I find it hard to accept that official version of events. How could my parents have made such a huge blunder? Why did two intelligent adults not at least scan the school curriculum before shelling out a king's ransom in fees – and, even if that was the case, how could four whole weeks have passed before the issue came to light?

Did something else happen that they never told me about? If it did, Graham certainly would never have confided it to me. Very strange.

Whatever the case, it was indeed me and me alone in the back seat of the car when my mother and father drove back into Joburg that Sunday. Normally one or the other of them would drop me at the entrance and turn the car around and leave, but this time they parked up, and both of them walked in with me. As it happened, the tall, skinny prefect who'd chest-punched me clear across the room a few days earlier came striding out the front double doors just as we arrived – and I had a fleeting moment of satisfaction when his eyes widened in fear, doubtless imaging that my parents were coming to lodge a complaint, or worse, that my father had come looking for him, personally.

Sadly, that was not the case. My parents were there to talk to the housemaster about Graham's situation, and to gather up his belongings in his giant steel trunk and take the whole lot back to Benoni, and the incident with the prefects and the bread never even cropped up in the conversation. Tall and Skinny didn't know that, however, and in the days that followed he was suddenly all smiles every time our paths crossed. He even threw me an orange at one point. And me being me, I wasn't too proud to eat it.

The bread strike was called off and life returned to whatever passed for normal in that House of the Damned. The following Sunday evening I received four of those arse-blistering strikes with the cane after notching up not three demerits but six, and for a variety of petty offences – one of which was being late to morning showers after being held back by Hitchcock again; a second was for forgetting to carry my khaki socks downstairs in the morning before school.

To add insult to injury, me and all the other new boys were told to stay behind in the main dining hall immediately after dinner to listen to a half-hour lecture from the housemaster – a heavyset, bald and bespectacled guy whose name I can't recall – about what a bunch of wimps we were, complaining to our parents about the most trivial of matters when we should have been manly enough to just suck it all up. "Have you ever read *Tom Brown's Schooldays*?" he demanded to know. "Anybody?"

I put my hand up but he ignored it. Question was rhetorical, apparently. "Those boys had it tough," he said. "You lot … ach!" He made a disgusted noise and dismissed us with a wave, but as we turned to leave he called out the name of one boy who had apparently earned his favour, and with it the right to join him for hot chocolate and biscuits in his personal study.

Perfectly normal. Just a middle-aged, single man and his favourite boy, cut out from the herd, sitting close around the fire getting to know each other a little better over drinks and nibbles. Hmmm.

Again, looking back, that sort of thing throws up all sorts of red flags but fortunately I wouldn't be around long enough to learn if it was as sinister as it sounds, because that week, it turned out, would be the last I would ever spend at Jeppe Boys' High. Liberation was at hand, because my parents had come to the decision that it simply wasn't worth the effort travelling backwards and forwards to Joburg just for me, and that if Graham and Christine were to be stuck back at Willowmoore High, I might as well join them (Christine had also quit her private school by then, though I don't remember why).

Which suited me just fine, let me tell you. Frrrreeedom!!! to quote William Wallace.

The following Monday morning I woke up in my own bed. I lingered over a huge breakfast and when it was over I crammed down a couple of extra slices of toasted cheese, just because I could, and because there was no one there to tell me I couldn't. After that it was time to leave for school, and I walked down to the bottom of Barbara Avenue along with my brother and sister. The three of us boarded the bus into town together and then walked the 15 minutes or so from the terminus to Willowmoore High.

My parents had spent every last penny they owned on the ill-fated private-schooling venture and it would be another term or two before they could afford to buy me my own mud-brown blazer and faded beige trousers, so I stuck out from all the other pupils like a sore thumb in my Jeppe uniform. But I didn't mind a bit. My six weeks of hard labour was over and that was all that mattered.

◆ ◆ ◆

Things had settled down quite a bit at Willowmoore after the chaos of that first year, with a host of new teachers, new rules and even a new principal – a Mr Cawdry, if I remember right – but academically speaking it still fell some way short of the excellence of Jeppe, and my school marks plummeted immediately.

One reason for that was that I was no longer compelled to do any homework, and so I didn't, not a word; a more compelling factor was that it simply wasn't cool in the eyes of the new friends I was making there to pass any class tests. And if you absolutely had to pass, the thinking was that you really shouldn't be scoring anything higher than the minimum 40 per cent.

Eager to fit in, I did what I could to lower my performance and fail as many tests as I could – and, hey, it turned out that that was one more thing I was reasonably good at doing. By the end of the first term I had worked my way down to the very bottom of the class.

CHAPTER FOUR

It was around this time that I had my one and only life experience of handling a gun, and by that I mean a humble pellet gun, rather than some kind of Kalashnikov assault weapon. A few of my friends owned one of these relatively harmless air rifles and they'd use them to shoot at streetlights or rows of cans, but I'd never really seen the attraction – until, that is, I read the Wilbur Smith novel *When The Lion Feeds*.

For anyone not familiar with it, it tells a rip-roaring tale of the Courtney family's adventures on the Highveld at the time of the gold rush, and later the Boer War, and it features all the hunting and fighting and action a boy could wish for, and even a few risqué passages that were enough to get it banned for a while by the ever-watchful South African censors. I was captivated from the first page.

I'd stumbled across a copy on a family outing to one of the many second-hand book exchanges that still existed in Benoni in those last days before the arrival of television. This was a long-standing tradition in the Weir household: once a month or so my mother and father would load up on novels by Agatha Christie and George MacDonald Fraser and the like, while Graham, Christine and I would get piles of *Archie* comics or books like *Tom Sawyer* or Enid Blyton's many childhood classics. We'd stop off at Mr Rooster or Dairy Den on the way home and pick up a takeaway meal and then spend a happy evening engrossed in our various works of fiction. A month later we'd return that batch of books and comics and pick out the next lot.

When The Lion Feeds was very different from anything I'd

read before, because the setting wasn't some quaint English seaside town or far-off American backwater, but the South African veld – which this Wilbur Smith guy obviously loved as much as I did! When he wrote about Sean Courtney and his trusty sidekick Mbejane creeping through the high grass, rifle or assegai in hand, stalking their prey, animal or human, I could picture it vividly, because I lived right across the road from one such veld. Hell, I didn't have to picture the hunt – I could live it! All I had to do was borrow a pellet gun.

I cycled round to the home of one of my buddies the morning after I finished reading the book (the first time, that is – I kept that copy, and re-read it three or four times more in the years that followed). The buddy in question was David L, a fellow Protea choir member and a generous guy who had, in fact, offered to lend me his gun once before, though I'd shown scant interest at the time. He was a bit surprised by my sudden request but he didn't think twice about handing it over. He even gave me a crash course in how to use it, along with a box of tiny lead pellets.

I cycled home again with the gun balanced between the crossbar and the handlebars, already feeling like a bit of a desperado, and imagining passing drivers nodding to themselves and thinking "ah, he must be a hunter!" or maybe "ooh, you don't want to mess with *that* guy, he's got a rifle!" Things like that.

I dumped my bike and grabbed a quick jam sandwich or three and then I headed out into the veld, pellet gun in hand and a steely glint in my eye. There would be something out here I could kill, I thought; maybe not an elephant, like Sean Courtney might have, but something. Anything.

I ducked through my regular hole in the fence and into the forbidden zone where, I reasoned, there was far less human traffic and therefore more wildlife. It was late summer, I remember, and the grass was green and tall and filled with the sounds of humming insects and rustling critters in the undergrowth, but nothing jumped out and presented itself as a target. I got myself entangled in the web of a giant garden spider at one point – scary-looking guys, but pretty much harmless – and the lower half of my jeans quickly filled up with hundreds of blackjack burrs, but after half an hour of stalking and hunching and wetting one finger and holding it up in the air to gauge the wind direction, I finally straightened up and wiped my sweaty brow and puffed out my cheeks in frustration.

I stared around me, and my eyes settled on a row of white wooden beehives that somebody had set up in the grove of giant pine trees a few months earlier, each of them perhaps 2ft wide and tall and deep. I'd seen them before, of course, and Shaun and I had even contemplated breaking into one of them at one point to see if we could find the honey, but we'd backed off pretty quickly when he was stung on the back of the neck and a cloud of angry bees began to form overhead. I hadn't wanted to get too close to those hives again ... but I had a gun now. I could keep my distance. And I needed something to shoot at.

I crept to within 30 feet of the nearest white box, and I got down on one knee and lifted the pellet gun to my shoulder and squinted down the rudimentary sights, like David had taught me to. I steadied the barrel for a second then I squeezed the trigger. The gun jumped back against my shoulder and – splat! – the pellet whacked into the side of the hive.

I held my breath ... but nothing happened. There was no reaction from the bees, so I swivelled a bit to the side and lined up the next hive in my sights. Splat! Nothing. I fired off a third and then a fourth pellet, and at last I could hear the gentle hum from within those hives picking up in tempo.

Quite a few bees started spilling out the sides, from all eight boxes, and the hum changed to something more like a low growl as they circled up into the air. I watched for a few moments, impressed by how many critters each of those boxes could hold, and I was about to take another pot shot when there was a sudden loud buzzing in my ear and a single bee appeared right in front of my nose. I batted it away, but it flew right back at me, joined by a second one a moment later. Then a third.

I was still wondering how the hell a stupid bee could have worked out that the splatting sound on the side of its hive was connected in any way to the small humanoid crouched in the grass 30 feet away when I felt a sharp pain in my right forearm and realised I'd been stung. I pushed myself backwards and landed on my arse, and suddenly there were four or five bees buzzing around my head and I became aware that the growl from the ominously darkening cloud gathering above the hives had swelled to a terrifying roar. It was time to leave. Quickly.

I sprang to my feet and swivelled around and sprinted away, suddenly scared, but the bees kept pace, maybe eight or ten of them whizzing all around me. I was stung again, this time on the right ear – *shit that hurt!* – and at that point blind panic took over. I tossed the pellet gun mindlessly to one side and threw my head back and ran like a madman, not thinking about which direction I was going or whether I was about to fall into one of the many open sinkholes that pockmarked the land, just windmilling my arms around my head and slapping myself in the face and howling in pain every now and again as another of those fiendish little bastards sank a stinger into my flesh.

I cannoned into the forbidden-zone fence at full speed – it's called blind panic for a reason – and the taut wire bounced me backwards like a trampoline. I landed flat on my back but I was up again in a split second, racing towards the hole which I'd spotted 40 or 50 feet away, and I took a running dive at it and rolled out on the other side. I staggered up and carried on running, wild-eyed and gasping for breath now as I headed in the general direction of my house – and, let me tell you, if I'd ever run like *that* at one of my Rynfield Primary sports days I'd have crossed the finishing line before the other kids had even taken a step!

I slowed down only when I reached my driveway and the

rational brain reasserted itself and pointed out that I'd finally left the bees behind. I was safe – but, man oh man, I was absolutely finished, exhausted, a spent force.

I sank to my knees and then just tumbled over on to one side and lay there panting and heaving like a freshly landed barbel for several minutes, dry-retching a couple of times. After a time I sat upright and started plucking out the bee stings with my fingernails, five in total. They hurt like hell. Especially the one on my frickin ear.

It was late afternoon before I was able to convince myself it was safe to venture back into the forbidden zone in search of the pellet gun, my eyes constantly darting in the direction of the beehives as I crept along, all my senses on high alert for the first hint of a buzzing sound, my legs still feeling all trembly from the over-exertions of the morning. It took me a long time before I finally spotted the gun lying up against the side of a huge termite mound, a fair distance from where I'd expected to see it.

I bent and picked it up and examined it for any obvious signs of damage. The barrel was clogged with sand but I was able to shake that out and it appeared to be otherwise intact, so I heaved a huge sigh of relief and turned to head home again ... trying not to think about how much better Sean Courtney would have handled things.

I'd told David that I'd return his gun the following day, and when I went to bed that night I was planning to do exactly that, first thing in the morning, no questions asked. But the resilience of youth is a marvellous thing, and a good night's sleep can give a whole new, positive perspective on life. Or maybe it's just that I've always been a bit thick. Whatever the case, by the time I jumped out of bed the next morning I'd decided to have one more go, so I pulled on my jeans, still coated in blackjack burrs, ate a couple of bowls of Coco Pops and ice-cream to get me properly in the mood and then slung the pellet gun over one shoulder and headed out into the forbidden zone again.

All appeared to be quiet over by the giant pines and the beehives but I steered well clear of them anyway, aiming instead for another wooded spot over on the far left where I'd almost stepped on a rinkhals once, a couple of years earlier. Again, I stalked around fruitlessly for ages without seeing anything to shoot at – until finally I heard a fluttering of wings overhead and a small mossie flew by and alighted on a tree branch a short distance away, maybe 25 or 30 feet. A target at last!

I knelt quickly and lined up the bird in my sights, eager to take a shot before it flew off. It hopped to one side. I repositioned myself and steadied the barrel. It hopped back to where it had been a second earlier. I swung the barrel back to the left and fired immediately, fully expecting to miss by a mile – but somehow, incredibly, call it beginner's luck, there was a soft *thwack* sound and the little sparrow dropped off the branch and fell like a stone.

I jumped up with a shout of triumph and ran over to claim my kill ... but that exhilaration evaporated in an instant when I saw my innocent prey up close and personal. The bird was dead, of course, sprawled in the dust, one wing thrown open, its claws grasping for nothing, its beak and half its face blown away, the other half leaking blood and gunge out onto the ground. I blinked at it a few times, horrified but unable to stop staring.

Overcome suddenly with guilt and a deep sense of shame, I grabbed a few handfuls of grass and covered up the scene of my crime and stood and turned to leave, but then stopped. It just didn't feel right. I turned back, and I knelt down again and thought for a second or two. Then I searched around me for a sharpish stone, and I used it to dig a little mossie-sized grave in the soil, just four or five inches deep, and I laid the bird down in it and covered it with sand. But I still felt horrible. Not like a proud hunter at all. Just ... horrible.

I trudged back home in a sober frame of mind. I gave the gun a wipe-down and then I mounted my bike and cycled back to David's place. He asked if I'd had fun and if I'd be asking my folks to get me my own pellet gun, so we could go shooting together sometime? I faked a smile and told him, sure, of course, but the truth is I've never had the opportunity to handle any kind of gun since that day, and nor have I sought out the chance to do so.

I'm no pacifist, I hasten to add. If, let's say, there was a knock on my front door one night and I opened it to find Vladimir Putin standing out there with a Molotov cocktail in one hand and he said: "Prepare to die, Gavski!" – well, I wouldn't think twice about kicking him in the nutsack and beating him to death with one of the little flower pots that Asha keeps out there. Kill or be killed. I'm alright with that.

But hunting for sport? Using dogs and a fast horse to run down a fox? Or buying a high-powered rifle to murder a drugged lion in some cosy canned hunt? Or taking to the deep seas with some high-tech fishing kit to hook a blue marlin, not to eat, but just so you can take a selfie alongside its corpse hanging upside down from a giant hook? Not for me.

I always want to say to those brave hunters: go, track a wild tiger in the bush armed with just a knuckleduster, or jump into the sea with just a breadknife in your hand, at a place where you know the great whites are swimming ... and if you still emerge the victor, I'll be the first to sing your praises. *Then* you'll be a man, my son, to quote Mr Kipling.

CHAPTER FIVE

The first cigarette I ever had was a Pall Mall, given to me by my old mate X one dark night when we were out prowling the neighbourhood on one of our regular jaunts. I was 13. We were out of sight behind some homeowner's side hedge, plotting our next move, when he unexpectedly produced not one but two cigarettes from his top pocket along with a box of matches. He placed one between his lips and lit up expertly, then he offered me the other. I took it, hesitantly.

"When did you start ..."

"Last week," he replied casually, exhaling a cloud of smoke and coughing only a little. Me, I coughed a lot when I drew in that first lungful of foul, acrid air, and like every single one of the hundreds of millions of other smokers around the world my first thought, on that first night, was: why the hell would anyone choose to do this to themselves? This was terrible! I felt like being sick on the spot!

I can't speak for those hundreds of millions of others, but the answer, in my case, was simple: peer pressure. You had to persevere; you couldn't try it once and walk away claiming you didn't like it. That simply wasn't acceptable.

Smoking was the done thing. *All* the kids were doing it. My mother and father were doing it, and so were all the other adults who used to visit our house socially or show up at the monthly choir committee meetings. My brother and sister were smokers. Half my friends were by then too, and so were their parents, and their brothers and sisters.

All the cool kids at Willowmoore would come into class in the mornings reeking of smoke, and they'd light up again during the lunch break, lying in tight groups facing inwards on the grass in the far corners of the playground, blowing the smoke down and fanning it simultaneously so it couldn't be seen by any curious teacher.

I remember one of the girls in my new class, Susan B, turning around in her desk one day and asking me directly: "Do you smoke?" I'd waggled my eyebrows a couple of times and given her what I hoped was a rakish smile that suggested "hell yeah" – but I'd come away feeling distinctly inadequate, because, no, I didn't smoke.

So when X pulled out those Pall Malls that night, filched from his mother's supply, I was more than happy to give it a try, and in the days and weeks that followed I was determined to get the hang of it, no matter how unpleasant an experience it might be.

I sneaked out with one of my father's Ransom Select cigarettes one morning and trotted over to the forbidden zone and lit it up, being sure to inhale all of the smoke with every single puff. I'd cheated a bit with most of X's Pall Mall on that first night, drawing the smoke into my mouth but blowing it out again without having breathed it into my lungs. This time, I did it *right* – sucking in huge, disgusting clouds of the stuff, coughing and spitting but pressing on determinedly until my head was spinning and I thought I was about to be physically ill.

I smoked that Ransom down to its distinctive filter – white, with two thin gold bands, I remember – but I hated every moment, and for all the years that followed that was the one brand of cigarette that I just couldn't stomach.

Remember those plastic baggies of cash that Shaun used to bury in the forbidden zone? Well, I dug one of them up a week or so later, and I walked over to the family supermarket and bought myself my first pack of Peter Stuyvesant cigarettes, which made me feel like a pretty big deal. I smoked one when

I got back to the veld, and it wasn't quite as bad as the first time. I buried the pack in the same plastic baggie, in the same spot, and I revisited it most days over the next few weeks until I'd worked my way through the lot and I knew I'd be able to answer a confident "yes" the next time somebody asked me: "Do you smoke?"

Admirable commitment, if I say so myself.

Of course, I didn't know it then – and probably wouldn't have cared if I did – but, as hard as it was to start smoking, I would find it a hell of a lot harder to stop, further down the line. I finally did, aged 22, but only after many, many failed attempts; only after an embarrassing incident one day when I had to run hard to catch a train, and ended up semi-collapsing and puking all over a crowded, rush-hour platform at the Benoni station, because my poor lungs had been shredded, tarred and feathered from nine long years of abuse; they could no longer provide even a stick-thin frame such as mine was back then with the oxygen it required.

The first cigarette was followed soon after by the first drink but, strangely, I have no recollection of the exact incident. All I can say for sure is that I must have started drinking about halfway through my Standard Six year, because I can remember going to a Friday night party at the home of one of the new friends I'd been making at Willowmoore, and taking with me two cans of Black Label lager – even though I knew very well that just one can would be enough to get me drunk (so, by that point, I'd obviously gotten drunk before). The second Black Label was purely for show; to make it known to my new mates that I was no amateur, that I was a two-can kinda guy.

I was desperate to fit in with the new crowd but it didn't help that I was the youngest. I'd just turned 13, but a couple of the others were already 14 and one of the boys, we'll call him

D, may even have been older still, because he was a foot taller than me and had to shave every morning before school. Me, I didn't even have hair under my arms yet; I knew, because I'd begun checking hopefully on an almost daily basis, but always in vain. D had a deep bass voice; mine hadn't even started to squeak, never mind break. I was still in the frickin choir, though I kept that information to myself.

I was hanging out with D during school lunch break one Monday when one of the other guys, Paul J, swaggered over and said howzit and announced that his folks would be going away for the weekend, and he would have the house to himself … so the plan was to have a little get-together. A *jol*. Were we interested?

"F***ing of course!" growled D.

"F***ing lekker!" I piped up. We did a lot of manly swearing in those days.

"Bring a six pack and a bird," Paul added. "We're going to jol hard, boet!"

I gulped. *Bring a bird? A … girl? For a weekend of hard jolling?* Where the hell would I get a girl? The six pack of beers wouldn't be a problem; my old mate Shaun was still stuck at Jeppe, so the supply of cash baggies buried in the forbidden zone was not being replenished, but I knew there was at least one still out there. I could dig it up and head on over to the bottle store at the Northmead Mall and buy six Black Labels, even though I was pretty sure I'd get sick and embarrass myself if I tried to drink them all in one session.

But that was by far the less problematic of the two requirements. *Bring a bird?*

Paul was staring at me closely. "Yeah?" he asked.

"Kiff ekse, zabra!" I replied confidently, speaking in Willowese – the Oxford English translation of which would be, "I say, that sounds marvellous old chap!"

He grinned with delight and produced a smelly, half-smoked cigarette from his blazer pocket that he'd saved from earlier in the day. He lit up and we passed it around for a couple of drags each, me being careful not to "piss-pot" the filter – wet it with my saliva, which was something a real man would never do – and then the bell rang and we headed back in for another period of biology or trig or some other subject that I was doing my level best not to grasp.

Which wouldn't be difficult at all on that particular day, because my mind was whirring, racing with the urgent problem: where exactly was I going to find a bird for a weekend of frenzied group sex and alcohol abuse? I couldn't say for sure, but I doubted any of the girls in the Protea choir would be up for it.

I spent an anxious week stewing about the problem but I was no closer to finding a solution by the time Friday rolled around, and when Paul approached me and D again at the same spot I felt that my number was finally up. I was about to be horribly exposed, but I was determined to keep up the pretence to the very last moment.

"You okes ready for tomorrow?" he asked brightly. "You've got a bird?"

"F***ing of course!" D said … and I wondered about that briefly, because I knew he didn't have a regular girlfriend, and we'd been hanging out together all week and he hadn't mentioned making contact with any new mystery woman. Hmmm.

Paul turned to me with an expectant look.

"You?"

"No problem at all," I assured him, supremely confident on the outside.

"How about *you*?" D asked … and a strange thing happened. Paul's shoulders slumped and his chin dropped. His eyes darted briefly to one side – and I knew at that moment, without any shadow of doubt, that he himself did not have a bird for the weekend!

My hobby, these days, is playing poker, either at our local casino in Milton Keynes or in Las Vegas once a year, and a vital part of the game is working out if the other guy is bluffing. I had no experience of that back then – but if ever there was a clear and obvious example of a failed bluff, Paul's reaction was it. He had obviously been hoping all along that neither me nor D would be able to source a nymphomaniac with unusually low standards, and that one of us would have to ask to call the whole thing off. Instead, both of us were raring to go, apparently.

He coughed a couple of times, then he mumbled: "F***ing toppie chooned me skeef, ekse!" Translation: "I say, my dear father misinformed me."

D: "Huh?"

Paul: "My folks. They're not going away this weekend after all. So … ah, we can't have the jol."

D: "No!" But he looked hugely relieved.

Me: "Damn!" Also hugely, enormously relieved.

Paul: "I'm sorry okes."

D: "That's kak man!" Expressing general disappointment.

Me: "Jou ma se moer!" – which may have been a little too strong, because I'd inadvertently cursed Paul's mother's vagina. I was still getting the hang of this Willowese thing. He reared back, shocked and angry.

I added quickly: "No! I don't mean that! What I'm saying is … um … f***sakes! You know?"

At which point the bell rang and all three of us dropped the subject with indecent haste, turning and hurrying back towards the main school block, for once eager to reach the sanctuary of the classroom, where there could be no further awkward questions about the weekend ahead.

Just three teenage virgins, all of whom had been tested and found wanting; none of them able, apparently, to produce a bird on demand.

CHAPTER SIX

One of the downsides to trying to prove your bad-boy credentials and competing for the title of Worst Pupil of the Year is that you have a lot of disagreements with teachers, which means a lot of trips to the principal's office and a lot of canings. Of course, I'd survived something similar three years earlier, when I was in Standard Three, so none of this was new to me – and it helped that I wasn't alone this time round. In fact, fully half the boys in class, like me, were using their school tie to keep a running tally of how many cuts, or "jacks", they'd received, adding a small notch for each one along the bottom stripe of the tie, and when that line was full, moving up to the next stripe. There was fierce competition to see who could work their way to the top of a tie.

It was a painful process, and I took to wearing a pair of PE shorts under my school trousers on days when where was a reasonable chance I'd be getting caned. I learnt soon enough, however, that one pair didn't make a lot of difference, so I tried adding a second pair of shorts. That helped a little, but not enough.

There was an enterprising boy in my class whose name I don't recall, but who gathered a bunch of us together at break one day for the grand unveiling of something he said would revolutionise the industry and preserve the arses of troublesome pupils at schools everywhere: a flapjack that you could stuff down your trousers to deaden the impact of the cane. I'd heard of such things before, of course, but this was the first time I'd seen one.

Made from the inner tube of an old car tyre, it was maybe 10 inches wide and six inches deep, and a quarter of an inch thick, but peppered with little holes all the way across to allow any trapped air to escape. Without those holes, so the story went, the rubber flapjack would produce a loud farting sound with each strike of the cane, thereby alerting the world to its presence. Truth or myth? You decide.

Did it work? I had the chance to find out for myself just a week later when I learnt that I'd be visiting the principal's office the following day for some infraction I've long since forgotten. I'd been sentenced to four of the best from Mr Cawdry, who'd earned himself the reputation of being a heavy hitter.

I borrowed the flapjack from the boy whose name I've forgotten, and I followed his instructions to the letter when I got dressed for school that morning:

Step one: Apply two pairs of underpants;

Step two: Insert flapjack between first and second pair of underpants;

Step three: Apply one pair school PE shorts to hold everything in place;

Step four: Apply school trousers as normal.

Hmmm. I bent over in front of the mirror and gave myself an experimental whack with the flat of one hand but I could still feel it, so I stripped everything off and started again, adding a third pair of underpants and a second and third pair of PE shorts (my brother's, a couple of sizes bigger). I thought about it for a second and then I also pulled on my denim jeans, only just managing to close the button at the top, and finally I squeezed into my school trousers again – but with considerable difficulty. I had to tug them up a couple of inches on the left leg, then a couple on the right, and so on. I was a skinny kid and those trousers generally used to hang off my frame like a scarecrow's, but not that day.

Bloated like the frickin Michelin Man, but only from the

waist down, I lumbered onto the school bus and stood all the way on the drive into town because it was just too uncomfortable to sit down. Once I got into class I had no choice; I had to sit down, so I wedged myself in at a 45-degree angle between the fixed wooden chair and the desk it was attached to, and I stayed in that position for the duration of the lesson, shuffling from side to side every now and again to get the blood flowing back into my toes.

About midway through the second period I became aware that I needed to pee, but I decided that that would be way too much hassle under the circumstances. I'd just have to wait until after my visit to Mr Cawdry's office at first break.

I knocked on his office door at 10am, as instructed, and he barked at me to come in. He was distracted with paperwork and he didn't look up, didn't notice that I'd developed an obesity problem in the bum area since the last time he'd seen me. He motioned towards the usual spot in front of his desk and carried on writing, then he stood up, still scanning whatever document it was he was working on and said to himself: "Okay ... Weir ... ah ... four was it?"

"Um..." *If I said two, would he go for it?*

"Four," he confirmed, and he stepped out from behind the desk.

I assumed the position. He reached for his cane. I gripped my knees and braced myself. He lifted the cane high and swung it down and as it connected there was a dull, flat *doof* sound, like a lead ball falling into desert sand. Decidedly fishy!

There was a brief pause, and I had time to wonder if he was about to take a closer look at my fattened toosh, but then the cane swished again, three more times in quick succession – *doof, doof, doof* – and it was over.

I straightened up and turned to leave, smartly, but as I reached for the door handle Mr Cawdry said: "Weir. The next time you come in here wearing who-knows how many pairs of trousers, you're getting six of the best, not four. And a week's detention too. Clear?"

I flushed guiltily. "Clear. Sir."

He nodded and went back to his paperwork and I went back to my classmates, who were gathered in a tight, excited bunch in the playground waiting to hear how the flapjack had performed. I gave them the update: a 25 per cent reduction in pain, by my expert reckoning, but at the cost of a morning spent in extreme discomfort and the embarrassment of being caught out, with possible additional punishments as a result.

So was it worth it, they demanded? I honestly wasn't sure, I replied.

I left them debating the finer points – two or four pairs of underpants? Jeans or no jeans? How much could they sell a flapjack for on the open market? – while I huffed and puffed and shuffled along to the toilets as fast as any Michelin Man had ever gone and then I finally, gratefully, tore off all that extra clothing and had that pee I'd been holding in all morning.

There was a horrible accident at Willowmoore that year involving one of my classmates, a studious boy by the name of Robert G, and it happened during the lunch break when a bunch of us were running around the rugby field while a school gardener was cutting it with a big petrol lawnmower.

The first half of the story, I have to admit, I'd forgotten all about until a couple of years ago when I made contact with some old school friends on Facebook, and they reminded me that someone, at some point, had come up with the bright idea that we play a game of chicken with that lawnmower; that we see who dared to get closest to its whirring blades.

I'd remembered only the second half of the story, the horrible accident itself, and those images are still very clear in my mind. I can still see Robert G running along with a big grin on his face but turning away too late and then falling into the lawnmower, one foot disappearing underneath it – with sickening consequences. He was carried from the field screaming, with blood spurting and gushing from that shredded foot, one hand clutched over his eyes to shield himself from the terrible sight.

He lost three of his toes that day, and although the surgeons managed to save the rest of the foot, what was left behind was not pretty. The pale white flesh was criss-crossed with red scars and deep gouges, and he would never walk freely again without favouring that side of his body.

He spent two or maybe even three months recuperating before finally returning to school, and as if things hadn't been bad enough, he then found himself being targeted by a bully on a daily basis. My new friend D.

D was a lot bigger than any of the other boys in the class and didn't really need for his victim to be in any way disabled but, for whatever reason, he began to pick on Robert in the weeks and months after his return to the classroom. He'd walk behind him in the corridors and clip his heels, causing him to stumble, or he'd sit behind him in class and flick his ears, or kick his chair, or tip out his rucksack on the floor.

I never joined in the bullying, but I'm ashamed to admit that neither did I try to stop it happening, which was something I definitely would have done back in my primary school days, when I'd been confident in my ability to protect the weaker kids, and not so desperate to fit in with the crowd. Me and my friends *were* the crowd in those days.

Anyway, Robert's father or somebody else must have told him that the only way to end things was to stand up to the bully, and after enduring a couple of months of abuse he certainly tried to do that. No one could question his courage, but Robert was a scholar not a brawler, and he had no experience at all of schoolyard punch-ups.

A bunch of us were sprawled in a group outside one of the classrooms one day when D directed some ugly insult at his victim, who was sitting just a few feet away. Robert jumped to his feet. He stared for a couple of long moments at his tormentor, clearly summoning up his nerve, and then, pale in the face, he said: "Stand up and say that again!"

D blinked. "Huh?"

"Stand up and say that again!" he repeated, curling his right fist into a ball and tensing up his whole body. Clearly, so very obviously, he was going to throw the punch he'd probably been dreaming of throwing for months.

D gave a soft chuckle and stood, and as he did so Robert swung with all his might – but of course every one of us sitting there could see the punch coming a mile off, and it whistled harmlessly through the air. D eased aside, then stepped forward and gave him a hard shove, sending him staggering backwards. Robert almost tripped over a couple of the other boys, managing, just, to stay on his feet, but any hope he might have had of felling his opponent with a single blow had evaporated.

He turned and walked away, trying to hold his head high, his limp painfully apparent. A couple of the other kids laughed but most of them just stared at the big bully, resentfully, because this was going too far.

Maybe D had some sense of the group turning against him, or maybe he was surprised enough by Robert's show of defiance, however unsuccessful, that he himself decided that enough was enough, because the taunting subsided from that point on and may even have stopped altogether. I don't remember any further incidents.

I learnt via my Facebook friends recently that Robert had died a couple of years ago, not living long enough to see his 60th birthday. I hadn't seen or heard from him for 45 years or more, but I still felt saddened by that news. He was a good guy. He didn't deserve any of the horrible stuff that happened to him at Willomoore.

I just hope he had a good life in the years and decades that followed his miserable time at the school.

CHAPTER SEVEN

Wow. If you're thinking that this story is starting to take on a darker tone, then you're probably right, but there's a good reason for that. My life was taking on a decidedly darker tone at around this time; in fact, by the start of my Standard Seven year I was already looking back with nostalgia at my primary school days and thinking just how much easier and better everything had been then.

Old friends like X had started to avoid me. I didn't understand why, but I do now, and I have to say I don't really blame them because, frankly, I was becoming a real pain to be around. That same need for attention that had gotten me into so much trouble back in Standard Three had resurfaced, and with a vengeance. I was always trying to say something funny, trying to not be ignored, trying to be seen all the way back there in the shadows being cast by Graham's rapidly rising star.

In 1976 Protea presented what was probably its most successful show to that point, a raucous, fun-filled production of *Joseph and the Amazing Technicolour Dreamcoat*. It played to a packed-out hall for a couple of weeks, and the highlight, for many people, was Graham's performance as Pharaoh, bursting out of a fake sarcophagus wearing a sparkled catsuit and Elvis sunglasses, swivelling his hips and belting out one of Andrew Lloyd Webber's catchiest tunes. My father captured that part of the show on his old 8mm cine camera, and although there's no accompanying soundtrack, that shaky, discoloured clip still manages to give some idea what must have been a joyful and carefree moment in my brother's life.

At home, Graham was having a lot of fun making prank phone calls, with me and my friend Bruce – remember the Lion from *Wizard of Oz*? – joining in sometimes. A lot of kids were doing the same thing in those days, calling up the local supermarket, for example, and asking if they had Van Riebeeck (coffee) in a tin, and then saying: "Well, you better let him out or he's going to suffocate!"

Graham tried a few different tactics. He would phone various teachers or shopkeepers and experiment with foreign accents, telling rambling stories that led nowhere, or getting the sweet little boy who lived next door to us at the time, Craig K, aged four or five, to ask them to go find his mother – prompting grave concern on the other end of the line.

At one point he phoned a family friend, Kim Y, who had started work as a sports reporter on the *Benoni City Times*, and told him: "I haff good story for choo!"

Kim responded: "Ah! Lemme grab a pen ... okay, what is it?"

"My son. He ees roonink."

"Roonink? Running?"

"Yiss. Iss what I say: roonink."

"Okay ... where's he running?"

"Round the dam."

"And?"

"Choo can write story. Choo haff exclusive. Yiss!"

"Has he won any races? Lots of races?"

"Oh Yiss. Me and heem. He win every time."

"Wait – there's just you and your son in the race? That's not a story!"

"But ees roonink!"

"Running!"

"Roonink fast!"

"No! I can't write a story about –

"Round the dam!"

Kim would get exasperated and hang up after a while, and Graham would call back a day or two later to let him know that his daughter was sweeming in the dam, or that his cousin was joomping over the dam wall.

Bruce would have a go, and he too was able to keep the person on the other end of the line guessing and we'd all have a good laugh about it. I came up with a few ideas of my own but they never seemed to work that well. The next day at school I'd tell my old mates like X all about it anyway, pressing ahead despite an ever-less-enthusiastic response.

Another thing that Graham used to do that, to my impressionable mind, seemed really clever and cool was to bum money from classmates and any other school pupils who were gullible enough to fall for his wretched tales about needing enough bus fare to get home, or to buy a pie from the school tuck shop because somebody had stolen his lunch. He'd get two cents here and five cents there, and eventually he'd have enough to buy a bottle of Marvel Orange and a couple of loose cigarettes from the shop at the Benoni Central terminus where we used to catch our bus back to Morehill every afternoon.

I followed his example and for the first couple of weeks it was a complete success. I was astonished by how easily my fellow pupils could be parted from their cash – but of course the longer it went on, the less popular I became, because nobody likes to see the same kid hanging around the school tuck shop hassling everyone in the queue for a few cents, day after day after day.

Sadly, I seem to have been surprisingly slow to grasp that idea. I can remember at a much later point being told candidly by Andy K, a kid who'd been a friend back in primary school days, that nobody really liked me anymore because I'd become like a pair of underpants: always on the bum.

He was wrong, I told myself. Graham bummed money all the time, and nobody called HIM a pair of underpants, did they? Many years later, Graham admitted to me that he'd been called exactly that, and worse, and that his antics had lost him just as many friends, and that he too had had a wretched time as a teenager. Hell, maybe we all do.

As I drifted away from my old friends I started spending more time with D which, in hindsight, was not such a great idea. He lived in the centre of town, and on many afternoons I'd walk back home with him rather than catch the bus to Morehill. We'd have a sandwich at his place and then head on over to the local pinball arcade in the new Cranbourne Ave centre, whiling away the hours smoking and swearing and spitting ostentatiously, trying to hassle the other kids for 10 cents at a time to play the machines and occasionally running up a number of free replays, and then selling them off one at a time to the next batch of boys who wandered in.

On one such afternoon a scrawny Afrikaans kid about the same age as me was playing on our favourite pinball machine, the *Spirit of 76*. He was doing well and after a few minutes the room resounded to a loud and familiar CLACK! sound – alerting him and everyone else that he'd just scored himself a free game. D and I left the corner where we'd been slouching coolly to take a closer look.

The kid was flipping the ball with expert timing and giving the machine a gentle nudge at all the right moments, hitting all the right targets and sinking the ball in all the right slots, but just as it seemed he was about to score a second free game, D, out of the blue, gave me a hard shove in the back. Taken completely by surprise, I was unable to stop myself stumbling forward into the side of the pinball machine, with a fair amount of force – instantly triggering the "tilt" mechanism within. The lights died and the music stopped and the silver ball dropped to the bottom of the table and disappeared into the hole. The Afrikaans kid swore and threw up his hands in despair and anger.

I apologised, and D assured the boy that it had been a mistake. He was sceptical, of course, but after muttering dark curses beneath his breath for a few moments he pressed the restart button for his free game and fired the silver ball back into play. Ten seconds into the game D did the same thing, again shoving me into the machine and tilting it.

This time the Afrikaans kid swung around with fists raised, ready to go to war, but common sense prevailed: he was outnumbered two-to-one, after all, and one of the two was D, who towered above him.

Swearing loudly, he stomped out the arcade. Me and D laughed loud and long.

Actions have consequences, however, and the follow-up to this incident came about a week later. It was a Friday night, if I remember right, and I was playing pinball at the Mexican Hat café, just down the road from the Cranbourne Centre arcade, when that same scrawny Afrikaans kid walked in with a smaller boy, presumably his little brother, in tow. He stopped dead in his tracks when he spotted me.

The pinball machines were located at the back of the shop, next to the rows of Coca-Cola fridges, and the owner had erected a few curved mirrors on the walls and ceiling to make sure that the groups of boys forever hanging around back there weren't helping themselves to a free drink from time to time. The Afrikaans kid approached cautiously, looking around him and checking those mirrors to make sure that D wasn't anywhere in the vicinity. Satisfied that I was on my own, he bent and whispered something in his brother's ear, and the little boy immediately turned and hurried out the shop.

I'd watched all this with a growing sense of unease, and my suspicions were justified a moment later when the Afrikaans kid stepped up alongside me and whacked the side of the machine, tilting it the same way I'd tilted his.

I swore and lashed out and he sprang away, assuming a fighting stance – at which point there was a loud shout from the Portuguese owner of the store: "Hey! No fighting in here! Get out on the street!"

Me and the kid exchanged a few pleasantries in his mother tongue on our way out – "P**s!" and "F** jou!" and "Jou ma se woer woer!" and so on. I may even have thrown in the odd Glaswegian taunt in the heat of the moment – "Awa an bile yer heid!" – though I doubt he would have understood.

We spilled out onto the pavement, with the store owner standing at the entrance to enjoy the show, and I let rip with a wild kick. The Afrikaans kid leapt backwards. I stepped forward and threw a punch. He leapt back again. He turned briefly to look down the road behind him and I rushed forward with another punch, but he was agile enough to take another step back, just in time.

This pattern continued for another minute or so, the pair of us gradually crabbing our way down the road without any contact at all being made, but with the Afrikaans kid turning every now and then to shoot a glance over his shoulder ... and if you're thinking to yourself at this point: gosh, it's almost as if poor Gav is being lured into some kind of trap, well, you'd be entirely right.

We were almost down to the corner when a small army of angry Afrikaners suddenly came charging into view, and not just kids like me: the little brother had obviously rushed back to their home nearby and summoned the whole frickin family! There were at least three grown men in that mob, one of them an oupa in his slippers and dressing-gown, along with at least four teenagers of varying height and size – and every last one of them was intent on catching the skinny rooinek and beating the shite out of him.

My opponent, emboldened by the arrival of the cavalry, jumped forward at last with a triumphant cry – which allowed me to sink one meaty kick into his guts – and then the mob was upon me. I ducked a wild haymaker thrown by the teen who was leading the charge, so close that I felt it raise the hair on the top of my head, then I turned and ran for my life, and at a more than reasonably good pace.

I whizzed passed the shop owner standing goggle-eyed in the entrance then darted unexpectedly to the right, shaking off the tenuous hold one of my pursuers had managed to acquire on my T-shirt. I weaved between a couple of parked cars then shot across the road in front of oncoming traffic, gaining myself a precious few seconds.

The arcade was just a hundred yards or so farther along and I headed towards it instinctively, hoping and praying that D would be there, and maybe a few other regular dropouts who might want to even up the odds a bit, but my heart sank as I burst through the glass double doors and saw that the place was deserted. Trapped like a fox, gasping for breath, I fetched up against one of the pinball machines and stood there panicking and wondering what the hell I was going to do.

The manager, a young, bearded man whose name I can't recall, stepped out from the tiny cubicle at the back that served as an office of sorts. "What's going on..." he began just as the Afrikaner army arrived. Assessing the situation in an instant, he stepped forward and raised an authoritative palm, like the wizard Gandalf telling the Balrog: "you shall not pass". More to the point, he swung the door shut in the face of the guy at the front of the mob and he turned the lock as the rest of them piled up against the glass, yelling and swearing and pointing at me, murder very clearly on the group mind.

"Get back! Get away!" the manager shouted.

"We want *heem!*" the front guy shouted. A couple of them started banging on the glass with flattened hands, enraged and frustrated in equal measure, able to see their prey cowering back against a pinball machine, sweaty and pale and trembling, but unable to exact the vengeance they so richly deserved.

"I'm calling the police," the manager shouted, and he stepped back in the direction of his office, making dialling motions with his fingers to underline his intent – and it was tribute to the respect the average Benoni resident still had for the authorities in those days that the mob stopped banging on the glass ... but they didn't immediately leave either.

The manager paused at the door to his cubicle and reached inside for the telephone receiver. He looked down and appeared to dial a few numbers on the old rotary telephone, but it was only when the mob could see him start speaking into the receiver – there was nobody on the other end; he was bluffing, but they didn't know that – that they finally, reluctantly, moved away, still swearing and shaking their fists in my direction.

I sank down to the ground, offering effusive thank-yous to my saviour as I heaved in great lungfuls of air, telling him how those crazy dutchmen had targeted me out of the blue, for no reason at all, as I was walking along just minding my own business and looking for old ladies I could help across the road.

"I don't like bullies. Eight against one? Or was it nine?" he asked.

"Easy. Maybe even ten. A dozen," I agreed. I fumbled out a cigarette from the crushed packet of Peter Stuyvesants in my jeans pocket and offered him one too.

A moment later there was a knock on the glass door, and I jumped up in fear, certain that the gang was back, but then I heaved a shaky sigh of relief: it was just my father out there, knocking again and checking his wristwatch and probably wondering why the door was locked. He'd agreed to pick me up at 8pm and it was maybe 8.10pm.

That, by the way, was another of my father's weird quirks: like most of the other parents in my friend group, he was willing to pick his kids up from the ice rink or the cinema or wherever, but he was always late to arrive; every single time, without any exception at all, over a period of several years. It was just a thing with him. We knew it and expected it, but on this particular occasion that quirk probably saved him a solid beating, because if he'd happened to show up on time that night, just as the mob was milling around outside the arcade, and if they'd realised he was my father ... well, I'm pretty sure they would have laid into him there and then.

Close call, for both of us.

My father didn't ask, on the drive home, why I was drenched in sweat and shaken up, and I didn't volunteer the information. Nor did he mention that he'd seen me holding a cigarette in my hand and expelling a lungful of smoke as I'd jumped up and stared over at the door.

It was only the following evening, when my mother and I drove around to the nearby Kentucky Fried Chicken outlet to buy dinner, that she said, very casually, out of the blue, as she was parking the car: "I'm telling your father to give you a hiding when we get home."

"Eh? What for?" I asked, mystified.

"He saw you smoking last night. At that pinball place."

My blood ran cold. He did? He had? But ... but why didn't he say anything at the time? And why did my mother wait until the next evening before telling me I was in trouble? And just before a KFC dinner too, that I'd really been looking forward to?

Contrast that with my parents' reaction on the night, a short while later, when they saw me drunk for the first time, at the cast party held at our house to mark the final performance of *Joseph and the Amazing Technicolour Dreamcoat*.

There were a dozen or so people milling around the swimming pool in the back garden and a couple dozen more crammed into the lounge, gathered around the piano and singing along to various ditties played by my father. At some point in the festivities I came crawling into the room on my hands and knees, mindlessly drunk and completely incapable of standing upright, but just about able to belt out the chorus to *There's One More Angel in Heaven* along with everyone else.

I fell silent for the last verse however, and anybody watching closely would have noticed my face turning ominously pale. I crabbed backwards into the hall, still on all fours, and made it to the toilet just in time before I started throwing up, and then I toppled over to one side and passed out on the cold, tiled floor.

I fully expected another close encounter of the painful kind the following day but there was no reprimand at all. Like the phone-box incident, my mother had a laugh about the whole thing.

Blurred lines, man.

CHAPTER EIGHT

I t was some time towards the end of my Standard Seven year that me and D cycled out to Willowmoore High on a sleepy Sunday afternoon, not with any concrete plans in mind but just because we had nothing else to do. There must have a caretaker somewhere on site, even back in those days, but there was no sign of him that day, so we cycled around the main quad for a bit doing donuts with our rear tires and revelling in the freedom of having the place to ourselves and the sense that we were somehow challenging the school authorities just by being there. Heady stuff.

At some point D wandered over to one of the classrooms and noticed that the sash window was open just an inch or so at the bottom, so he gave me a leg-up and I clambered through, then I turned back and helped him over the sill.

We stared around us. We were in one of the maths classrooms. D headed straight to the teacher's desk and started rifling through the drawers; me, I strolled over to a filing cabinet against the wall and did the same, tossing aside piles of papers and books in my search for anything of value. I came up empty-handed, but D was more fortunate: there was a big manila envelope in one of the drawers and it had dozens of coins swishing around in the bottom of it, 50 cent and 20 cent pieces mostly, along with a list of names of people who'd bought a ticket in some sort of school fund-raising raffle.

D laughed out loud and tilted the envelope to one side and emptied the coins onto a desk and swept them into his pocket, then he crunched up the list and threw it into a nearby litter bin. "Let's go," he said. "We'll count it later."

We tipped a few desks over for good measure then we slid out through the window we'd come in, mounted our bikes and cycled off to the nearest café and bought a couple of packs of cigarettes each.

I half expected some sort of announcement at school assembly the following day, maybe an appeal of sorts for anyone who knew anything about the break-in to come forward, but there was nothing at all, no acknowledgement of the crime. Maybe the teacher who'd left the cash in the drawer – seven rand, if I remember right, so not a huge sum – had decided just to meet the shortfall himself, rather than admit that he'd left it unguarded in an unlocked drawer. Whatever the reason, we were emboldened enough by our success to revisit the school a couple of weekends later.

We tried all the windows of the classrooms on the ground floor but this time they were all locked tight so we cycled around a bit more until D pulled up with a stylish wheelie outside the tuckshop. It too had a sash window, maybe five feet above the ground, and it was also locked ... but sitting there in plain view on the other side was a full box of Fizzer bars; long chewy strips of sweet stuff that I personally was a big fan of.

"Gimme one of those rocks," D said, pointing to one side, where a school gardener had been working with a pile of soil and plants.

"This one?" I asked, hefting one in my hand the size of a grapefruit.

"That'll do," he said, taking it and lobbing it at the lower pane in one smooth motion. The glass shattered and he reached inside carefully and pulled out the box of Fizzer bars, maybe 15 or 20 of them.

Just then there was a loud shout from the general region of the school office block and I looked up to see an aging and overweight man, the caretaker presumably, shaking one fist in the air and lumbering towards us, shouting at us to stay right where we were ... which, of course, we weren't about to do. We fumbled as many of the Fizzer bars into our pockets as would fit then we peddled away at top speed.

CHAPTER NINE

You may have wondered at some point in this story why it is that my sister Christine has received only a passing mention here and there, and the reason is quite simply that I don't remember us having too much to do with each other in those early years. There was none of the conflict or hostility that marked relations with my brother but neither was there any particular affinity between us; she minded her business and I minded mine.

We became closer for a time as young adults, when we would often sit and chat through the night over countless cups of coffee, and I learnt that she too had been struggling with various issues as a child and teenager, chief of which was a chronic lack of self-confidence and a sense that, like me, her needs took a back seat to Graham's in the family dynamic.

She had talents outside of the singing and acting line that she would later choose to follow as a career, and she was good enough at sports to be named Victrix Ludorum at Willowmoore High one year after winning a bunch of track and field events at the school sports day. But the inter-high competition that followed soon after provided a perfect example of the self-doubt that had plagued her throughout her childhood: she told me that she was crouched on the line waiting for the starter's gun when she decided that all the other girls would probably be a lot faster than her, so when the pistol sounded she deliberately stumbled and went to her knees ... allowing her to stand up a moment later and give a helpless shrug as the others went racing off towards the finishing line. That way, she wouldn't have to suffer the embarrassment of coming in last.

Would she have won if she'd committed herself to the challenge? Maybe, maybe not ... but this way she had an excuse.

That theme persisted throughout her twenties when, as a struggling actress and singer, she would consistently oversleep and miss important auditions, or suddenly come down with laryngitis on opening night. By the time she hit her thirties she'd gotten a handle on the situation and was starting to find success on the stage, but by then a decade or more of what should have been her best years as a singer had passed.

I can remember a couple of fights between her and my brother in our teenage years, when Graham had begun taunting her about her still-developing figure, branding her with a cruel nickname which I won't repeat here but which used to drive her nuts every time he said it. I remember her chasing him – and me, because I'd joined in, of course – from the kitchen one afternoon with a breadknife in her hand and a glaze of insanity her eyes, and I hate to think how that would have ended if she'd managed to catch us.

Me, I had just the one big physical altercation with Christine as far as I can recall, but it was a big one, and it happened on a busy morning when the whole family was trying to get ready for school or work at the same time.

For some reason we didn't own a toaster, but the kitchen hob was equipped with a large solid hotplate that, once heated, could toast a slice of bread to a lovely golden brown – but it did take a few minutes each time, and there was fierce competition every day to get to it first.

Food being my prime motivator, I was usually in the kitchen ahead of everybody else. On the morning in question I already had four slices of bread spread out on the hotplate, toasting at least the inner quadrant of each, when Christine came flouncing in, demanding to know how much longer I was going to be. She did a lot of flouncing in those days.

"I dunno. Till all the pieces of bread are ready," I said.

"Looks like they're ready now!" she shot back.

"Well, they're not. And I've still got to do the other side, so it's going to be a while."

"Hpmphh!"

She moved to one side long enough to cut a couple of slices of white bread for herself and then she stepped up to the stove again, shifting her weight from foot to foot and sighing impatiently. She gave it another moment and then she flounced back to her bedroom – only to reappear barely a minute later, her patience apparently exhausted. She reached out an angry hand and simply brushed all four slices of my half-toasted bread off the hob and onto the adjoining tabletop.

"Those are ready," she declared. She placed her two pieces on the hob.

"No, they're bloody well not!" I replied, and I swept *her* pieces of bread aside in exactly the same manner and replaced mine.

"They're brown! They're almost burnt!"

"That's how I like them!"

"THEY'RE F***ING READY" she screeched, and she grabbed my four slices of bread up in one swift motion, her fingers digging into one corner of each simultaneously, and she turned and hurled them at the far wall with all her might. At which point I leapt forward and kicked her in the stomach, and she flailed at my face with her fingernails and we started bouncing off the tabletops, grappling and swearing and kicking and biting and sending butter containers and jars of jam and anchovy fish paste crashing to the floor.

The family dogs, two cross-collies called Brandy and Sherry, and an old mongrel mutt called Rusty, came running in, barking like crazy, followed by my father close behind, his chin still wreathed in shaving foam. He pulled us apart and floored me with a hard whack to the back of my head. Christine was screaming and crying and I was yelling out my side of the story, infuriated by the sight of my precious breakfast being so horribly abused. My father, for once, began shouting at the top of his voice for everybody just to shut up! Just shut up! Just shut up!!!

At which point Graham snuck into the kitchen and slipped two slices of bread onto the hotplate, sparking another round of furious shouting from both me and Christine.

Crazy morning. All families have them, I'm told.

CHAPTER TEN

By the close of my Standard Seven year the powers that be down at the Benoni Council had made a few changes to the school zoning rules, and pupils from the suburb of Morehill were told they could make the switch from Willowmoore to the new Benoni High if they wanted to. Christine and I both took up the option; me starting in my Standard Eight year and her in matric. Graham, of course, had just finished his schooling and had enrolled at Wits University to study drama, intent on pursuing a career on the stage.

The change meant that I quickly lost contact with D, which was definitely for the best because I would probably have gotten into more trouble, and of an increasingly serious nature, in the years ahead if I'd remained under his sway. As it was, I never saw him again.

I was reacquainted on that first day at Benoni High with several of my old buddies from Rynfield Primary, and that filled me with hope that there were better days ahead – but it didn't take long at all for me to realise that the dynamic that had existed back then had altered fundamentally, and not in my favour.

I'd been somewhere near the top of the social hierarchy back in primary school, mostly popular with the other boys and sure of my place in the world. Now every last one of my classmates seemed to have somehow leapt ahead of me in the race towards manhood. They were louder and brasher, more muscled and hairier, confident with girls. Half of them were already riding motorbikes while I was still tooling around on my old Raleigh three-speed bicycle.

I'd always been skinny; now, approaching my 15th birthday, I was positively skeletal, the skin stretched tight over my bony nose and jawline and my face and shoulders producing a fresh crop of horrible pimples every day without fail. My fingers were stained from the 12 or 15 cigarettes I was smoking every day and I'd developed a wet and thoroughly unpleasant cough. The other guys were smoking just as many, but without any apparent side effects.

I tried out for the school football squad one afternoon, cheered on by former Rynfield team-mates like Steve V and Andy K and Richard V who'd assured the coach that I was halfway competent, but whatever little ability I may have had back in the day appeared to have deserted me. I did my old trick of sprinting down the left wing with the ball but somehow lost control of it every time I stopped and turned and tried to boot it into the centre. I missed the ball entirely when I jumped for headers and my spindly legs were no longer able to propel me across the field faster than whoever was marking me. Stamina had been one of my strong points with the Rynfield team, but now I was out of breath ten minutes into the session.

Needless to say, the coach didn't ask me back for a second try and my old team-mates didn't try to convince him otherwise.

I was experiencing similar setbacks on the badminton court. I'd always loved the game, more so than football in fact, and me and Shaun F had been getting steadily better as the years went by. I'd begun playing one or two evenings a week in the Benoni adult leagues, often beating full-grown men in the singles matches. But as that Standard Eight year drew on I found myself losing most of those matches, and even being beaten by kids I'd been outplaying easily for years.

The smoking and occasional drinking binges were taking their toll. I had become acutely conscious, every time I stripped off my tracksuit trousers, of just how stick-thin my legs now looked in my badminton shorts. My diet was terrible, consisting mainly of ice-cream and cereal, or toasted cheese sandwiches, or chips and hamburger patties; not exactly the food of champions.

All of that was bad enough – but there was something else going on too, and it made itself known towards the end of that year when I realised that I was struggling to read the words that the teachers were writing on the class blackboard.

I shared my fears with my mother one night after dinner. "Mom, I think I might need to get some glasses," I said.

"Rubbish!" she replied without a pause. "Nobody in this family has ever had to wear glasses. We've all got good eyes. You're absolutely fine."

Whew, that was a relief, I can tell you. There was me worrying that I might have some kind of visual problem but my mother had been able to clear things up in an instant. I was absolutely fine.

Except she hadn't cleared anything up at all, and I was a long way from absolutely fine. There *was* a problem with my eyesight, it turned out, and it wasn't, sadly, something as straightforward as me being short-sighted. I learnt soon after, when I finally visited an optician and then a specialist, that I was afflicted with something called keratoconus, and that it was a gift that would keep on giving for all the days of my life to come.

I have a cheerful motto (which I believe I came up with myself, although it is possible that I read it somewhere) and it goes something like this: no matter how bad things are, they can always get worse. You always have to work hard at making your life better, but it can get dramatically worse in the blink of an eye, and with no effort from you at all.

A brief aside, just to put things in context:

Keratoconus, according to my good friend Mr Google, hits about one in 2,000 people, and for no good reason that science has been able to determine. It affects the cornea, the clear jelly at the front of the eye, causing it to grow thin and bulge outwards in a cone shape, distorting the vision and often creating a sensitivity to glare. There's no cure as such, but most people afflicted by it can get along well enough with just a pair of spectacles or, in more severe cases, hard contact lenses that provide the smooth surface necessary for light to pass through the pupil undisturbed.

However, for one in five of those one in 2,000 – one in 10,000 people, in effect – there comes a point at which contact lenses and spectacles can no longer produce any clarity of vision and they find themselves permanently looking out at the world as if through a frosted-glass bathroom window, and the only remaining option is to undergo a corneal transplant.

I had my first transplant at the age of 21 (right eye) and my second when I was 30 (left eye), and in the years since I've had laser surgery on both eyes and experimented with literally dozens of new-fangled contact lenses and specialised spectacles as my corneas have continued to shape-shift with depressing consistency.

With the help of some expert practitioners (big shout out to Claire Ranger in Milton Keynes, and Allon Barsam in London in recent years!) I've usually been able to find some combination of glasses and contact lenses that have enabled me to live a mostly normal life – but there's no denying how vulnerable I feel when I pop that lens out at night and wake up, say, at 3am to a suspicious sound downstairs, or out in the garden, and I have to shuffle out with my frosted-glass vision to investigate the cause.

Of course, I'd never have been able to live much of a life at all without the operations and the countless lenses and spectacles I've had, but I've often paid a high price for all of that (and I'm not talking just about the tens of thousands of pounds I've spent over the years). There've been many times when I've lost a lens at the most inconvenient or dangerous moment: riding a big wave on a paddleski in the Durban surf or speeding along a busy motorway at 90mph; building a campfire in the remote Namib desert or looking dreamily into the eyes of my beautiful wife-to-be on our first date. I've blinked at just the wrong angle, and the bastard thing has popped out my eye and vanished into thin air, leaving me pawing myopically at my chest.

I'm eternally grateful to the two anonymous individuals who donated their corneas to me all those years ago. The one in my right eye has been going strong now for almost 40 years, and whoever it belonged to originally might have been 60 or 70 when they died, making that small wedge of jelly a hundred years old or more. However, my eye specialist mentioned recently, as an afterthought almost, that "at some point it's going to fail" ... which will involve me having a second transplant, with reduced chances of success due to my advancing years.

Also, as I get older and my eyes naturally get drier it's becoming ever harder to find a lens that is both comfortable and does an adequate job. My left eye can't handle a lens at all these days so I rely on my right eye for reading and driving etc, and I've become so sensitive to glare that I'm forced to wear a baseball cap pretty much all the time, even indoors. I daren't venture outside without sunglasses.

At home, the curtains and blinds are always drawn and we use table lamps rather than overhead lights. Many TV shows are simply unwatchable, especially those funky ones with shaky, handheld camera images or sudden flashes of bright light, and when we go out to a restaurant I always have to position myself carefully to be sure my back is to the window or, if it's night-time, that we're not seated directly under some bright light.

When I work at a computer I have to remember to take frequent screen breaks or pay the price of a migraine headache an hour later, and when I lay my weary head down to sleep at night I know I have to wake up within a couple of hours to insert drops into my eyes to stop them drying out, and then repeat the process throughout the night. Which is one of the reasons why I sleep so badly these days, meaning I spend two or three mornings a week stumbling around with what I call zombie brain, unable to add two and two together until I've had a midday nap. Exhausting, right?

But every cloud has a silver lining. For me, it's the fact that all of this has made me such a pain in the arse for my employers that they've agreed to let me work from home permanently in these last few years before I finally fade away into retirement. When the pandemic eased up everybody else was told to go back into the office, but I've been allowed to do what I do remotely ... which is a huge deal for me, because I no longer have to endure that three-hour round-trip commute to London that was slowly but surely squeezing the life force out of me.

And finally, every time I'm having a bad day, and cursing my fate, and wondering why it was me who had to be the first Weir on record to get stuck with keratoconus, I remind myself of a salient fact: that there are, quite literally, tens of millions of completely blind people in the world, brave souls who you'll see striding along confidently with just a white stick to feel for obstacles in the path ahead, or with a guide dog at their side to show them the way. I remind myself that every single one of those people would cry with happiness if they could have the vision that I have.

At which point I tell myself to stop being such a wuss and to just get on with it...

CHAPTER 11

When a specialist in Joburg confirmed that, yes, I did indeed have keratoconus, the first question I asked was: what caused it? A popular theory doing the rounds at the time was that it could be triggered by a hard blow to the head at some point in your teenage years – and I didn't have to look too far to find one such glaring example. Christine had taken up with a new boyfriend a few months earlier, a likeable if overly cocky 17-year-old joller by name of Roger M. He'd drop by the house in the afternoons after school and the two of them would disappear into her bedroom for hours on end, supposedly to study. Of course, our house wasn't that big, and the muffled sounds of teenage passion could be heard up and down the passageway, so it was no surprise when Roger appeared at my bedroom door one day with the key to his motorbike in one hand and said: "You want to take her for a spin?" Obviously hoping to buy himself a half hour of uninterrupted loving time, though I was too naive to realise that at the time.

"Your bike? Of course!"

"Cool. You've ridden a bike before, right?"

"No."

"But you know how to?"

"No."

"Ah shit." He grimaced and turned away.

"You can teach me," I said quickly. "Just show me how to start it up."

"I dunno ..."

"And what button to press to make it go really, really fast."

"Sorry kid. I don't think I should..."

Christine called out from down the hall: "Rog? Are you coming back?"

To his credit, he did at least pause for a moment ... but then he gave in to temptation and said: "OK Gav, lemme show you real quick," and he hustled me out to the driveway where he'd left the bike. It was a 150cc, if I remember right; not an especially powerful machine, but it was an old model and so heavy that I could barely hold it upright with my puny biceps.

He raced through the basics: "You kickstart it like this ..." – *vroom* – "and you pull in the clutch here then put in in gear like this... " – *clickety-click* – "and the same again when you want to change gear..." – *clickety-click* – "and you accelerate like this..." – *vroom vroom VROOM* – "and when you want to stop you squeeze this lever and press down with your heel here ... got it? Right."

"Um ..."

"Put this on." He forced his full-face crash helmet down over my head, flattening my nose in the process.

"OK, I'll just go round the block," I said, revving the engine a couple of times.

"No, go for a proper ride. A long, long ride," he replied, and he turned and sprinted back inside the house without a backward glance.

You can probably guess what happened next, but I'll give you the finer details: I revved the engine a couple of times and then stalled it when I tried to put it in gear. I succeeded on the second attempt then stalled it again when I tried to change gears, and almost toppled over as I slowed to a stop. On the third attempt I was able to coast all the way up to the top of Barbara Avenue, and then right into Norman, right into Pamela, right into Dale, then right into Barbara again, staying in first gear all the way.

I drew up outside the house again, thrilled with my progress and eager to share my success with Rog, who I'd decided was the coolest guy on the planet, but when I parked the bike and ran to the back door I discovered it was locked.

Hmm. Strange. Almost as if Rog and Christine didn't want to be disturbed.

I shrugged. Rog had said to go for a really long ride ... so maybe I should?

I started the bike up again, stalled it, restarted it, and then crept up to the top of the road, still in first gear. I completed a second circuit of the block at a snail's pace and then, feeling braver, shifted into second gear after turning into Norman. As I rounded the bend into Pamela I clicked into third gear and turned the accelerator with gusto and the old bike leapt forward, picking up speed at an astonishing pace.

The sound of the engine was roaring in my ears but I kept the throttle open anyway and hit fourth gear, terrified and exhilarated in equal measure. The intersection was suddenly racing up to meet me at an alarming rate so I throttled back and decided to brake ... but was it the right heel or the left heel I was supposed to press down? Or click up? Left or right? Up or down? Or was there something on the handlebar I was supposed to push or squeeze or twist? Panic set in and shit-shit-shit no-no-no I couldn't remember!

I clicked and pressed and squeezed and twisted all at once and then, out of time and out of road and still with no idea of how to slow the behemoth between my legs, I simply froze up, watching like a passenger as the bike screamed into the T-junction at the bottom of Pamela Avenue. The front wheel hit the pavement and I was catapulted through the air at high speed, smashing head-first into a solid wooden gatepost. I blacked out.

I don't know how long I lay there. When the world finally came swimming back into focus I had no clue at all what had just happened, or why I was flat on my back staring up at some clouds scudding by overhead. I became aware of an intense pain in my neck, and then my right wrist, and when I tried to sit upright I almost blacked out again.

After a few more attempts I was able to stand and assess the situation and it dawned on me at last that I'd crashed

Rog's bike. I stared down at myself. My T-shirt was torn and splashed with mud and blood that, I worked out later, must have come from my nose. The crash helmet had been knocked clean off my head by the impact and was lying up against the homeowner's fence, but it had at least done its job: it was cracked down the middle and my skull was not.

The bike itself was lying off to one side, the front wheel crumpled back in on itself, the handlebars twisted at an odd angle and the massive frame covered in mud, with oil or petrol or some other dark liquid staining the grass all around.

I stumbled across and tried to pick it up, but a bolt of pain in my wrist forced me to quickly drop it. I stood there for a few moments longer, still dazed and uncertain, then I turned and headed back to the house, walking at first and then running.

I was shouting out Roger's name at the top of my panicked voice by the time I drew near and he came hurrying out to meet me in the driveway.

I blurted out what had happened, fully expecting him to throw a fit – or maybe even a punch – when he learnt that his beloved bike was a wreck, but he waved aside my concerns. Was I OK, he asked? Was I hurt? Where did the blood on my shirt come from? And then: did anyone need to know about this? I didn't really have to tell my parents, did I?

"Of course not! You're not going to tell them, are you?" I shot back. I wasn't exactly in the habit of sharing my day-to-day misadventures with my mother and father.

He breathed a sigh of relief. "No man. Of course not. So ... just how bad is the bike? Can it be ridden back?"

I shook my head miserably.

He nodded and looked around him. We had an open carport rather than a garage in those days, with various boxes and gardening tools stacked up against the walls. In one corner was a wheelbarrow, and Roger grabbed the handles and spun it around and started trundling it down the driveway. "C'mon Gav. Let's go get it," he said.

"You're not pissed off? With me?"

"Nah. It's not a big deal, man. F***sakes, I crash bikes all the time! C'mon, let's go. Before your folks get home."

I fell in step alongside him and we walked back to the crash site, me marvelling all the way at his laidback attitude. I'd destroyed his bike and he didn't hate me! Didn't want to punch my lights out, didn't tell me what a loser I was! What a guy! *This* was the sort of big brother I'd always wanted, I thought to myself. How come I got stuck with Graham?

Sadly, things fell apart between Christine and Roger in the months that followed, with all sorts of drama and heartache and crises playing out, none of which I feel at liberty to talk about here. He was finally banned from our house after a showdown between him and my father, and for a time I acted as a courier and a go-between for the star-crossed young lovers, arranging illicit meetings between them against the orders of my parents and carrying messages and generally doing anything I could to help. Eventually they parted ways anyway and Roger quit coming around, and I probably missed him as much as Christine did.

Good big brothers are hard to find.

A few years later, when I was visiting one of the many, many eye specialists I would consult over the course of my life, I was asked if I'd ever suffered a hard blow to the head during my teenage years; the sort of thing that might have triggered the keratoconus – and I said, why yes, I had a bike crash when I was 15.

The specialist nodded and said: "That was probably it."

Of course, that theory has since been discounted, but for a couple of decades afterwards, whenever somebody would ask how it was I'd ended up with keratoconus when no one else in my family had ever had it, I'd reply: "Well, my sister had a boyfriend called Roger, and he had a motorbike and ..."

CHAPTER 12

If there's one thing my real big brother did for me it is this: he introduced me to the game of poker when I was 15, and it would prove to be an endlessly fascinating hobby that has provided me with countless happy hours in the decades since. I'm talking about playing live poker, by the way, not the online version, which is hopelessly rigged, and which I definitely would not recommend. Graham and his buddies used to gather in our living room on a Friday night to play cards for a handful of small change; one and two cent pieces mostly, with the occasional five or ten cent piece thrown in by the big spenders. The gang was usually six or seven strong, and they were happy to let me join in. We played a variety of games – Queenie, Blackjack and so on – but it was the poker sessions I particularly enjoyed, some of which would carry on well into the early hours of the morning or, during school holidays, all the way through to sunrise.

There'd always be music playing in the background on our family's old record player – *Tubular Bells* was a favourite, along with various Jethro Tull albums and Fleetwood Mac – and the room would be wreathed in cigarette smoke and the floor littered with Lion or Castle beer cans. At some point in the night the door would invariably swing open and my father would stick his head in and make a twiddling gesture with one hand – "turn the music down!" – and Graham would comply but turn it up again five minutes later.

I make no claims, today, to be any kind of poker maestro and I lose almost as often as I win on my annual trips to Las Vegas.

But my love of Texas Hold 'Em, the main variant of the game, is genuine, and it's not just a gambling thing. I've got no interest at all in sports betting, or roulette, or craps, or any of the other games on offer in the casinos.

For me, and for most poker players, the thrill lies in the strategy of the game: calculating the odds of success as they change with every card dealt; trying to assess the ranges of the cards held by the other players at the table; determining whether that cool customer opposite me with the hoodie and shades is bluffing or not; interacting with the many and varied colourful characters you meet at the table (especially in Vegas!).

I love it all, and I can thank Graham for that, because my own set of friends in those years had no interest in cards. Motorbikes were more their thing.

As Standard Eight became Standard Nine, and one by one we celebrated our 16th birthdays, we were finally of a legal age to qualify for a licence and every last one of the teenage boys in my circle immediately went out and bought themselves a 50cc mean machine (or, more accurately, pressured their parents into buying them a 50cc mean machine).

My mother finally agreed to get me one too; second-hand, admittedly, but I was very fond of my Yamaha MR anyway, despite never having exhibited any kind of petrolhead tendencies before (or since). White petrol tank, red stripe with the Yamaha logo, a speedo that lit up a warm green at night … I have a single snapshot of that bike in an old photo album, and it holds some good memories.

Most of the other guys – Craig T, Richard V, Steve V, Derek T, Ian S – also had second-hand machines, but Bruce's dad had bought him a brand-new Suzuki, and he was the envy of the pack. His bike was faster than everybody else's, it never broke down and it offered a smoother ride – which, now that I think about it, kind of summed up Bruce's life: he appeared to be enjoying a far smoother ride in general than anybody else in the group.

His dad was cooler than all the other dads. He had more money, which he didn't hesitate to splash around when he took us all to the TA54 steakhouse for a T-bone and waffles, and he was one of the first in Benoni to buy himself a CB radio when that craze took off ("Ten-four good buddy" – remember that?).

He was funny and great at telling the sort of dirty jokes we weren't used to hearing from adults, and he even returned from a business trip to Europe one time with a tie for each of us boys that had a picture of a naked woman on the inner lining. As far back as our primary school days, if me and Bruce were camping out in a tent in his backyard he'd sometimes appear with his own sleeping bag and join us for the night.

I was really envious of Bruce. He'd always been a pudgy boy but by the time he hit 16 he'd shaken off that puppy fat and emerged as a good-looking and unusually confident teenager, one of the leading lights in the Protea society, which, by then, had pretty much completed the shift to theatrical productions fulltime. He didn't seem to suffer any of the acne issues or gawkiness or self-doubts that the rest of us so patently did; in fact, he could charm just about any girl he had a mind to, while I still found myself completely tongue-tied and incapable of producing anything other than shy grunts and shrill cackles whenever I found myself in the company of any female I found even remotely attractive.

Bruce had always been a frequent visitor to the Weir home, and he began spending even more time with my family at around that time. He and I would ride home from school together on our motorbikes. We'd get a bite to eat, maybe listen to a bit of Rodriguez's Cold Fact and smoke a cigarette or two, then we'd hook up with a few of the other guys and buzz around for the rest of the afternoon on our noisy 50cc machines like a plague of flies, settling at one girl's house after another for coffee and smokes and endless braggadocious chatter.

Those girls included Anne W (the Protea star who'd played

Dorothy in *The Wizard of Oz* a few years earlier), and an English girl called Helen who'd caught the eye of most of the boys when she cut her hair to look like Purdy (Joanna Lumley) from *The Avengers*, and Terry D, a petite girl who'd also been a Protea member for a time. Bruce had his pick of them all, and he eventually dated Terry for a month or two.

On Friday nights a bunch of us would sleep over at someone's house, most often Richard's, whose mother didn't mind us smoking, and we'd scrape together a bit of money from somewhere to buy enough beer or brandy to get mindlessly drunk. We'd almost always end the night puking energetically, because our still-maturing bodies simply weren't equipped to deal with the amount of alcoholic abuse we were subjecting them to, and I have one especially disgusting memory which I'm going to share with you here ... but be warned: if you're eating your dinner while reading this, now would be a good time to look away.

Bruce, Craig and I were at Richard's place on one of those Friday nights and, as usual, we'd all collapsed into a drunken coma by the time midnight rolled around. Richard had made it to his bed but the rest of us were sprawled on or under sleeping bags on the floor nearby.

I awoke at some point in the early hours of the morning, my head spinning and the nausea building, bitter experience telling me that I was about to be violently ill. I started trying to get up and make my way to the toilet down the hallway but I was out of time: my stomach convulsed and the puke came spraying up from my innards, two, three, four times ... and even as I lay there, retching helplessly on the parquet flooring, Richard gave a horrible groan and leaned over the side of his bed and started vomiting all over my head! True story – and probably the grossest thing I've ever experienced in all my life! I was so far gone I couldn't even get out the way; I simply passed out again.

When I woke a few hours later, covered not just in my own dried puke but Richard's too, I almost started throwing up all over again.

Squinting into the dawn light, I made my way on tottering legs down the hall to the bathroom and I climbed into the tub (there was no shower, sadly) and I just sat there shivering and shaking for a while, incapable of further action. Eventually I turned on the taps and sank down into the tepid water, groaning to myself and trying not to notice the little bits of semi-digested carrot or chewed-up chicken that came floating by my bloodshot eyes every time I moved.

Vile, man. Absolutely vile.

On another occasion a group of us decided to camp out on the big mine dump for a night. We climbed to the top as the sun was going down and the shadows were lengthening, and the first thing we did was to collect a huge pile of old and dry branches from the many blue-gum trees growing wild up there and build us a campfire.

We packed only the bare necessities for survival in the wild: matches, knives, sleeping bags, torches, packets of sausages and bread rolls to make hotdogs, and several bottles of Paarl Perle, the cheapest and nastiest wine on the market. It cost just 69 cents for two litres and it came with a cast-iron guarantee of a crippling hangover the following morning, assuming of course that you consumed enough, preferably on an empty stomach, to render you drunk as a monkey with a learning disability the night before. Which we did.

I have a hazy recollection of lurching around the campfire at one point with a breadknife in my hand and then stumbling over the outstretched leg of one of my comatose friends who had collapsed perilously close to the hot coals and very nearly skewering myself through my right eye with that knife as I went crashing to the ground.

I wonder, sometimes, how any of us survived those years...

The high-pitched whine of a 50cc motorbike was a constant soundtrack to life in Benoni back then. They were everywhere, because just about every teenager in town seemed to have one. Some of the older boys formed themselves into a gang called The Black Helmets, imagining themselves as apprentice Hells Angels as they tore up the Benoni High playing fields on a Friday night or organised drag races through the centre of town in the early hours of the morning.

Me and my friends didn't go quite that far, but we did occasionally ride out to the local Greyhound Drive-in and sneak in through the back gate without paying, or descend en masse on the CR Swart park at Rynfield Dam with our haversacks packed with beers and get too drunk to ride home – and then ride home anyway. It's something of a miracle that not a single one of us ever had a serious accident, though I have hazy memories of coming perilously close more than once. My guardian angel was a busy guy.

The Black Helmets were pests, but there were a couple of real gangs operating in Benoni in those days. One of the worst was The Lebs, a group of 15 or 20 teenagers and young men, maybe more, all of Lebanese origin – hence the name – whose idea of a fun Friday night was to gate-crash any teenage party they could find and beat the crap out of all the boys (and sometimes the homeowner too), trash the place for good measure, and then move on to the next target.

I myself nearly fell foul of that gang of orcs one night. Ian S and I had watched a movie at the Greyhound and stopped off at the Luna Plaza roadhouse on the way home for a Dagwood sandwich and a milkshake, removing our crash helmets to eat but still sitting there on our bikes. He finished his food while I was still working on the extra portion of fries I'd ordered, then he started up his 50cc and said his goodbyes and zoomed off into the night.

I crammed the last chips into my mouth and strapped on my crash helmet and was about to follow suit ... when two cars came speeding into the roadhouse parking area, music pounding and tyres squealing. They pulled up right alongside me. The Lebs.

I gulped. I tried to kickstart my Yamaha ... but it didn't take. I tried again. And again. The car doors opened and eight or nine of the bastards spilled out and immediately surrounded me.

"What's the hurry, zabra?" one of them demanded.

"Hey? Nothing, man. Was just about to leave," I said.

"On this piece of shit?" a second guy laughed, aiming a kick at my back tyre.

"You're going nowhere, bra," one of his buddies said, and he grabbed the seat from behind and lifted it – and the back wheel with it – clear off the ground. Someone swore at me, and out of the blue the first guy swung a punch. I ducked my head instinctively, and his fist bounced off the top of my crash helmet – which seemed to infuriate him. He roared some Lebanese curse at me and pulled his fist back for another shot but just then one of the mob stepped in front of him and shouted: "Wait wait wait hold it hold it ... I think I know this oke!"

I blinked. I stared at my saviour – and that's not too strong a description, believe me, because once that pack of mad dogs started with the kicking and punching, they generally didn't stop until the victim was bleeding and unconscious on the ground. It took an instant to recognise that particular Leb, because I hadn't seen him for a couple of years ... but, yeah, it was a kid who'd trained alongside me at a karate dojo near the Mexican Hat café back when I was in Standard Seven.

Man, was I happy to see him again! I'd taken those karate classes for only a few months before dropping out, but they'd proved to be the most effective self-defence classes ever: they saved my life that night, albeit in a very roundabout manner!

"Hey, long time no see," I said in a shaky voice, wishing I could remember his name. The first guy was still looking at me like he wanted to crush my skull and feed it to the Luna Plaza rats, but my newest best friend managed to pull him away and calm him down, but not all the way. The first chance he had, my karate buddy turned back to me and whispered urgently: "F*** off. Get out of here quick, boetie."

I needed no second invitation. My bike started on the third kick, and I eased past a couple of the gang while they were arguing among themselves about something. I turned on to the road and I sped off as fast as my little Yamaha would go ... but only for a couple of hundred yards before the blasted thing spluttered and died and coasted slowly to a stop. I pumped the kickstart repeatedly, in vain, casting frantic looks over my shoulder every time I heard a car pull out of the roadhouse, convinced that the Lebs had glanced over and seen me stalled there in the middle of the road and had changed their minds.

Eventually I jumped off the bike and began running alongside it, pushing it all the way home, at least three or four miles. Which was a long way to push a bike for a scrawny teenager as out of shape as I was in those days.

CHAPTER 13

For all its apparent advantages, life at Benoni High was pretty much the same as it had been at Willowmoore – for me, at least. I still did the bare minimum in all subjects, I still fell out with most of the teachers and was regularly sent to the principal's office, and I still bummed money at the tuck shop and parroted Graham's quips to kids who weren't interested in hearing them. I'd taken to bunking off school from time to time, most often when a big test was due or when I knew a hair inspection was coming up, and quite a few of my classmates were doing the same thing. We were able to get away with it for a surprisingly long time thanks, in large part, to the efforts of Karen Y (remember the peppermint liqueur girl?) who provided a steady supply of sick notes for all of us, supposedly from our mothers. They said things like: *"Dear Mr Xxxxx – Gavin was unable to attend school yesterday because he was up all night with an upset tummy … a raging fever … a terrible headache … a ghastly bout of gonorrhoea"* (ok, not that last one – but you get the picture).

The system worked well until the day I really *was* sick, and my mother sent in a genuine note explaining why I'd been off for a couple of days … at which point one of the teachers noticed that the handwriting was markedly different from the half-dozen other notes that "Mrs Weir" had supplied earlier in the year.

Busted! And not just me but all the other boys too, when the various teachers got together and compared the letters they'd received that year and realised that the vast majority of them boasted that same distinctive handwriting style perfected by Karen Y.

The whole lot of us were shipped off to Mr Lotter's office to face the music. That was bad, but things could have been a lot worse: we could have been sent directly to Mr Robson, the principal at the time, a universally despised man who took a downright sadistic delight in caning pupils, never administering just two strokes when he might give four, or four when he might give six.

Mr Lotter was vice-principal, and a very different man. He was loved and respected by pretty much everyone, because he actually cared for the wayward kids under his control and was far more likely to try to talk some sense into them than beat it into them.

He was no pushover, however, and this particular transgression was of a serious enough nature that he had no choice but to reach for his cane. But as he lined the five or six of us up for a couple of brisk cuts each I noticed something very strange: the strokes of that cane were becoming lighter with each one administered. I was the last to bend over and grip my knees, by which time he was barely making any contact at all, and when I straightened up and looked back at him I realised he was genuinely upset. *Jeez – he looked like he was on the verge of tears!*

"Sir?" I asked, hesitantly.

"Please … please stop, boys," he said softly, addressing all of us. "Just stop. I hate having to do this. I really, really hate it."

There was an awkward silence. Then somebody said: "I'm sorry sir. It won't happen again."

Somebody else said: "It won't sir. Promise." And the rest of us all chimed in, offering similar assurances, every last one of us robbed of our bravado, suddenly shame-faced, shuffling our feet and looking down at the ground. I can't speak for the others, but I know I felt so damn bad about making *him* feel bad that I actually made an effort to stay on the straight and narrow for a long, long time thereafter.

Well, for a month maybe. Okay, a couple of weeks. But, hey, that was a longer period of good behaviour than any six-of-the-best from Robson ever produced, from me or any of the other troubled young souls at that school.

Brian Lotter. The real deal. Benoni's Mr Chips. He later became principal of the school and apparently ruled over a just and scrupulously fair kingdom for many years before passing away, and if you log on to Facebook and find the *Benoni's History Now and Then* pages you can read the tributes left to him by many of the thousands of boys and girls whose lives he touched in the best possible way.

Rest in peace, Sir. Rest in peace.

The names and faces of most of the teachers from that time have pretty much faded from my memory but there are a few that stand out, and for different reasons.

There was a Miss Hillbrook, fresh out of training college and filled with an earnest enthusiasm for the job, but who had zero control over the rowdy mob that made up my Standard Eight cohort. Her science class was about as disciplined as a street riot, with groups of boys kicking a football around the back of the lab or shouting and arguing among themselves or using that little thingie with the wheels, a ticker timer, if I remember right, as a skateboard. Ian S used to sit at the back in his own world, sipping regularly from a hip flask filled with some kind of alcohol, and a couple of the boys went so far as to light up a cigarette back there from time to time.

Me, I wandered up to the front of the class one day while Miss Hillbrook was writing something on the blackboard that no one would read anyway, and I picked up a giant glass container on her desk that was filled with thousands of tiny iron ball bearings, presumably intended for use in some science experiment. I hefted it in both hands, testing its considerable weight, and for some reason I turned it upside down – at which point the lid fell off and those thousands of tiny balls crashed to the floor and sprayed far and wide, sending kids slipping and sliding and falling on their arses as they tried to jump clear of the flood.

Miss Hillbrook squeaked at me to go straight to Mr Robson's office, and I shrugged and complied: she sent half a dozen boys to the principal every other week, but none of us ever went: we'd simply wander around the school hallways for 10 or 15 minutes and then return to wreak more chaos.

By Standard Nine I'd absorbed virtually nothing at all from the Standard Eight science syllabus and I paid a price for my ignorance. The new teacher was a sturdy young man whose name I can't quite remember but who made a big impact on me, quite literally: when I flunked a test or misbehaved he didn't bother sending me to the principal's office, preferring to administer the punishment himself ... with a size 14 tackie filled with concrete! True story! I'd bend over, he'd swing that giant shoe down like a wrecking ball, and I'd go spiralling clear across the little lab at the back of the class, windmilling into the wall on the other side at about 90mph. He never needed to give six of the best. One was always enough.

A colourful character on the staff was the accountancy teacher, Mr Esterhuizen, an Afrikaner with a limited grasp of English whose threats to the unruly became the stuff of legend: "I will frow you by the window out!" he would yell, or "Did you heard my footprints coming up the stairs?" If he was writing on the blackboard and some kid behind him began misbehaving he'd demand to know: "What noise is coming from my backside?"

Another Afrikaner who made a name for herself, but by very different means, was Miss Oberholser. She was young and hot and would occasionally sashay into school wearing a short skirt, sparking fierce competition among the boys for the seats at the front of her class, in the left-hand row specifically, which offered a clear and unobstructed view of her legs whenever she sat down behind her desk to do a bit of marking.

Finally, there was Miss Hogg, my Standard Nine English teacher who inadvertently set me on course for a career in newspapers simply by reading out one of my essays to the rest of the class one day. That was no big deal; she regularly read stuff out to the class, but that was the first time she'd ever used one of my hastily scribbled compositions to make a point about the sophisticated use of metaphor or hyperbole or some such thing (which, of course, I had no clue I'd done – I certainly hadn't intended to!).

When she looked up at the end and gave me a warm smile, and said an earnest thank you for brightening her day – well, I was hooked, because I hadn't had that sort of positive attention since those halcyon, fleeting days as a blue-eyed boy back in primary school.

I started putting a bit of effort into my English classes; not so much, mind you, that I became brave enough overnight to use the word sesquipedalophobia in a sentence. My participles, when constructing a sentence, would still dangle in embarrassing places and I continued carelessly splitting my infinitives. But it was a start, and the seed that Miss Hogg planted that day would one day bear fruit, even if she didn't know it at the time.

CHAPTER 14

At some point towards the end of my Standard Nine year my parents sold up our house at 23 Barbara Avenue and moved us all into a flat in the centre of town, and I had to say a sad goodbye to that beloved patch of veld across the road where I'd spent so many happy and carefree hours as a boy. I was pretty miserable about that at the time but many, many years later I finally began to appreciate just how big a sacrifice they had made in coming to that momentous decision.

They'd arrived in South Africa as a young couple with three demanding children and very little money but had worked hard to get a foot on the property ladder and by the close of 1978 were the owners of a lovely home (DIY disasters notwithstanding) with swimming pool on a big plot in a beautiful suburb; the sort of luxurious surroundings that, for my mother particularly, raised in a tenement in a poor part of Glasgow, would have been beyond her wildest childhood dreams.

They gave it all up that year to pay for their children's further education, despite a decidedly doubtful commitment from all three of us to that noble cause. Graham had flunked out of his drama degree at Wits University at the end of his first year but was still hoping to make it in the acting world, so my mother looked around and found him an alternative: a three-year diploma course at the Pretoria Technikon.

He had a better time of it there and passed his first year without too much difficulty, at which point Christine, who had enrolled in some sort of secretarial college after her matric year, but also flunked out, decided that she too would pursue a life on the stage, and announced that she wanted to follow in his footsteps. She started year one at Pretoria Technikon on the same day Graham was starting year two.

Pretoria lies about 40 miles north of Benoni, too far for the pair of them to make the daily commute, so my parents decided to pay the rent on two flats for them in the same apartment block near the Tech. Along with two sets of tuition fees, of course.

All of that must have cost a pretty penny, and as if that wasn't enough of a strain on the Weir family budget, they agreed at the same time, the start of 1979, to send me to a private college for my matric year. My school marks at Benoni High had turned out to be no better than the dismal ones I'd been earning at Willowmoore High, and it was beginning to look very unlikely that I would gain even the bare minimum required to secure a place at university the following year.

Of course, the truth is that there was absolutely nothing wrong with the quality of education being offered by Benoni High; the problem was with me, not the school, and what they should have done was simply sit me down and tell me to get my shit together or they'd confiscate my Coco-Pops. *That* would have been a powerful incentive.

Instead, I joined Bruce and Ian and Steve V and even Margie S and a bunch of other overly privileged kids at Gramco College, a hip private institution in the centre of Benoni, revelling in the freedom to wear colourful shirts and ties rather than a school uniform, and grow my hair to shoulder length, and smoke and play ping-pong in the common room at lunch breaks, and chat with the teachers with an informality that would never have been tolerated at a government school.

Did my school marks shoot up, you ask? Did I start scoring distinctions in all subjects, from day one, and quickly guarantee my spot at one of the land's leading universities? Ha! You probably know me well enough by now to guess the answer to that one ... and it's a resounding NO!

The main reason for that, of course, was my inherent laziness, a glaring character flaw that I would finally recognise and take concrete steps to overcome only when I hit my mid-twenties, but there were a few other things going on at the time that ensured that I would keep bumping along reliably at the bottom of the class throughout my final year at school.

First and foremost was my obsession with a football-themed game I'd created using nothing more than a standard deck of playing cards and several school exercise books, and which I played for an hour or two every single afternoon after school (while everyone else, presumably, was doing their homework).

I split the deck into ten football "teams" of five cards each and devised a series of complex rules dictating which cards out-pointed which when two teams squared off. Each of the squads would play against all the others, home and away, in a league format, with points and goal differences deciding the finishing positions at the end of each season. The results would be entered into the record books and the pack would be reshuffled and new players dealt to each team, but with the winning teams always getting first pick of the aces and the tens (a big advantage) to offer some consistency from one season to the next. The bottom two teams were relegated and replaced with new ones each season.

Those exercise books quickly filled up and overflowed with row upon row of intricately detailed records, in my barely legible handwriting, as I worked my way backwards all the way into the 18th century. The results of every one of Manchester Albion's epic clashes with Benoni United were recorded for posterity, Colchester City's enduring rivalry with Tottenham Powerlines laid bare for pundits everywhere to analyse.

Bored already? You almost certainly are; jeez, I'm dozing off right now just thinking about that completely pointless pursuit – but for some reason it consumed me throughout my final year in school, and if I'd deployed even half of the mental energy in the classroom as I wasted on those league tables I might well have scored a couple of distinctions at the end of the year.

When I wasn't working on my leagues I was strumming away on the strings of the guitar I'd been given for my 17th birthday and composing some of the shittest and most pretentious songs the world has ever heard (or, thankfully, *not* heard). The first had a simple but very catchy chord sequence that I was pretty proud of, and I was thinking that I might even have composed the world's next Number One hit when Graham wandered into the room while I was playing it one day and said: "*Smoke On The Water*? Cool!"

"What? No, that's *my* song," I said indignantly. "I wrote it myself. I call it *The Only Lonely Eagle*."

"Hmmm. Sounds a hell of a lot like *Smoke on the Water*."

"No. Listen, I'll play the main chorus again." And I thumped those strings hard and belted out the chorus at the top of my voice, with pride and passion and sincerity:

> *"One lonely eeeegle*
> *His girlfriend up and died*
> *(now he)*
> *Cries like a seeeeee-gull"*

At which point the guitar sequence kicked in: Da-da-daaa, Da-da-DA-daaa, Da-da-daaa-da-da

Graham hooted: "Ha! Those are the exact same chords, and that's the exact same tune. That's *Smoke on the Water*."

"It's not! It's my song! It's *original*! It speaks to the anguish of avian bereavement and subsequent hopeless isolation in a pre-apocalyptic, humano-centric reality!"

"Kuk man! You've copied it, and you don't even know it. Sing it again, and I'll sing the Deep Purple song at the same time, and you'll see what I'm talking about."

So I did, and he did, and … and damn he was right! I *had* copied it, inadvertently; that's why those chords had sounded so familiar the first time I played them to myself! Sob! It was back to the drawing board.

Thankfully, the rest of toe-curling lyrics to *The Only Lonely Eagle,* along with all my other lame compositions, have been lost to the mists of time, and none of them will ever trouble humanity again. Verily, the Lord is merciful.

My keratoconus, meanwhile, was kicking up a gear as the months went by, and my eyesight was deteriorating slowly but steadily. I finally had to start wearing contact lenses in addition to my spectacles – and these were rigid plastic contact lenses, mind you, not the wafer-thin, super-comfy silicone softies available today that you can pop in your eye and forget about for a month.

I remember the first time I tried them on, sitting there in my optician's room and gripping the sides of the seat tightly as she delicately inserted them, thinking to myself that if I had to start each day like this, dropping what felt like a little lump of molten lava into each eyeball ... well, it might just be easier being blind; at least that way I wouldn't have to bother with matric exams, and university and the rest.

Of course, I was over-reacting, and after the first few moments the pain lessened to discomfort, and then a mild irritation, but I was still very, very glad when she popped those lenses out again after a few minutes or so. I'd get used to the sensation, she assured me. After a week or two I wouldn't even know they were there.

She went through the whole procedure with me a couple of times – put the lenses in, take them out, drop them into the little plastic container; rinse hands and repeat – and it worked just fine while I was sitting there in her consulting room. I was reasonably confident I'd be able to do it on my own later that night.

It started well, certainly. I inserted the lenses without too much bother, left and then right, and then I sat and waited for half an hour, as per instructions, to let the corneas begin to adjust.

By the 30-minute mark I was thinking, hey, maybe this isn't actually that bad after all ... until I started trying to remove the lenses and discovered that I couldn't budge the blasted things. I blinked and looked left simultaneously like my optician had shown me; I pulled the eyelid up and then down, I looked right and blinked again, furiously, and titled my head over my knees; I lay flat on my back and poured half the bottle of saline solution into my eyes ... but those little pieces of plastic had glued themselves onto my corneas, it seemed, and could not be shifted.

Panicky and frustrated, I smashed my fists into the wooden dining-room table a few times but that didn't really change anything, and my mother finally had to lead me out to the car and drive me down to the nearby Glynnwood hospital, where a nurse laid me out on a gurney and plucked out the lenses with the help of a tiny rubber suction-cup thingie. Massive, massive relief!

I did, of course, get used to wearing those hard contact lenses, like millions of other people, and I would be reliant on them for decades to come, but those first few years were decidedly unpleasant, in part because nobody realised back then – my optician certainly didn't – that you really should change the contact lens solution in the holder every morning, at least. I was doing it maybe once a week, and the impurities and tiny particles of dust or whatever tended to build up as the days went by, meaning I'd spend the first hour or so of every day with red, streaming, irritated eyes, with the risk of serious infection an ever-present danger.

No o'er bright, as my mother would say.

CHAPTER 15

Protea staged what was almost certainly its best show ever that year, a powerhouse production of the hit musical *West Side Story*. It played to sell-out crowds and rave reviews in Benoni, drawing in audiences from the surrounding East Rand towns of Springs, Boksburg and Brakpan too. It even caught the eye of a prominent theatre producer in Johannesburg, Mannie Manim, who immediately began negotiations to move the entire show, lock, stock and two smoking barrels, to the Market Theatre, one of the top venues in the country. Sadly, however, this was at the height of the cultural boycott of South Africa, with the world pushing the apartheid government to rethink its policies, and Manim was unable to secure the necessary performing rights from the United States for what would then have been classed as a professional production in a profit-making venue, so the idea had to be shelved.

Looking back, it's no surprise that the show did as well as it did, because it was, in fact, pretty close to being a professional production already. Four of the five stars – Graham, Christine, Bruce and the girl who played the key role of Maria, Jenny D – would go on to be pro actors and singers in the years that followed, and the fifth star, Tony S, who played the other key role, Tony, was a few years older than the others and was already a semi pro. All five were at the peak of their powers; all good looking and young and confident, their singing voices strong and pitch-perfect.

The director of the show was Dennis Watson, a

schoolteacher from Springs who was widely acknowledged as the best in the amateur theatre business on the East Rand, and he brought with him a bunch of talented kids from his regular productions. Choreography, another essential element of this particular story, was handled by a dance-teaching whiz called Lynn Clarke, who was able to train even flat-footed apes like me (I played one of the Jets gang members) to rock-and-roll and cha-cha-cha without tramping on my partner's feet more than a dozen times per performance.

These days, everything under the sun is videoed and captured for posterity on a million smartphone cameras but back in 1979 there was none of that, and there is no recorded performance of that show anywhere at all that I'm aware of; nothing to offer a reminder of just how good it really was. Such a shame.

Bruce was in the habit of returning to the Weir flat with the rest of the family after rehearsals or performances, and as often as not he'd stay the night, because it was easier than riding all the way back to his home in Rynfield on his 50cc; also, our flat was close to Gramco College, and the pair of us would head off to school together the following morning. He got along well not just with Graham and Christine, but with my parents too, and was pretty much a sixth member of the family by then. Graham and Christine were both living in Pretoria at the time but making frequent trips back to Benoni and sleeping over whenever their schedules allowed, making for some crowded but usually jovial times in that three-bedroom apartment.

On one such morning, a school day, I remember, I got up a few minutes before everyone else to make myself a bit of breakfast. Graham, Bruce and I had crammed into one of the bedrooms the night before; me and Graham sleeping on the two single beds and Bruce lying on a mattress and a sleeping bag on the floor between us.

I slipped out to the kitchen and made myself a couple of toasted cheese sandwiches and a cup of tea, and when I was done I checked the clock on the wall and decided it was time to start getting ready for school, so I headed back to the bedroom.

I swung the door open and stepped inside – and then stopped and stared. Graham was propped up on one elbow, leaning down over the side of his bed. Bruce was reaching up towards him from his mattress on the floor. The pair of them were embracing passionately, their hands in each other's hair. They were completely oblivious to my presence.

I stared a moment longer, puzzled, just trying to make sense of what I was seeing. It was an image that I can still conjure up in my head to this very day.

I said: "What are you guys doing?"

They broke apart like they'd been cleaved by a bolt of lightning; two faces swivelling in my direction, shocked and despairing. Graham recovered first and aimed a playful punch at Bruce's shoulder. "Wrestling! Ha ha. Just wrestling!" he said, but Bruce's reaction told a different story: he collapsed back onto his pillow, staring up at the ceiling and repeating to himself, over and over again: " Of f***! Oh f***"! Oh f***!"

I opened my mouth to say something but no words came, so I shut it again and just stood there for a long moment. I turned and left the room.

The school day passed in a daze for me, my mind in a whirl. I stared at the blackboard without really seeing what was written on it; I joined the rest of the students in the common room for a smoke between classes; I exchanged a few words with a couple of the other guys during the lunch break without listening to what they were saying.

Graham and Bruce? Together? Obviously NOT wrestling? But ... but what exactly HAD they been doing? It looked like ... nah! Not possible. Couldn't be.

Bruce approached me as the lunch break was ending, biting a fingernail, uncharacteristically nervous. "Can we ... will you ... do you want to come back to my house after school? Can we talk about it?" he said.

I nodded woodenly. "OK."

We rode to his home on our motorbikes, but not side by side as we usually did. When we got there he made us a cup of coffee each, and we smoked a couple of cigarettes and listened to Rodriguez to fill the awkward silence. Then after an hour or so I said: "I should probably get going," and he replied "Ah ... ok." And I got back on my bike and left without a word being said about what I'd seen that morning.

By nightfall, however, the shock had pretty much worn off and I was forced to admit what I'd been denying to myself all day: Graham and Bruce were ... they were ... well, they were *queers*! As ludicrous as that thought would have been to me a day earlier, there was no denying it: they were *queers! F***ING QUEERS! BOTH OF THEM!!!*

Before you rush to judgment and cast me as a bigot and homophobe, dear reader, let me remind you of this: the year was 1979, and this was apartheid-era, small-town South Africa, and I was a naïve boy of 17 with zero exposure to the wider world. Sixty-year-old Gavin has a mainstream approach to such matters; he says "meh" to the sexual preferences of the world at large as long as there are no children involved, and all parties are willing participants. Seventeen-year-old Gav had a decidedly narrower viewpoint, but one that was mainstream in that time and that place.

Yes, I was aware that there were a few "queers" around the town, but everybody knew who they were, because they stood out from the crowd and their handshakes were limp, right? Graham couldn't be one of *them*! He'd never displayed any feminine characteristics; didn't giggle or squeal loudly and hug everybody like *they* did – and neither did Bruce, for that matter! Hell, Bruce had had several girlfriends – so he couldn't be queer, right?

Wrong, apparently.

Recognition was followed quickly by resentment and anger. How long had this been going on, I wondered? Had Bruce *ever* been my true buddy, or had our friendship been nothing more than a cover story all along for his forbidden relationship with my brother? He'd been a part of the family for years. He and I had shared a bedroom as far back as our primary school days; hell, I'd changed into my pyjamas or swimming costume a thousand times in front of him, and the thought of that made me feel suddenly very self-conscious.

And getting back to Graham: I'd pretty much based my whole personality on his, copying his mannerisms and his jokes, his habits good and bad, no matter how unpopular it had made me. I'd hated him at times and fought with him constantly, but I'd always wanted to be like him, because he was Mr Popular, the star of the family. And all along ... all along, he'd been *queer*! And to cap it all, he was now angry with me, for being angry at him!

The Weir household was a very tense and unhappy place in the days that followed that bombshell moment in the bedroom. Bruce stayed far away, showing up for rehearsals for the show but heading off to his own house immediately afterwards. An icy silence fell on the lounge if Graham was there and I walked in, and vice versa. Conversations would die in mid-sentence if my mother, or Christine perhaps, asked: "where's Bruce today?"

After maybe a week of this my mother cornered me in that same bedroom one day and demanded: "Right: what's going on?"

"What d'you mean?" I countered.

"You and Graham. You can cut the atmosphere with a knife. What's happened?"

"It's nothing. We had a fight."

"About what?"

"Nothing."

"About what!!!"

"Nothing! Ask him!"

"I did! And he won't tell me." And for maybe the first and only time in my life I saw something approaching fear in her eyes; a vulnerability that was completely out of character. "What happened," she asked. "Please. Just tell me."

I paused, and I took a deep breath. "You'd better sit down," I said. People say that in the movies all the time, but that's the only time I've ever said it.

She sat down on the edge of one of the beds and waited.

"Graham and Bruce," I said and then stopped, because I couldn't quite get the words out. "They're … queers. I saw them."

I was expecting shouting, some kind of angry outburst, an accusation that I was lying … but she just kind of sagged a bit lower on the edge of the bed. After a second or two she nodded, more to herself than to me. "I think I've always known," she said.

She swore me to secrecy, and that wasn't a problem. I'd been about to swear *her* to secrecy – that's how big a deal it was, in 1970s Benoni, to have a son or a brother who was gay.

The show had to go on, of course, in this case, quite literally. When the curtain rose on *West Side Story* on the opening night a few weeks later there was no hint publicly of the bitter undercurrents still swirling around backstage and within the Weir household between me and Bruce and Graham. I have a vague memory of my mother calling Graham and me together at some point and sitting us down and telling us that we had to patch things up, because even my father, as remote as he was from day-to-day life at home, was bound to notice the angry, silent war playing out right under his nose, and might start asking about the cause.

How would he have reacted if he'd learnt the truth? Hard to say – but if he ever came to recognise that his elder son was gay, he refused to acknowledge it, to his dying day. In the years that followed, when Graham and Bruce were living together and my brother's acting career was taking off and he was becoming less concerned about public judgment of his lifestyle, he appeared in several militantly pro-gay productions. My parents went along to watch them, as they did with all his shows.

Graham would drop by the family home to visit the following weekend, but within just a few minutes he and my father would become embroiled in a blazing row, every single time – about politics, or religion, or a hundred other topics, but never about the one subject that neither of them dared to raise.

On an evening after one of those troubled visits, following another of those provocative stage shows, my father appeared at my mother's side as she was washing up the dishes. It was evident, she told me later, that he had something big on his mind.

"Graham ..." he began tentatively, and then stopped. "Is Graham ..."

My mother paused her dishwashing, a coffee mug in one hand, a soapy cloth in the other. She waited. She was going to tell him, she had decided. He just had to finish asking the question.

"Graham and Bruce," my father tried again. "Are they ... is he ... are they ..."

My mother drew in a deep breath and opened her mouth to reply – but my father turned on his heel and walked away quickly. He would never broach the subject again, but he had his answer, I think, and the proxy rows between father and son would continue for several years afterwards.

Again, it's easy to rush to judgment but again I feel compelled to point out: this was a very different time and a very different place to the world we live in today. It's just so very sad that it took all of us – not just the Weir family, but the western world at large – such a long time to change.

CHAPTER 16

Outright hostilities with Graham eased up a bit after the sit-down meeting between us organised by my mother, and in the weeks that followed things began to return to normal. It took a bit longer, somehow, for me to move beyond the bitterness I felt towards Bruce, however unfair or illogical that might have been, but we did eventually get back to the point where we could talk about this or that without any awkwardness.

Things would never be the same again, of course, but all three of us moved on with our lives – but I was now living with a secret that I wasn't able to talk about with anyone other than my mother, and she and I didn't really do a whole lot of talking.

That secret began to weigh heavily on me as the months went by.

I'd struck up a friendship during that time with a guy called Mark H, who was one of the other *West Side Story* cast members and also a fellow Gramco College pupil. As that matric year drew to a close he told me about a magical cottage on the eastern Cape coastline where he and his family spent their holidays every year, and he asked if I'd like to go along with them that December? I said yes, he said cool, and we spent a happy few hours at his kitchen table in the weeks that followed plotting the 700-mile route we would drive in his little Datsun 120Y, his father looking on approvingly and offering suggestions from time to time on where to stop for petrol, and which campsite to sleep at overnight.

Mark was a mostly sober-minded and conservative young

man. He'd get drunk occasionally, but nowhere near as often nor as recklessly as I did. He didn't smoke and he wasn't much given to backbiting and gossip; something which, sadly, had become an all-too-common theme between me and Bruce and the rest of my high school crew (with me being probably the worst of the bunch, to be honest).

One afternoon when he and I were sharing a few beers by the side of his swimming pool, listening to Jethro Tull and shooting the breeze about various things, Bruce's name came up in the conversation, possibly because Mark had begun dating Terry D – who'd been Bruce's girlfriend for a time (did I mention that Benoni was a small town?). Anyway, whatever the circumstances, I decided that it was time to tell someone the truth about Bruce.

Big mistake. I really should have kept my mouth shut.

Out of some twisted sense of loyalty to my brother, I told Mark only half the story: I told him that Bruce was gay, and that I'd seen him with another guy, but that I wasn't at liberty to say who exactly that other guy was ... and from that moment on, things with Mark got downright weird.

Our trip to the coast was just a week away, and there were still a few details to iron out, which we'd planned to do on the final couple of nights before we left, but he called off those meetings abruptly and I barely saw him again until the morning we were due to leave. I showed up anyway at his house at the scheduled day and time, and we packed the car under his father's watchful eye and then drove off in the direction of the road which would take us south. The conversation was stilted and the laughter was forced.

After maybe eight hours we stopped for the night at a small town called Aliwal North, known for its mineral springs. We followed the signs to a local campsite and when we got there we unpacked the two-man tent and hammered a bunch of pegs into the dusty ground and fitted the tent pole and secured the guide ropes. I stepped inside and laid out my sleeping bag on the groundsheet ... and then noticed that Mark had laid out his sleeping bag on the outside of the tent. Weird.

More stilted conversation followed that night, despite several beers a-flowing.

We got cracking early the following morning and reached the holiday cottage in a rustic resort at the mouth of the Mpekweni river, near Port Alfred, an hour ahead of schedule because Mark was driving fast. His mother had travelled down a day or two earlier with a bunch of cousins and family friends, and she met us at the cottage door, bustling about and helping us to unpack and carrying things inside.

She went to lay out Mark's sleeping bag atop the thin mattress on one of the two beds in the small room where we'd been billeted, but he told her no, I'm going to be sleeping in the other room. She asked why; he mumbled some excuse and carried off the bag himself and deposited it in the adjoining room. Weird.

The resort filled up quickly that day and the next with three or four different extended families, all of whom knew each other well because they had been visiting this idyllic spot for Christmas every year for decades; a happy crowd of 25 or 30 adults and children and teenagers who talked endlessly of shared experiences and funny escapades and close encounters from holidays gone by. I plainly wasn't part of the inside crowd and Mark made no effort to include me in the conversations, preferring to spend time with a couple of his cousins and leaving me to my own devices.

On the second or third day his father, maybe noticing me sitting apart, said to him: "Didn't you say you were going to teach Gavin to fish?" Mark hummed and hawed, but his father fetched a couple of rods and hooks and things and shooed us off in the direction of the beach, and he had no option but to go through with it.

I'd never handled a fishing rod in all my life so Mark baited up the hook on the end of my line and showed me how to cast into the crashing waves – and then picked out a spot for himself about a hundred yards away. Weird.

Five minutes in, I was already thinking that fishing was a highly over-rated exercise when the rod suddenly jerked in my hands and the line went taut. I had one! Complete beginner's luck, of course, but I tugged the rod up the way I'd been shown and started winding the reel furiously ... and lo and behold, a fish came flopping out of the water, flapping and twisting its way up the beach towards me as I carried on winding. How big? About 15 inches. What kind of fish? No idea, mate. And I had no clue what to do next.

"Mark! Hey Mark – I've got one!" I shouted excitedly. He turned and frowned in my direction, but he came across and helped me to get the hook out the poor creature's mouth. He told me to take it back to his mother at the cottage, who would help to prep it for dinner, and then he went back to his spot and began casting again, with a grim determination. Over and over again.

I hurried back to the cottage and handed over the catch of the day with a big grin. Mark's mother and the other ladies – friends and cousins, and a few maids for good measure – all made a big deal of it, and for the first time that holiday I began to feel a bit cheerful.

Lunchtime came and went, but there was no sign of Mark, and it was late afternoon before he reappeared, empty handed, because the fish hadn't been biting, he said. He didn't look at all happy about the fact that the beginner – me – had hooked one within minutes.

His father, apparently unaware of any tensions, insisted on fetching his camera, and retrieving my fish from the fridge before the ladies began gutting it along with a few others that had been caught by the rest of the group. He set the camera up at the front of the cottage and he told me to strike a pose, then he clicked the button and captured an image which I still have to this day in an old photo album. It shows a long-haired, skinny youth wearing a baseball cap and an uncertain grin as he holds aloft a fair-sized fish of indeterminate species. And in the background you can see Mark sitting up against the cottage wall, glowering at both me and the fish with an unsettling intensity.

So ... what the hell was going on, you ask? Why did Mark react so very badly to me telling him about Bruce being gay? I thought about that long and hard, and finally decided that because I'd told him only half the story, and never identified who exactly Bruce's mystery partner was ... well, he must have come to the erroneous conclusion that that partner was me! And if I was queer – well, there was no way he was going to share a tent or a bedroom with me!

Homophobic times indeed – and, weirdly, I'd been given a taste of the very prejudice I myself subscribed to so whole-heartedly back then, albeit just for the duration of that summer holiday.

All of that happened in December 1979, but we need to backtrack briefly, just a couple of months, because I've inadvertently skipped past an important milestone in this story: the end-of-year matric exams, the results of which would determine whether or not I qualified for a place at university in 1980.

Did I know which university I wanted to go to? What degree I wanted to take and what career I saw myself following in the years and decades ahead? Nope. Not a clue. I hadn't given it a thought. But my mother had, and one afternoon after school she dragged me down to a government building in the centre of town where they offered aptitude tests for baffled boys like me which would hopefully point the way to a suitable vocation.

I filled in a bunch of forms and answered a series of questions in a complex process that seemed to drag on for hours. The testers took everything into account, presumably including my crappy attitude to anything requiring effort and my dismal school marks in absolutely every subject over the past decade. Their assessment was that my best bet would be to find a very high building and jump off it, but assuming I failed at that too I might want to try some career that would involve writing.

The very next day my mother began scouring the prospectuses of various universities and before too long she settled on Rhodes University in Grahamstown, because it offered a degree in journalism.

"How does that sound?" she asked me brightly. "You'd be writing every day. Can you see yourself as a journalist?"

"Nah," I said.

"You'd get to interview famous people. Maybe film stars or singers. Or politicians like John Vorster."

"Who?"

"He's the prime minister, for heaven's sake!"

"Never heard of him."

Sigh. "Okay, so you steer clear of politics. But you could be an investigative journalist. Seek out big scandals and expose them, that sort of thing?"

"I dunno. I don't really care about scandals."

"Sports? You used to be good at sports?"

"I know about soccer and badminton. But nothing else."

"Financial journalism? You track the stock markets and write about company profits and losses?"

"Boring."

"Travel writing? Visit exotic places?"

"So much packing. And unpacking."

"Consumer journalism?"

"Sounds like hard work."

"Theatre critic? Film critic? You get your popcorn free."

Pause. "Oh really?"

"Yep. Or how about this: food critic."

My ears pricked up.

She pressed her advantage. "You eat at all the top

restaurants, and then you write about it and tell the readers to choose the steak but avoid the soup. That sort of thing."

"Wait – that's all you do? You *eat*? And somebody *pays* you for it?"

"Well, there's probably a bit more to it than –"

"I wanna be a journalist. Sign me up."

She sent off an application to Rhodes right away and they wrote back to say they'd be very happy to enrol me on their prestigious journalism course ... but there was still the small matter of passing my matric exams at the end of the year, which was by no means a done deal. I'd barely opened a text book all year and time was growing short, so I waited another month and with two weeks to go before the first exam I started my studies.

It was too little, too late, of course, and on the December day when I went into college to pick up my results I was told that I'd scored a miserable tally of two C's, a D, an E, an F and a G – not quite enough for that all-important matriculation exemption. My uni plans were a bust. The dream of being paid to eat was dead.

I remember my mother greeting me at the front door with a cold, hard stare when I got back home with my results that day: she and my father had shelled out a very big bundle of cash for a year at Gramco but I could have achieved those same crappy grades at Benoni High, and it wouldn't have cost them a penny.

Things were looking a bit bleak until we learnt that Rhodes would be gracious enough to accept me anyway, albeit with something called a conditional exemption. The reasoning was a bit obscure and I can't remember all the details but all it meant, in effect, was that I had to take Geography (for some reason) as one of my four subjects when I started there in January 1980.

That wasn't a big deal, I reasoned. I'd probably need a bit of geography in the years ahead, when I was a morbidly obese food critic jetting from one country to the next to eat at all the world's best restaurants...

CHAPTER 17

The future looked bright. Rhodes promised a fresh start, a new life away from the dramas and miseries of my troubled teenage years in Benoni, but there's one final incident I need to mention before we leave the Seventies behind forever, and it's a strange and sinister one. A week or so after I'd left for that holiday with Mark and his family in the eastern Cape there was a knock on the front door of my parents' flat one evening, and my mother opened it to see a well-dressed stranger standing there with a briefcase in one hand. Her first thought was: Jehovah's Witness! She was already starting to push the door closed when he said: "Mrs Weir? Mary Weir?"

She paused. "Yes?"

"May I come inside?" the stranger asked. His speech was clipped, his accent Afrikaans.

She frowned. "Um … why? Who are you?"

"I need to talk to you about your son, Gavin."

There was a time, of course, back in my troubled primary school days, when there'd been strangers knocking on the front door every other day demanding to speak to my mother about her son Gavin, but this didn't appear to be one of those situations. Her eyes widened.

"Oh no! Has there been an accident?" she asked. "Has something happened?"

"Nothing like that, I assure you. He's absolutely fine."

"Then …"

"Perhaps if you allow me in, I can explain."

"Gavin's not even here. He's away on holiday."

"Yes. Mpekweni. With his friend Mark. He'll be back next Friday. We know."

We know? *We* know? Who the hell was *we*? Mystified, she stepped aside and allowed the stranger to cross the threshold. He followed her into the dining-room and accepted a seat at the table, then he snapped open his briefcase and pulled out a few sheets of paper.

My father, dozing in his lounge chair, roused himself and joined them at the table. He asked for the man's name, and the stranger offered something bland and forgettable. He worked for the government, he said, but declined to say which department exactly.

"So, why are you asking about Gavin," my mother ventured.

"He's going to Rhodes University next year. He'll be studying journalism." He checked his documents. "He'll be staying in the Jan Smuts hostel."

"Eh? How do you know – "

"You're probably not aware, Mr and Mrs Weir, but the journalism school at Rhodes is a hotbed of communist activity. Anti-government agents. People working to tear down our society. We need somebody on the inside who can keep an eye on some of those people."

"What? Keep an eye ... what does that mean?" my mother demanded.

"We'd like Gavin to be that person on the inside."

"Who's 'we'?"

"As I said, I work for the government."

"Well, yes, but doing what? Police? Security?"

The man thought for a second, then agreed. "Yes. Security."

The penny dropped. So did my mother's jaw. "You want Gavin to *spy* on someone? You're with ... BOSS?"

He refused to elaborate, but he didn't have to. My parents had never been politically active; being British passport-holders rather than South African citizens they'd never had the chance to vote in any of the whites-only elections that had put the National Party in power in 1948 and kept it there ever since. But they'd heard about BOSS, of course, the Bureau for State Security. A secretive intelligence agency with vast resources and questionable ethics, it worked behind the scenes to dismantle any threat to the apartheid state, by any means, fair or foul. Very foul, in some cases. You didn't mess with BOSS. Not if you were in your right mind.

The man continued, unperturbed. "We don't want a spy, Mrs Weir," he said. "We just need one of the journalism students at Rhodes to be on the alert for anything that might pose a danger. Just watch some of the professors. And, yes, some of the students. The radical ones. And report back to me, or one of my colleagues."

"But we're not interested in politics."

"We know."

"And neither's Gavin. He doesn't even know who the prime minister is."

"Exactly. That's why he'll be valuable to us. No one would suspect him."

"But –"

"Of course, we'll cover all his expenses. Your expenses. Tuition fees, hostel fees, petty cash. And, perhaps more importantly, when Gavin graduates we'll make sure he gets a job working in one of South Africa's top newspapers. Where he can keep an eye on some of the radical editors and journalists."

My mother gaped again. "You can do that?"

"We can do many things, Mrs Weir. Many things."

My parents talked it over after the stranger had left, but not for long. As attractive a proposition as it was to have an all-expenses-paid ticket to Rhodes, they reasoned that, if the stranger had the power to pull strings and boost my career in the years after graduation, he also had the power to pull strings and hamper that career. More to the point, if there was any truth to the stories that were beginning to surface at about that time of abductions and torture and death squads linked to that same shadowy agency … well, it would be wise just to stay far, far away from all of that.

The following day they phoned the telephone number the stranger had left them and told him that they weren't interested, and that Gavin wasn't either (I heard about it all only after I'd returned from my holiday, but I agreed wholeheartedly with their decision). He thanked them politely and hung up and they never heard from him again.

But the question remained: how the hell had he known as much as he did about me and my movements? Had he bugged our telephone? The whole flat maybe? Was there some family friend of ours who had secret affiliations to BOSS; somebody close enough to know where exactly I'd gone on holiday, and with whom and for how long? We never did learn the answer to that very unsettling question.

BOSS, as I say, didn't trouble us again but that didn't mean they'd lost interest in the professors at the Rhodes journalism school. The story broke early the next year that they'd recruited quite a few young students to spy on the department – one of whom, I would learn decades later, via Facebook, was among the group of friends I would go on to make during my year at university.

CHAPTER 18

The keener-eyed among you will have noticed that I said "year" rather than "years" at university, so I may as well end the suspense right now and tell you that, yes, although the B.Journ degree (Bachelor of Journalism) that I'd signed up for was a three-year course, I personally did the abridged version; the one-year cram course. Which is to say that I crammed a whole lot of drunkenness into my time in Grahamstown and played an astonishing amount of ping-pong with a bunch of new buddies, but barely opened a book and was asked politely to leave at the end of the year.

At which point, back in Benoni, in a cubicle in a basement of an obscure government building somewhere, the man from BOSS must have heaving a sigh of relief and saying to himself: thank God that idiot Weir kid turned us down, because he'd just have wasted all our money!

Which was probably what my parents were thinking at about the same time; in fact, the three of them would have had quite a bit to chat about if he'd called them up again at that point. ("Gavin finish his B.Journ? You must B.Joking! Ha ha!" That sort of thing).

Anyway, I'll tell you a bit about my time at university – the little I can remember, at least, that wasn't lost to an alcoholic haze.

Rhodes was a prestigious and generously funded institution and it had a wonderful campus boasting dozens of well-equipped lecture halls, top-notch sporting facilities and handsome old student residences. The streets were wide and clean and lined with ancient and beautiful jacaranda trees that bloomed a riot of purple in the spring and early summer, while the adjoining botanical gardens showcased nature's grandeur all the year round.

The university had an extensive main library and several smaller, specialist ones, though personally I never felt the need to visit any of them. For me, coursework was something that could always be put off until the following week, and lectures were an optional extra. And as the months went by I opted to attend ever fewer of them. I preferred to simply wander around the campus, day after day, barefoot, with my long hair flowing over the shoulders of my tatty old RAF greatcoat and my guitar slung over my back, troubadour style. Bit of a moegoe, really.

I had a room on the ground floor (second door on the left as you step in via the back entrance) of the Jan Smuts hall of residence, a solid and handsome block that looks exactly the same today as it did 40-odd years ago. I know because I looked it up on Streetview recently and, remarkably, nothing at all appears to have changed.

I'd just finished unpacking on the first day when there was a tap on my door, which I'd left ajar, and I looked up to see the kid from the room next to mine standing there. I'd nodded a hello to him ten minutes earlier as I lugged my case through the wide hallway.

"You want coffee?" he asked abruptly.

"Uh – yeah. Yes," I replied.

He disappeared. I waited for a moment, not sure if he was about to reappear with a pot of the finest Java and a tray of cupcakes, or if he was going to walk me down to wherever the student café was, but then I heard a rattle of cups and teaspoons next door, along with a tuneless whistle, so I stepped out my room and into his.

The kid was squatting on the wooden parquet floor, spooning sugar and Frisco instant coffee into two slightly grimy mugs. He stood and filled them both with cold water from the handbasin tap and then he sat back down and plunged some sort of handheld electric immersion heating element into the first of the mugs. After barely 30 seconds he pulled it out and gave the contents a vigorous stir and slid the mug across to me, before transferring the element to the second cup. Thirty seconds later his own brew was ready, and he took a sip, gave a satisfied nod and sat back on the floor with a pleased grin.

Worst cup of coffee I've ever had, anywhere, at any time, in any country. Lumps of coffee powder floating on the surface. Stone cold. But it was a warm welcome, and it was very much appreciated by me, and I would learn soon enough that what Hew D (for that was his name) lacked in social graces, he more than made up for in character and sheer oddball personality. He would become my best buddy in that year at Rhodes.

The student life was a pampered and privileged one, with pretty much all our needs taken care of to allow us to focus our efforts on our studies (ha ha!). The bedrooms in the residences were small but more than adequate, with a basin and a mirror and an old electric bar heater that kept things cosy on the cold, eastern Cape winter nights.

There was a huge shared bathroom on each of the three floors and several common rooms equipped with comfy sofas and card tables. There was even a large games room in the basement, which was where I would spend at least an hour a day throughout that year pursuing excellence in the pointless field of table tennis.

Clothes were collected once a week, washed and ironed and returned to our bedrooms without so much as a sock ever going astray. Meals were provided in a dining-hall a two-minute walk away, and the food was generally pretty good, and plentiful. Urns of tea and plates of biscuits appeared at 10am each morning and 3pm each afternoon on various lawned areas dotted between the lecture halls and the residences.

The social calendar was a busy one, with some kind of party or festival on offer every weekend, and there were smaller, private societies too, offering companionship for those with shared interests in a huge variety of fields: Chess Society, Tennis Soc, Guitar Soc, Running Soc, Squash Soc, Astrology Soc, and so on, even a bunch of rival religious groups such as Cath soc and Meth soc (Methodist, that is, not Methamphetamine; there were a few groups on campus doing drugs but they were a bit more discreet about it).

Looking back, I'm not sure what exactly I would have been able to report to the man from BOSS if I had taken up his offer, because there wasn't a whole lot of anti-government activity happening in the journalism department, not that I was aware of anyway. Maybe I would have been expected to ingratiate myself with any suspicious professors or get to know the outspoken Year Two or Year Three kids who ran a couple of student newspapers. They used to carry articles every other week calling for lecture boycotts as a show of solidarity with anti-apartheid campaigners everywhere, or demanding that the chancellor open the gates to black students (universities, like the rest of South Africa, were still strictly segregated back then) and protesting over any kind of police presence on campus.

Did that qualify as seditious activity? Or merely the sort of angry-young-man activism you can find on any university campus around the world? Fortunately, I didn't have to make that choice.

BOSS may have been a little overzealous in policing the Rhodes journalism department, but it was an approach that had proven brutally effective on the wider front. You'll have heard the name Nelson Mandela, I wager? Well, I hadn't, and I was 17 and I'd grown up in South Africa!

True, I had no interest at all in politics, but even if I had, I probably still would not have been familiar with the name Mandela, because it was banned by the apartheid government. Newspapers weren't allowed to print it and radio stations weren't allowed to utter it, and the South African Broadcasting Corporation, the only television service in the country, offered the government's interpretation of the news, local and international, and nothing else. Any reporter or editor who dared to challenge the party line was arrested and shown the error of his ways; any publication that persisted in defying the government was banned.

The result was that a whole generation of kids like me had grown up in South Africa with no knowledge of the Rivonia trial in 1964, arguably the most influential in the country's history, and the one at which the man who would become one of the most recognised faces on the planet was found guilty of sabotage and locked away for 27 years.

In fact, the first time I ever heard the name Mandela was when I was visiting the student café near the residence one day, maybe a month or two into the academic year, and I saw a poster on the noticeboard with the words: "FREE MANDELA!". Somebody had come along later and added a few words, tweaking it to read: "One FREE MANDELA with every item purchased!".

The lecture boycotts and occasional protest marches organised by the student newspaper guys were generally poorly attended, because the Rhodes campus was a far more conservative place than that of, say, Wits University in Johannesburg, or UCT in Cape Town. Part of the reason for that was the high number of Rhodesians studying there; I can't give an exact figure, but it felt like every second student you spoke to was from Rhodesia, the neighbour to the north which, like South Africa, had been ruled for decades by a white minority.

All of those Rhodesian students were white, of course, and many of them were embittered, because their country was in the process that year of handing over power to the black majority and changing its name to Zimbabwe. Most of the guys had spent time in the Rhodesian army before beginning their studies at Rhodes, fighting a bloody war that they were winning on the battlefield but losing on the world stage; a situation much like South Africa itself was beginning to confront. A lot of those guys still had their army-issue haircuts and their anger issues, and they didn't like the look of long-haired hippie-types like me – but we'll get to *that* incident shortly. Don't go anywhere.

The friends I made that year were all very bright young men and women, tackling a range of courses from law to pharmacy and economics, and managing (unlike me) to spend enough time with their books outside of regular party hours to achieve the grades required to make it to Year Two and beyond. But there was one who stood out from the crowd. We'll call him Bradley, though that's not his real name.

Bradley was Rhodesian, and a year older than the rest of us but probably ten years older in terms of maturity. Me and Hew and Paul F and Alan K and the rest were still kids at heart, but Bradley was a young adult, smoothly confident and seemingly wise in all manner of things. He was a practising Christian, but with a devilish sense of humour; he didn't smoke or drink but seemed to be loving life without those crutches; he played a mean guitar and he had a good singing voice and had even written a handful of his own songs which were actually pretty good.

He was a talented cartoonist too, which I discovered early in the year as I sat alongside him during a Sociology lecture one morning. All the other students were taking notes as the lecturer did his lecturing but Bradley was doodling absent-mindedly on his workpad, coming up with a really funny image of a little Japanese guy in karate gear kicking down somebody's door. To all intents and purposes, he hadn't heard a word the lecturer had said, but he must have been taking it all in anyway, at some level, because when the half-year exams rolled around, he emerged as the top student in the whole year group.

And it wasn't like he was cramming in the studies after hours; you could drop by his room at pretty much any time of day or night and there'd be a group of people in there chatting and drinking coffee and generally having a good time.

Bradley was probably the most intelligent and charismatic

individual I'd ever met by that early stage of my life, and I fully expected him to go on to achieve something really big in life. For many years after I'd left Rhodes, whenever I'd haul out my old photo albums and reminisce about what a fun time I'd had in 1980, I'd pause and wonder what he was doing now, and how come his name hadn't emerged in some prominent field or other, maybe politics, but there was nothing.

Until maybe five or seven years ago, when I learnt through a Facebook friend that Bradley had gone into the world of teaching and had been doing very well until stories began to emerge about him practising some kind of rudimentary hypnotism on one of his pupils and then sexually abusing him. He apparently fled to the UK at that point before criminal charges could be brought.

Many years later, he was teaching at a prestigious private school in England when that same pupil tracked him down and alerted the authorities to his shady past, and he was forced to do another disappearing act, never to be heard from again.

Such huge potential. Such a depressing outcome.

CHAPTER 19

Rhodes was the beating heart of Grahamstown and many local businesses survived on the custom generated by the 3,000 or so students – bookstores, corner cafés, a cinema and, of course, the discos and the pubs. There were several drinking establishments within lurching distance of the campus but there were two in particular that me and my buddies tended to support enthusiastically on the weekends, and the occasional weeknight too.

One was called The Graham and the other the Vic, but although both tried to keep their prices down so as to remain competitive, it was still a bit pricey to spend a whole night there. What we tended to do instead was to buy a 5-litre box of el cheapo wine to share – Autumn Harvest, if I recall correctly – and have a mug or two of that each in Hew's room, maybe while listening to a Monty Python tape or a bit of Chris de Burgh, and only then head out for the evening, already listing several degrees to port, with our spirits high and our judgment severely impaired.

I have a memory of one night that was probably replicated many times over in one way or another: me and four other guys are carrying Hew back to his room in the early hours of the morning, all the way up the Grahamstown high street and then through the campus, each of us holding a foot or a hand and slinging him along between us like a heavy sack of grain while he belts out the Pink Floyd classic *We Don't Need No Education* at the top of his voice.

On another such night – or, rather, the morning after –

I woke up with no contact lenses in my eyes, but with no recollection of having taken them out either. That was a worrying development, because my optician was all the way back in Benoni, and replacement lenses would probably have taken a month to reach me. As crazy luck would have it, I found the left lens stuck to the side of the plastic bottle containing my saline solution, and the right lens on the side of the washbasin, beneath the small mirror where I'd presumably removed them the night before and was trying to place them in the small plastic holder when I lost interest and passed out.

That was a wake-up call, let me tell you, and I determined to change my ways immediately from that day on. Which is not to say that I stopped getting stupid drunk; only that I started taking out my contact lenses *before* we went out drinking, rather than after. That wasn't ideal, because I couldn't really see where I was going, but I reasoned that by about 9pm I wouldn't be able to see where I was going anyway, so it didn't make much difference.

I had to wear spectacles as well as contact lenses in those days, at the same time, to achieve clarity of vision. Using one without the other didn't really make much sense, but I carried on wearing my spectacles anyway on those drinking nights because I'd gotten used to having them perched on my nose and somehow felt bare without them. Anyone who wears specs fulltime will know what I'm talking about.

Anyway, one chilly Friday night in June, Hew, Paul, Alan and I were down at the Vic trying to shout at a group of girls above the deafening music when a bunch of those embittered Rhodesians with the army-issue haircuts I mentioned earlier decided to pick a fight with us. It would have been a lopsided mismatch even under the best of circumstances: there were six of them and four of us; they were hardened soldiers fresh from the battlefront, we were lanky boys, all already hopelessly drunk, me with my frosted-glass vision further reduced by the effects of the alcohol. It was never going to end well.

I have only the haziest of memories of the whole incident; a series of vivid flashes, each one a little more alarming than the one before it:

Flash: I'm surrounded by a hostile group as we step out onto the street outside the Vic. One of them swears at Hew and shoves him, and he responds by telling the guy that his mother still owes him change. Which makes the guy a bit angry.

Flash: somebody jostles me and gets me in some kind of headlock, and I break free and try to knee him in the groin but miss. There's a fair amount of shoving and swearing at that point, and I end up on the pavement somehow.

Flash: I'm standing upright again – swaying, actually – but holding my spectacles in one hand, spitting mad because they're broken. I'm asking: "Whash the meaning of thish outrage! Who broke my glashesh?" Somebody tells me that we've just been jumped by a gang of Rhodesian army guys. I say: "What? When? Lesh go find the bashtarsh!" (A terrible idea, of coursh – sorry, course – but it seemed like a good one at the time).

Flash: I'm loping up the high road in the direction of the campus, vengeance on my mind. Hew is close behind but Paul and Alan are no longer with us for some reason.

Flash: We've managed, very unfortunately, to track down the Rhodesians. They're standing on the small bridge near the Jan Smuts residence which spans the aptly named Kotch (vomit) Creek, a tiny stream running maybe 20 feet below. I'm shouting: "Which of you c**** broke my glashes???" I start trying to pull off my jacket but it's a real struggle because my arms are somehow tangled in the sleeves behind my back. I'm standing there unsteadily, wrestling with that jacket and trying to look over one shoulder to figure out how to unstick it when one of the Rhodesians steps out of the group and punches me right between the eyes. BOOOOM!

Flash: I'm flat on my back. Seeing stars.

Flash: I'm grappling with the Rhodesian. We tumble over the side of the bridge and go rolling down the bank, just like in the movies, to the edge of Kotch Creek. He gets on top and starts strangling me. He tells me: "I haven't killed anyone for SIX MONTHS!!!!" – and that's verbatim; he actually says that. I remember those words very well.

He adds: "D'you give up? D'you give up?"

I reply: "Gurgle! Splutter!" because the blood from my broken nose is pouring down my throat, which he's simultaneously squeezing, and I'm drowning and suffocating at the same time. A bit like water-boarding, I imagine, but with blood. Somebody appears alongside us and pulls him off, and I'm able to draw breath again.

Flash: I'm back on the bridge helping Hew to his feet, because one of the other Rhodesians has taken the opportunity to sucker-punch him and knock him senseless while everyone else is watching me being strangled.

Flash: The two of us are searching around the bridge and down by Kotch Creek for my room key, which has fallen from my pocket and been lost at some point in proceedings.

Flash: Hew is helping me up the stairs to the first floor of Jan Smuts residence, and along the hallway to Bradley's room. He's had first-aid training and has offered to let me sleep on his floor, as I'm still unable to get into my own room …

… and the next thing I remember is waking up the following morning feeling a thousand times worse than I'd ever felt before (or since, it's probably safe to say). My head was pounding and my stomach was churning – which, admittedly wasn't unusual for a Saturday morning – but this time my nose was also blocked with dried blood, and twice it's normal width, with the bottom half now sitting a couple of millimetres to the left of where it had been a day earlier (it's still skew to this day; check my profile and you'll see what I mean).

I had aches and pains everywhere, in every part of my body. I had a cricked neck, and a big black eye, and the fingers on my left hand were all purplish and very painful to move, and when I groaned and tried to roll over onto one side I realised my right knee was swollen and unbendable. I coughed and there was a stabbing pain from my bruised ribs. Man, I felt f***ing terrible.

Wrecked. Fubared, in the fullest sense of the word.

We saw those Rhodesians again later that very same day, and at the same spot on the bridge over Kotch Creek where the confrontation had played out. That wasn't surprising; they were living in the same residence, after all, and they were walking up towards the dining hall for lunch at the same time we were. They were all looking pretty hungover too, but it's a measure of just how drunk I'd been the night before that I didn't even know which one of them it was who'd almost killed me.

I stopped and fumbled out my broken spectacles and balanced them on my swollen nose for a moment. I peered at the group through the cracked glass covering my one unblackened eye: "Who f***** me up?" I croaked.

One of them shuffled his feet and answered: "Um – that might've been me." Pause. "Sorry." A bit sheepish.

He wasn't a big guy; in fact, he looked like a bit of a geek, and I learnt later that his nickname was "Duck". Not terribly threatening. But appearances can be deceptive, as they say, and, as he himself had pointed out the night before, he'd been out and about killing people just six months earlier.

I nodded and hobbled on by. I still, at least, had all my teeth. I should be able to eat lunch without too much difficulty, I told myself.

Quite a few Rhodes students went on to excel in the South African media world, but the professors in the journalism department would probably point to Shaun Johnson as their greatest success. He had graduated the year before I arrived, and he rose to become executive editor of what was then the biggest English-language newspaper group on the continent, and then left to write a few books and lead various anti-apartheid initiatives, before founding the Mandela Rhodes Foundation aimed at giving poor black kids a better start in life.

Another student who did exceptionally well was Shona Bagley, and she was in my class, and from Springs, the town next door to Benoni. I'd sit beside her at lectures whenever the opportunity presented itself – she was very pretty, but also pretty damn intelligent, and easygoing – and she'd occasionally cheer me on when I played my guitar and sang for a handful of students in the café or the botanical gardens (I had, by then, learnt to stick to recognised favourites like *Streets of London*, or *Piano Man*, because people tended to clap for those tunes, rather than leave halfway through *The Only Lonely Eagle!*).

Shona won a prestigious scholarship to the United States and quickly rose through the ranks on her return, emerging a few years later as the young and vivacious launch editor of *Elle* in South Africa, before editing and group-editing a bunch of other top publications. Tragically, both she and Shaun Johnson died relatively young; he at 60, she at 57, and both from cancer.

Would my life and career have been any different if I'd applied myself to my studies with the same dedication, and gone on to achieve that B.Journ degree? Or if I'd taken up the offer from BOSS? I very much doubt it. I had, after all, signed up for a career that I had no particular interest in, and that hadn't changed by the time I left Rhodes. I still had no clue at that point what I wanted to do with my adult life, and although I did later somehow stumble into the newspaper world anyway, back in those days you didn't really need a degree to get started in that line of work, and the fact that I didn't have one was never held against me.

Until I came to England, that is, almost twenty years later. (We're drifting off-topic here, but I'll explain quickly and then we can get back to the story):

By the turn of the millennium my wife Asha and I and our young son Jordan had moved to England and were living in a rented, semi-detached house in the gritty suburb of Edmonton, north London. I was doing subbing shifts at any national newspaper that would take me, desperate to land a staff job so that I could earn more money and finally get a foot on the property ladder.

One of those newspapers was the *Daily Mail* (as I said, I wasn't fussy). I'd done a handful of shifts in the features department, and the chief sub, a laidback guy who I won't name here, liked me enough to tell me that he wanted to put me on the fulltime staff. Fantastic news!

I went home that night and drew up my CV like he'd asked me to. I tucked it into a neat folder and took it into the office the following day and handed it to him, then headed back to my desk and started subbing a story. He appeared alongside me ten minutes later and handed it right back to me. "Bring me one of these that says you have a university degree," he said.

I paused. "But ... I don't."

He shrugged. "Just say you have. Nobody's going to check. The *Mail* won't take you on if you haven't got a degree."

I agonised over that decision, let me tell you. I talked it over with Asha and then I agonised some more. On the London newspaper scene you're treated very much as a second-class citizen if you're one of the so-called casual sub-editors, a temp. You're underpaid and overworked, forever at the whim of whoever it is that draws up the rotas, overly careful not to piss off the chief sub, or the revise sub, or the news desk, or the night editor, or even the frickin janitor. It's a horrible way to make a living. Life is a whole lot better if you're on the staff of one of the big papers.

I really, really wanted that job – but if I lied on my CV, and if somebody *did* ever investigate further, and if that led to me being fired on the spot ... could I live with the shame? More to the point, would I ever get a job at another London newspaper? I couldn't take that chance.

I told the *Mail* features chief sub no, I couldn't give him that alternative CV, and he picked one of the other casuals to fill the spot instead. But my honesty was rewarded just a couple of months later when I phoned *The Times* to see if there were any shifts going, and a man by the name of Dennis Rink answered, a South African who'd been living in London for several years. Dennis told me *The Times* already had its full quota of casual sub-editors and wasn't looking for any more, and he was about to hang up when I said quickly: "Is that a South African accent I hear?"

He said: "Yes, it is. And I was wondering about your accent?"

"Part-Scottish – but I grew up in Benoni."

"Benoni? Ha! I know it well." Pause. "Okay, lemme look again." Pause. Shuffling of papers. "Hmm … yeah, ok, I can get you in next Friday if you like?"

I liked.

I took that shift, and then another one, and another one after that, and shortly afterwards the managing editor, Simon Pearson at the time, called me in to his office to tell me he had a job for me. A few months later I was a staff member on *The Times*, and I'm still there today, 20-odd years later … and probably the only person on the whole paper, and maybe the entire London Bridge office, who doesn't have a university degree.

And with that, let's get back to Grahamstown, where I should have been working flat-out to achieve that degree...

CHAPTER 20

Failing four out of four half-year exams in June would have given the average student a bit of a nudge in the direction of the library but, as we've established, I was a less-than-average student. I shrugged and told myself I'd put in a big burst of effort later in the year, and I told my parents that the half-year exams had been called off due to a lack of interest from all parties involved. That was the plan, at least, but they never actually asked me how things had gone, and I never volunteered the information. Don't ask, don't tell.

I'd made the long trip back to Benoni for the Easter holidays, and again in July, sharing a car and the petrol bill with three or four other students each time, but I decided to stay on campus for the September break. Things would be very quiet, because the majority of students would be going home for a couple of weeks – even the hordes of Rhodesians, who had a thousand miles or more to travel – and with none of my buddies around to drink or play table tennis with I'd have nothing else to do but study.

I had good intentions, but I was nothing if not resourceful when it came to *finding* other things to do. I went jogging the first day, pounding down the deserted streets of the campus at a reasonably good pace until I realised just how out of shape I was thanks to the pack-a-day of Chesterfields I was smoking, at which point I stopped and walked back, and didn't try again the second day.

I spent a lot of time in the botanical gardens playing my guitar. I read a couple of novels. I slept a lot and I even got drunk by myself a couple of times in my room, turning up the volume to ten on my little tape recorder and yodelling along at the top of my voice to the Pink Floyd classic *Great Gig in the Sky* because there was no one around to hear me. Very liberating – you should try it.

I got talking to another work-averse kid on the first floor who hadn't gone away for the holidays and who, I discovered, also liked table tennis, and that accounted for another couple of hours every day ... and before I knew it the September break was over and I hadn't quite gotten around to opening a single text book or visiting the library.

Hew was back. Alan was back. Paul was back, along with a bunch of other friends – Tommy E, Clive S, Greg V, Phil T, and Bradley – and that called for a celebration down at the Vic, and then a second, and a third.

And so it continued. September became October, and October became November, and I noticed at some point that students all around me were getting their heads down, my friends among them, and preparing for the end-of-year exams.

With a week to go before the first paper I rummaged through the piles of beer cans and empty cigarette packets that covered the desk in my room and I found the couple of writing pads I'd used earlier in the year to take down a few notes during lectures ... but there was no semblance of order to them, and the writing was so untidy I could make little sense of any of it. A graphologist might have commented on just how tiny that handwriting was, and drawn conclusions about my low self-esteem, but, whatever the case, those lecture notes were useless to me, so I concluded that there was only one course of action remaining to me: I would have to visit the main student library.

I picked up a Bic ballpoint and a fresh writing pad and even put on a pair of shoes, which showed just how committed I was to the task, and I screwed my courage to the sticking point and made the short walk across campus.

I had seven days to cram in a year's worth of learning, but

I thought I might still be alright if I could employ the "spot" technique with the same level of energy and blind luck that had carried me through high school; that is, to pick one or two areas of the curriculum and study them hard, and hope to hell that they featured in the final test paper.

I collected half a dozen big and very bulky history textbooks from the shelves and carried them over to a desk in the corner but my heart was already sinking, because I was realising already that I may have underestimated the sheer scale of the task at hand. That massive pile of books covered just the Byzantine period, one of a dozen different topics that might come up, and it would take me a week just to read them, never mind study them in depth. And if the Byzantine period didn't feature in the exams after all, well, I might as well not have bothered "spotting" it at all. The one-in-12 odds just weren't good enough to justify the effort.

I sat back and thought for a moment. I knew I needed to pass a minimum of two of my four subjects to be allowed to return to Rhodes for Year Two ... so maybe I should abandon History and focus all my energies on the other subjects? Good idea. Great idea.

I returned the half-dozen history books to the shelves and headed over to the Sociology section. I'd pretty much stopped attending Sociology lectures halfway through the year because ... well, I couldn't really remember why ... but whatever the case, there was very little in the second huge pile of books that I carried to that same desk in the corner that looked even vaguely familiar. Again, there was simply too much to take in and too little time to do it.

Hmmm. Might have to narrow things down a bit more, I thought. Maybe focus just on Geography and Journalism. I could really, really go to town on those two subjects.

Geography should be easy, I reasoned. I knew where stuff was. I'd toured South Africa with the Protea choir, after all, and I knew about Britain thanks to the Weir family ties, and I could probably learn all the rest of it by looking closely at the big globe over by the entrance to the library and memorising the names of a few capital cities and mountain ranges ... right? Right?

Wrong. Turned out geography at university level was not quite the same as geography at Standard Two level, which was the last time I'd paid any attention to it. The lectures that I hadn't shown up for had apparently included a whole bunch of stuff you wouldn't (OK, *I* wouldn't) expect to find under that classification: urban planning, and geomorphological process, and biophysical diversity and a host of other crap that I'd never heard of. All of which was talked about at length in another dozen textbooks that I had no hope of getting through in a week. Ack!

That left Journalism. Even if I scored a 100 per cent mark in the exam it wouldn't matter, because one pass out of four subjects was still a fail. So was there any point in me returning to the library shelves and seeking out the Journalism textbooks, I wondered? Not really. Not at all, in fact.

I left my Bic Ballpoint and notepad on that desk in the corner, thinking that maybe a *real* student would be able to put them to good use. Shoulders slumped and spirits low, I headed for the exit.

There was no miracle turnaround and the exams went about as badly as expected. I didn't bother attending the Geography or Sociology ones, as there was no hope at all of success, but I did at least show up for the first of two History papers, and I probably did enough to scrape through – but the second, for which I was expected to write two essays from four topics presented, was a complete bust, because I had no knowledge at all of any of the four topics on offer. I shuffled the papers around for a bit and left after ten minutes.

The same thing happened in the Journalism exams: I was able to spout enough general knowledge in the first of two papers but came up against a brick wall in the second and bowed out gracefully long before the three hours was up.

My university life was over. A bust. Finish and klaar. It was back to Benoni, a year older but no wiser.

I remember my mother greeting me at the front door with a cold, hard stare.

Hew travelled back with me to visit for a week or ten days, because he'd never seen the bright lights of nearby Johannesburg and I'd offered to show him around. When that was over I said my goodbyes to him at the Joburg station and he stepped aboard the same southbound sleeper train I'd used a year earlier and he headed home, and I've never seen him nor any of my other university buddies since.

We connected on Facebook a few years ago – Hew, that is – and I discovered that he's also living in England now, out in Somerset somewhere. We've talked about getting together sometime for a beer, but you know how it is: he says he'll give me a shout next time he's in London; I say I'll look him up if I ever pass through his hometown, but it never seems to happen. Life gets in the way.

CHAPTER 21

Hindsight is 20/20, they say, and many of us make decisions that we question later in life. I've made my share, and then some, but there's one that stands out head and shoulders above the rest, one choice that is the dumbest and most bewildering I've ever made, and it is this: I signed up the following year for the drama diploma at Pretoria Tech, following in the footsteps of both Graham and Christine. Why? God only knows. I certainly don't.

Had I discovered a magic pill among my Christmas pressies that December giving me a sudden boost of acting talent? And a second one offering brash self-confidence – both of which, let's face it, are essential for anyone contemplating a life on the stage? Not that I recall. I think I'd have remembered that.

Had I forgotten the humiliation my 11-year-old self had suffered at the *Wizard of Oz* audition, and the fact that I actually preferred a bit of anonymity in the chorus to the spotlight of the centre stage? Apparently. I was happy enough by then playing my guitar and singing for small groups of people, but take that guitar away and stand me up in front of an audience and I was as awkward and insecure as I'd ever been … so why exactly did I think it would be a good idea to become an actor?

Looking back, I can only think that I was swept up in the continuing obsession within the Weir family with all things theatrical; the glamour and excitement of opening nights and cast parties and press reviews, the promise of fame and fortune, the heady drug of public adulation. Graham had just completed his drama diploma and had secured his first acting contract with the Performing Arts Council of the Transvaal; Christine was in Year Three and dreaming of hitting the big time; even Bruce was in Pretoria and doing the drama course, in Year Two.

Back in Benoni, my mother was loving life at the head of Protea, directing a couple of amateur shows a year and thriving on the attention, while my father was still involved in his Gilbert and Sullivan productions in Springs and rather enjoyed hob-nobbing with the theatre crowd in the lobby on opening nights, especially when somebody would turn to him and say: "Wow, so you're Graham's father!"

There were regular trips with family and Protea friends to professional shows in Joburg's many theatres, and endless discussions over drinks afterwards about the high points and low points of the show, or the talents of the star performers, and talk of who had visited London or New York to see the latest hit on the West End or on Broadway. Intoxicating stuff.

So when one day, bored and restless back in Benoni, and still with no clear idea of what path to follow in life, I said to my mother: "Hey, how about I also do the drama course?" she said hey, why not.

On a January morning in 1981 I moved into a residential hotel called The 224, about a 15-minute walk from the Pretoria Tech, where I stayed for a few weeks while I looked for somewhere more permanent to stay. On the first day of term I attended an induction ceremony at the nearby Loftus Versfeld rugby stadium along with a few thousand other first-year students, most of them Afrikaans and strait-laced, and signing up for far more sensible courses like engineering or teaching. The day after that I met my new classmates for the first time.

The Pretoria drama department was a small one; in fact, my year group consisted of only seven students doing the English-language version of the diploma and another seven or eight on the Afrikaans side, and it's fair to say we stuck out from the other students like sore thumbs, thanks to our funky hairstyles or alternative clothes. *Moffies en hoers*, they called the drama kids – gays and whores.

The coursework included a few formal classes on the origins of Greek tragedy and Stanislavski's method acting and so on, but the emphasis was on the practical. It was all about developing the sort of clear diction and powerhouse voice that would reach the back row of a crowded theatre, projecting an aura of belief in your role that would convince the audience, exercising the diaphragm and correcting the posture and *being* the character you were trying to portray up on that stage.

An essential part of the actor's trade, we were told, was to shuck off all traces of inhibition, to feel no sense of embarrassment in any situation, and we had regular improvisation classes that were a big part of that.

The idea was simple: the teacher, a stout lady by name of Betts P, if I remember right, would tell us to spread out across the room, standing a metre or two apart, and to imagine we were, say, a bee trapped inside a ping-pong ball or a leaf floating down a lazy river. We'd bounce off the walls or off each other, or wriggle along the floor in undulating waves.

If she asked us to be a tree, some of the kids would start swaying gently in an imaginary breeze, fingers trembling towards the heavens, while others would find themselves being bent over backwards by an invisible hurricane and struggling to stay upright.

Anything was acceptable and nothing was wrong, but I tended to sneak a peek sideways, anyway, just to see what the other students were doing before "expressing myself", to be sure I didn't look foolish (or any more foolish than anybody else, at least). I was sceptical at first, but those improvisation classes may actually have had some effect, because I started easing up a bit as the weeks went by and losing some of my inhibitions.

One morning Betts P told us to assume the identity of the most evil creature we could think of, and I quickly dropped to all fours and started snarling and snapping my teeth at the kids around me like a rabid baboon. *Be* the rabid baboon! Grrr!

I was surrounded by lurching hunchbacks and cackling witches and flapping pterodactyls, and there was suddenly a real sense of menace in the air. One of the other students was a skinny and intense young guy called Toni C, proud of his part-Italian heritage and with a wild look in his eyes at the best of times. I spotted him slithering across the floor towards me with deadly intent – he'd turned into some kind of ravenous python-alligator hybrid – so I gave a guttural roar and swung around to confront him … but I'd somehow forgotten that there was a very solid grand piano sitting there, slap-bang in the middle of the room, and I smashed my head into the corner of it with full force, producing a loud and reverberating *boingggg* from within, and splitting the skin in the centre of my forehead.

I sat back on my arse, momentarily stunned, as the blood came gushing down my face and my fellow students shrieked in horror and came running over to help. Betts took one look and rushed me off to see the nurse in the Tech sick bay.

She was a miserable old tannie, I remember. She put three stitches in the cut and told me to blerry look where I was going next time man!

"I wasn't *going* anywhere," I said, a bit offended. "I was attacked by an alligator. In drama class."

She paused mid-stitch. "An … alligator? In drama class?"

"Yes! Well, not a real one. It was Toni. But he was *being* the alligator. It was very realistic."

She muttered something under her breath. It sounded like: "Moffies en hoers!"

That incident reshaped my face for the second time within a year. If the Rhodesian army guy had given me a hook nose where my pointy one used to be, the piano gave me a single deep indent between my eyes where once I'd had twin frown lines. Plastic surgery on a budget. And my nose would be reshaped again a decade later during a karate tournament in which my opponent caught me off-guard with a foot-sweep and spinning reverse punch.

All of which means that when I pitch up at the Pearly Gates one of these fine days St Peter is going to have a bit of a job reconciling my battered face with the photo he has on file ...

CHAPTER 22

I moved to my own studio flat a couple of months into the academic year, in the exact same apartment block around the corner from the Pretoria Tech where Graham and Christine were already living. I was on the fourth floor; Christine was on the third floor, and Graham and Bruce were sharing a one-bedroom on the fifth floor. On the first floor was yet another Benoni boy who was doing the drama course, Robin P, a talented pianist with a sharp wit who, on a bad day, would joke about flinging himself from the window of his not-so-highrise apartment … onto the ledge directly outside.

I had almost nothing in my flat at Caledonian Mansions besides a bed, a single brown-leather bean bag and a pair of mismatched curtains. I never felt alone though, because I had the constant companionship of a few thousand giant cockroaches; fearless bastards, some of them two inches long and with six-pack torsos and gang tattoos on their hind legs who would try to stare me down if I dared to enter my own kitchen, and only run away when I started stomping them left, right and centre. Messy business.

Their numbers started to drop off after a couple of months, not because I was getting any more accurate in my stomping, but because they had started to realise by then that the new inhabitant of No 401 was way too lazy to ever do any cooking for himself and tended to eat out most days: burgers and chips, or sometimes just half a loaf of bread washed down with a 500ml Coke. That meant there were rarely any crumbs or leftovers for them to feed on.

On those nights when I did cook something in the tiny kitchen the roaches would gather around the stove in excited clusters, chattering among themselves and jockeying for position and whinnying with delight ... but a collective groan would go up when they saw me pull out yet another packet of taste-free Smash (instant mash potato – just add hot water!) and plop yet another Fish-in-a-Bag into a pot of lukewarm water. Their little antennae would droop and they would turn away and shuffle off, depressed, towards the cracks in the linoleum floor that they'd emerged from.

To this day the descendants of the survivors probably still talk about the Great Famine of 1981, when 401 Roach Colony had to disperse to greener pastures in Flat 402 or Flat 403; when they had to send desperate appeals for food parcels down to the fast-food café on the ground floor where, it was whispered, their ancestors had come from decades before.

That terrible diet wasn't doing me any good either and I was probably skinnier then and in worse shape than I'd ever been in my whole life. I was still smoking heavily and getting drunk regularly, and the only exercise I ever got was the five-minute walk to the Tech, Mondays to Friday.

Also, I had discovered marijuana, and although I never became a committed user – I smoked a joint once a week at most – it probably didn't help. I had a couple of wonderful experiences playing my guitar and feeling like David Gilmour, with a chorus of angelic voices in my head seeming to provide heavenly harmonies, but I also had a couple of not-so-wonderful ones in which I got really paranoid and started thinking the man from BOSS was back, spying on my every move and about to swoop in and arrest me. God knows what horrors my fevered imagination would have thrown up if I'd ever tried LSD. I never did, fortunately.

Toni, when he wasn't *being* the alligator, was a guitar player like me, and although neither of us were especially skilful we tried our best to make up for that with sheer youthful enthusiasm. We discovered that we shared a love of Pink

Floyd and when we gave an impromptu duo performance of *Comfortably Numb* at a drunken student party one night, and got a big cheer for it, we decided to try working together on a few other songs too.

A month or so later Toni pulled me aside with some exciting news: he'd arranged for us to perform on the coming Sunday night at a bar and restaurant called the Midnight Grill. We'd get ten rand each per hour, a king's ransom for a couple of penniless students. Fantastic! But on the Sunday morning he showed up at my apartment to tell me he couldn't go through with it: we simply didn't have enough songs prepared, he said, and he had a croak in his throat, and … and, well, he'd decided we weren't ready.

I said: "Toni! Buddy! We'll be fine – come on!"

"Gav! I don't want to embarrass you!"

"You won't have to – I'll embarrass myself!"

But he'd made up his mind. He wouldn't perform, he said, but if I wanted to do the gig by myself I could still use his 12-string acoustic guitar and, crucially, his amp and mike. He'd be there to offer immoral support, he promised, and to set up the equipment and to lead the cheering section (we'd promised a dozen of our fellow students a free beer each to come along and clap loudly). I thought about pulling out, but not for long: twenty rand was a lot of money for a drama student and, anyway, I rather fancied the idea of playing to a paying crowd for the first time.

So at 8pm on a cool autumn night in March 1981 I stepped onto a raised section of the floor in the Midnight Grill with Toni's guitar in one hand and my heart in my throat. I tapped the microphone and said hello – and the four tables over in the corner full of rowdy drama students cheered like I was some superstar who'd just performed his latest chart-topping hit. They knew a thing or two about acting, after all.

I opened with *My Sweet Lord*, and my fan club whooped and hollered. I played *Piano Man* and *I Wonder* and *The Sound of Silence* and half a dozen other songs I knew, and the drama students went wild every time, and quite a few of the regular customers got caught up in the mood and started cheering too.

Before I knew it, the two hours was up and I was packing away Toni's guitar, and the manager of the Midnight Grill was pushing twenty rand into my sweaty paws and telling me he'd see me again the same time next week because, man, the crowd really, really loved me!

I left on a wave of euphoria, already dreaming of the day in the not-too-distant future when I'd be filling every seat in Madison Square Garden ... but that performance, sadly, proved to be the high point of my one-man-band career. It was downhill all the way from then on.

I showed up as scheduled the following Sunday night but this time I was on my own. I still had Toni's sound equipment and his 12-string guitar, but Toni himself couldn't make it, and none of my sponsored fan club were there either. The beer wasn't *that* good, even if free.

I played the same songs, and I got a polite round of applause each time, but nothing like the rapturous reception of the week before. The manager paid me my twenty rand at the end of it but he wasn't looking quite as happy.

I'd planned to practise hard during the week and come up with another few songs that I could perform on the third Sunday but me being me I never got around to it, so I trotted out the same tunes as before. More muted applause. That was a bit discouraging, so I sang a little louder and strummed a little harder – but things took a turn for the worse when, midway through *Streets of London*, one of my 12 strings suddenly snapped and wrapped itself around the neck of the guitar, producing a discordant *twanggggg*!

I stopped and untangled the blasted thing, then re-started with a Rodriguez classic. I sang:

"Sugarman, won't you hurry, cos I'm –" twanggggg!!!

Dammit! I stopped again. Removed the broken string. Tried

again:

"Sugarman, won't you –" twanggggg!

I pressed ahead grimly but I was down to seven strings on that 12-string guitar by the end of the song, and I could hear the distinct sound of sniggering from one or two nearby tables.

The problem, I realised as I untangled the fifth broken string, was the plectrum, the small piece of plastic used for strumming. I normally played with a lightweight, red Sharkfin but I'd somehow misplaced it that evening and had had to substitute it with one of the rigid ones preferred by bass players. It was way too heavy for the thin acoustic strings – with predictable consequences.

I eased up on the strumming and I was able to play out the rest of the two-hour session without further mishap, albeit with a somewhat reedy and threadbare tone from the guitar. As I stood up after the last song, to listless applause, and prepared to start packing things away the manager appeared at my side and asked if I'd mind if *this* guy – he pointed to a young man sitting at a table close by – played a quick tune before I unplugged the mike.

I said: "Um ..."

"Thanks," he replied.

He nodded to the guy, who sprang up from the table and immediately started twiddling with the knobs on the amp and re-positioning the mike in a professional and frankly intimidating manner. He took the guitar from me and tweaked the tuning knobs ever so slightly. He looked at the plectrum with distaste and said: "You should be using a red Sharkfin."

"I *know* that!" I replied testily, but he'd already dismissed me, positioning himself on the bar stool that I'd vacated and pulling the microphone closer.

I sat down at the table where he'd been sitting a moment before, and I watched and listened with a sinking heart as the stranger crooned and finger-picked his way through a flawless rendition of *Sultans of Swing*, a song that I'd experimented with but ultimately abandoned because the guitarwork was way too complex for me to perform with any confidence. He managed it just fine, and with seven strings instead of 12.

When I showed up at The Midnight Grill on the fourth Sunday night, my guitar in one hand and Toni's little amp in the other, I found that same stranger already sitting there, in my bar stool, surrounded by a bank of amps and mikes and auto-drum boxes and other high-end stuff. He didn't even give me a second glance, but the manager at least looked a little sheepish as he told me he wouldn't be requiring my services again. He gave me ten rand instead of 20, and I turned around and trudged back to my lonely and unwelcoming flat.

I was feeling a bit down about the whole experience the following morning as I headed over to the Tech for the usual Monday classes but I was enough of a realist to recognise that the stranger, whoever he was, was a hundred times better than I would ever be. But Toni, 50 per cent Italian and 100 per cent loyal to his friends, was not so quick to forgive. He went absolutely nuts when I told him what had happened. He was ready to charge on over to The Midnight Grill right there and then and twist the f***** manager's head all the way round on his f****** shoulders till he was staring down at his own syphilitic pimpled arse! "The f***! The f****** f***!" he roared.

"Toni – I'm okay. It's all okay. And that other guy was a pretty good guitarist anyway."

"Let's get him too! The f***** f***!"

He raged some more, saying he would sprint back home there and then and change into his old army boots and hunt down the pair of them and give them both the kicking of a lifetime, but after ten minutes or so he finally started to calm down a bit – but, hell, he said, me and him were going to ditch our classes for the morning and just go get drunk in the bar around the corner, okay? I didn't usually drink before 11am, but I didn't really have much choice on that occasion. I said okay. And, truth be told, I felt a lot better for it afterwards.

CHAPTER 23

Performing to a live audience was, of course, a big part of the Tech drama experience and we staged a series of shows throughout the year in a small, purpose-built theatre on campus, allowing the students to hone their skills and showcase their talents to family and friends, and to the wider public. That was well and good – but just a ten-minute walk down the road from the Tech was the brand-new State Theatre, a vast, sumptuously equipped complex that was the largest in Africa, and there was great excitement when we learnt one day that auditions would be held there for the first professional staging in South Africa of the Lloyd Webber hit *Evita*.

At least 10 or 12 Tech drama students from Year One through to Year Three turned out on the day in question, all of us dreaming of landing a role in the show and taking a shortcut to stardom. We joined several hundred other hopefuls queuing outside the complex waiting for the doors to open, and when they did we surged inside, queuing again to fill in a couple of forms and collect a ticket with a number on it, and then join a nervy, excited mob milling around waiting to be called into a cavernous rehearsal room where the audition would take place.

Toni was standing next to me in that mob, shifting his weight from foot to foot and staring around him anxiously. *Evita*, of course, is a rock musical, and the first thing the producers wanted to know was: could we sing? Toni could; in fact, he had a strong bass voice, and he was armed with a piece of sheet music, as per instructions, which he was ready to hand over to the pianist when it was his turn to take the stage. But he wasn't feeling at all confident.

"I'm gonna forget the words, Gav," he confided. "I just know it!" His song was *Pick a Pocket or Two*, from the stage musical *Oliver!*

"You'll be fine," I reassured him. "You've sung it a dozen times this morning! You haven't forgotten once."

"Yeah but when I get up *there* ..." he flicked his head in the direction of the audition room. At that moment a young woman walked past with a pen and clipboard in hand, one of the organisers, and Toni's eyes lit up. His eyes always lit up when a young woman walked past – did I mention his Italian heritage? – but on this occasion he was after something different. "Hi," he said, quickly falling in step alongside her and flashing his most charming smile. "Could I borrow that pen? Just for a moment?"

She handed it over, and he spent a frantic couple of minutes writing out a few key lyrics from *Pick a Pocket* on his palms. Just as he finished, and handed back the pen, the big double doors leading into the rehearsal room up at the front opened and somebody stuck their head out and yelled: "Number 78! Number 78!" Toni's eyes bulged. "That's me!" he said.

"Go!" I told him. "Break a leg, buddy!"

He stepped forward tentatively. He was ushered inside and the doors closed again behind him. I elbowed my way towards the front of the crowd, hoping to hear what was happening in there, but there was too much of a babble all around me; people joking nervously or practising their vocal scales or singing their lines to themselves.

A few minutes passed. I was no longer thinking about how Toni was doing, but about how I was going to do, because I was next, and the nerves were building fast. The doors opened again and somebody yelled "Number 79! Number 79!" – and there was a brief moment when I considered crumpling the ticket in my hand and just easing away towards the exit, but a buck-toothed stranger standing next to me poked me on the shoulder and pointed. "Hey, that's you, boet," he said.

It was indeed. I gulped, and I forced my trembling legs to carry me through the double doors. Inside, that same somebody pointed me towards a piano at the foot of a small stage. "Give your sheet music to the pianist then take the stage," the person said. I can't recall if it was a man or a woman, young or old. That's how nervous I was.

You've seen *Pop Idol*? *Britain's Got Talent*? Well, they had a very similar set up back in 1981. A long-haired guy was sitting at the piano and he was extending a hand towards me expectantly. I handed over my music. In the middle of the room was a long table strewn with papers and Coke cans and ashtrays, with three people sitting behind it discussing something among themselves, maybe Toni's performance moments earlier.

One of them, a middle-aged woman with horn-rimmed spectacles, I remember – not at all glamorous or funky, as I'd expected – shuffled the papers in front of her then looked up at me and said: "Gavin? On the stage please. Start whenever you're ready."

I climbed the few steps and walked to centre-stage and cleared my throat a few times then nodded down to the piano player, who was apparently able to sight-read pretty much any song and perform it at a moment's notice. I'd chosen *One Hand, One Heart*, from *West Side Story*. He eased into it like he'd played it a thousand times before.

I gave it my best shot, hitting the high notes and starting to relax and thinking that maybe I might be doing okay, but as I drew a deep breath to start the second verse the bespectacled woman held up a hand and said: "Thank you – that'll do," and gave a half nod in the direction of the exit on the far side of the room. She and the two others began comparing notes again, and I stood there uncertainly for a moment and then I climbed back down from the stage. The pianist stood and held out my sheet music towards me and I collected it and left, unsure if I'd made the grade or failed miserably.

Toni was waiting out there.

"Gav! How'd it go?" he demanded.

"Man, I'm not sure," I said. "I thought I was doing okay – but she cut me off halfway through."

"You got halfway through? That's good! They only listen to a couple of lines from most people."

"Really? How about you – did you remember the words?"

He gave a hoot of laughter. "No! I blanked out! But I held up my hands like *this*, as if I was, you know, looking at something that I'd pick-pocketed, and I read a few of the words and the rest came back to me!"

"Fantastic!"

"Yeah, but the woman in the middle, the one with the glasses – she told me at the end: Toni, next time memorise the words so you don't have to write them on your hands! Ha ha!"

I clapped him on the back and we shared a laugh, relieved that the ordeal was over, whatever the outcome. "So now we wait?" I said.

"Yeah. When they've seen everybody they'll put up a list of all the people they want to come back tomorrow for a second audition."

It was 5pm before the list went up on a noticeboard outside one of the rehearsal rooms, with copies distributed on nearby doors and walls too, and there was a mad crush as everybody craned in close to see if they could spot their names. There were quite a few whoops and triumphant cheers, but many more disappointed groans, and it was a good five or six minutes before I could push my way to the front.

When I finally did I saw two separate lists. The first, directing the lucky candidates to rehearsal room C the following day, had maybe 60 or 70 names on it. I spotted Toni's name right away but there was no sign of mine, sadly. I scanned the second list with fading hopes – but hey there I was, just a few places from the bottom! Yeah, baby, yeah! I had to report to rehearsal room D the next day!

Toni was due at back at the State Theatre at 10 o clock the following morning, and me at noon. We speculated about why there were two separate lists, but only briefly. We were happy just to have gotten the call-back.

I showed up at rehearsal room D with a couple of minutes to spare, feeling a bit anxious, a bit excited – but I realised as soon as I stepped inside that something was amiss. There was no piano, like the day before, and no table in the centre of the room and no middle-aged woman with horn-rimmed spectacles directing operations.

Instead, a 30-something man with a lithe figure and a Freddie Mercury moustache appeared to be charge. He was wearing black tights and a black leotard, and he was surrounded by 30 or 40 other people in similar outfits. Dancers, obviously.

Half a dozen beautiful young women with leg-warmers around their ankles were stretching out their thighs on a barre mounted along the length of one wall. A mixed group were doing the splits on the floor nearby, the guys every bit as limber and flexible as the gals. Over in one corner a young woman was standing topless, pausing casually to chat to somebody as she changed her top.

I gaped – not just at the topless girl, but at the whole bunch of them. Why was rehearsal room D full of dancers? More to the point: why was I here?

The man in charge clapped his hands together a couple of times to get everyone's attention. "Good morning boys and girls," he called out. "Let's jump right in. We've got a lot to get through this morning. We'll take eight of you at a time."

He produced a list – the same one that I'd seen stuck on the noticeboard the day before – and he read out eight names. One of which was mine.

Seven dancers stepped forward and began positioning themselves in the centre of the room. I hurried across to the guy. "Hi," I said. "Um."

He was slotting a cassette into a big boom-box tape recorder and he ignored me for a moment while he fast-forwarded to the spot he wanted. When he looked up I said:

"I think there's been a mistake. I'm a singer. Not a dancer."

He rolled his eyes. "Your name's on my list, sweetie. That means you're a dancer."

"No – I auditioned with the singers yesterday. And my name was on the list telling me to come back today. To sing."

"To dance," he corrected. "The singers were here at 10am."

"No!"

"They're done for the day. We're just getting started. Take your place on the floor and we'll see how you do."

"But – "

"It's your only shot, sweetie."

I should have accepted defeat there and then but didn't. Instead, I stepped over to join the others, all of them in tights and ballet pumps, me in blue jeans and takkies. I had a moment to wonder how it was I always seemed to find myself in situations like this before a pounding rhythm blared out from the boom box and Freddie Mercury shouted above it: "Okay boys and girls – you remember yesterday's sequence? Step right, spin around, step left, spin around, shake-shake-shake it up, whoop whoop whoop and ... grand jeté! Three-two-one: let's go!"

And with that the dancers leapt into action all around me, jumping and kicking and spinning with perfect synchronisation while I shuffled clumsily alongside them, trying desperately to see what the girl nearest to me was doing and keep up. If I'd at least known the routine that they'd spent the previous day perfecting I might have been able to lurch along with the rest in some kind of hideous parody of modern dance, but the fact I had no clue what they would do next reduced the whole thing to farce. They turned right, I went left; they spun around, I tripped over my own feet, they ended with a graceful grand jeté, I waved my arms around and grinned sheepishly.

Freddie Mercury hit the stop button on the boom box and

held up a hand and pointed at me, but before he could even say the word I turned and began trudging off the dance floor. The girl next to me – the one whose moves I'd been trying to ape – gave me a squeeze on the shoulder and a sympathetic smile as I left.

It seemed a long walk back to my flat that day, my mind a whirl of confusion and disappointment. What the hell had just happened? How had I ended up with the blasted dancers? My first thought was that there had been a simple mix up. Somebody, somehow, had put my name on the wrong list, and that was downright tragic.

Later I came to a more likely conclusion: the judges must have been unconvinced by my audition. Toni, for example, had acted out the part while he sang his song, even if he'd had to read the lyrics from his hands, but I'd simply stood on the stage in the one spot, unmoving and wooden, and given a choirboy rendition of *One Hand, One Heart*. It wasn't enough. The judges must have decided that, while the singing was okay, there was no evidence I could act – but if I could at least dance, they would find a place for me in the show.

I couldn't. They didn't. So it was back to improv class with Betts P and the rest of my classmates.

Toni, by the way, was the only one of the dozen or so Pretoria Tech drama students who had auditioned for *Evita* to actually make the cut. He won a place in the chorus, and while that didn't exactly give him a shortcut to fame and fortune, he was at least the envy of all of his fellow students for months to come.

CHAPTER 24

Unlike Rhodes, there were no formal half-year exams at Pretoria Tech, but I didn't need them to know that I wasn't doing terribly well. My classmates were getting positive feedback from the lecturers and from family and friends for their performances in the regular student productions on campus, and rightly so, but my limitations and my inhibitions were exposed every time I stepped on to that little stage. I was beginning to suspect I'd made a horrible mistake in signing up for the course.

Nights in my studio flat were becoming desperately lonely. It wasn't like at Rhodes, where I could pop into the room next door and see what Hew was up to or grab Paul or Alan for a game of table tennis or go hang out with the crowd in Bradley's room. Here, when I said goodbye to my classmates at the end of the day and I headed back to the flat I'd be on my own for hours. I'd maybe listen to a Pink Floyd cassette on my tape recorder, or strum my guitar, or walk over to the nearby deli and play one of them new-fangled video games like *Space Invaders* or *Pac-Man* until my money ran out, but after that there'd be nothing to do, and all night to do it.

Sure, Graham and Bruce were up on the fifth floor, and I could in theory go visit, but although we'd long since gotten past the awkwardness of that morning in 1979 when I burst in on them, they weren't especially interested in hanging out with me. Christine was on the fourth floor, and I did start dropping in on her from time to time, but she had her own issues to deal with. We had started getting along quite well, in fact, for the first time in our lives, but she was notoriously moody and you never quite knew which Christine was going to open the door to you.

As for finding a girlfriend, or a sequence of hot and steamy one-night stands: well, I'd have loved nothing more on God's good earth, believe me, but the sad truth is that I was still striking out regularly on that front, because the attraction was never mutual. By which I mean the girls I fancied never fancied me, while the ones who did show an interest simply weren't my type. Very frustrating. Very depressing. Very isolating.

It was around this time that I started listening a little more closely to what Charlotte B was saying about the Good Lord, and how she'd committed her life to Jesus, and how beautiful it was to wake up each day knowing that she had the unconditional love of the heavenly Father who was watching over her and guiding her on life's path.

Charlotte, bespectacled and with a warm and kindly face, had been a fellow drama student in Graham's year group and she was still a close friend of his and a regular visitor to Caledonian Mansions, meaning that I'd bump into her from time to time. She always seemed to have a smile for me and for everyone else too.

I got talking to her one day, and she suggested that I might like to tag along the next time she went to her church; I said I wouldn't mind that at all; she said how about this weekend; I said yeah sure ... and so it came to pass that, on a Sunday evening in June or July, I stepped out of her old Datsun and into the parking lot of the Rhema Family Church in Randburg, a 45-minute drive from Pretoria.

The place was absolutely humming, with large groups of people calling out to friends or hugging and sharing a joke as they streamed towards a huge, converted warehouse with a giant cross above the entrance. Charlotte introduced me to her sister and her sister's boyfriend, and a bunch of their friends, and they immediately welcomed me into the circle, which felt pretty good.

We joined the throng pushing towards the warehouse and through the wide entrance. Music was being piped into the auditorium within, but not the stuffy hymns or organ recitals I'd been expecting; this was soft rock, with a surging, compelling beat and a gospel twist. There was a queue over in one corner where someone was selling Bibles and T-shirts with the Rhema logo, and tape cassettes and LPs (remember them?) showcasing the music of dozens of Christian bands.

A second stall had a TV mounted to one side showing an American preacher ministering to the masses, and two young guys were doing a brisk trade in selling videos of that preacher, and similar ones featuring the muscular Ray McCauley, the founder of this particular church. Legend had it that McCauley, 30-something and very charismatic, had been a nightclub bouncer and a champion bodybuilder before he found Jesus.

The mood was festive and welcoming. I was already thinking how cool all of this looked as Charlotte led our group to a row of seats as close to the stage as we could get ... which was more than half the way back, because the place was already mobbed, and filling up fast. I'm not especially good at estimating crowd numbers, but there must have been a thousand people crammed into that hall, maybe more.

There was a stage on an island in the centre surrounded by endless rows of chairs, with a live band up there playing more of that captivating gospel rock, backed by a chorus of eight or ten girls and young women in jeans and Rhema T-shirts. Rows of tinted spotlights overhead cast the performers in a warm glow. There was a photographer walking around and a camera crew setting up at the foot of the stage, presumably ready to produce another Rhema video to join the small library on sale in the auditorium. It felt like the preamble to a rock concert, with everyone already on their third happy pill and having the very best day of their lives.

A stir went through the crowd as McCauley came striding confidently up one of the aisles towards the stage, people reaching out to touch him as he passed, some crying out

"Hallelujah!" or "Praise Jesus!", others turning and hugging their neighbours excitedly. Charlotte reached over and squeezed her sister's hand. The show was about to begin.

McCauley opened with a cheerful greeting to the crowd and then an impromptu, almost informal prayer to God above, pulling the microphone close with one hand while hoisting a Bible heavenwards with the other, smiling and closing his eyes briefly in reverential bliss. A thousand worshippers answered with "Amen!"

He cracked a joke, he complimented the singers, he told his wife, standing alongside him, how much he loved her and he praised God for giving him a second chance, and he told an anecdote about his bodybuilding days.

Then he got down to business, thumbing open his Bible and quoting a line from the New Testament and offering his interpretation of it; I don't recall which one exactly, but I remember thinking that what he was saying made a lot of sense. He took another line and offered more insights and again I found myself nodding in agreement, but it was when he started talking about God having a plan for each and every one of us sitting there in that hall – including lost, lonely, insecure me – that I really began to feel the mood.

God had a plan for me? That was a compelling thought, because I certainly didn't!

The band had started playing a soft tune, way in the background, almost imperceptible, and the singers joined in with a soothing, angelic, almost hypnotic chorus. McCauley closed his eyes again and prayed, a heartfelt appeal for God's guidance this time, his voice shaking with genuine emotion, and I noticed that several people around me were swaying in their seats, whispering an amen, stretching their hands above them as if to touch some palpable presence, all of them swept up in an invisible but intense wave of emotion pulsating through that vast hall.

McCauley took a moment to compose himself and then he spoke of how Jesus had called not the righteous but the sinners to repentance ... and he wondered aloud if there was anyone here tonight, in this hall, right here, right now, who could feel the Holy Spirit moving within them? The band picked up the tempo a tad and the angelic chorus started hitting a few higher notes.

Was there anyone in the crowd, McCauley asked, who was ready to open their heart to God's love and acceptance and forgiveness? Right here, right now? Anyone who was ready to change their empty and meaningless life for something better, to embrace the warmth and leave the loneliness behind? Was there anyone, he demanded to know, who was ready to find their purpose, to be loved, *truly* loved, for the first time in their life ... and, yes oh yes, there was one: ME!

McCauley cried out: "Come on up to the stage, my brothers, my sisters, right here, right now – come on up and be saved! BE SAVED!" – and I shot to my feet, icy shivers rippling all the way from my scalp to my toes, the most intense and alien and wonderful sensation I'd ever had. I forced my way past Charlotte and her friends, desperate to reach the aisle, all of them clapping me on the shoulder, a couple of them even jumping up and giving me a hug as I barged by.

I wasn't alone; there were maybe 25 or 30 others who fetched up at the foot of the stage that night, men and women, boys and girls, all of them very emotional, most of them in tears. Me, I was sobbing my eyes out and I didn't know why. A kindly older woman in one of the Rhema T-shirts stepped towards me and gave me a warm embrace and a handful of tissues to wipe my streaming nose, and that simple act of human kindness made me start bawling even harder.

I was an emotional mess – but so were all the others alongside me, and that made it okay; better than okay, in fact. I felt ... released, freed at long, long last of the dreadful, choking misery that had been building up inside me for all the years since I crossed that continental divide between my happy childhood and my tormented adolescence.

Brothers and sisters, I felt saved.

I was light-headed on the drive back to Pretoria, excited at the thought of what tomorrow would bring and all the tomorrows after that. Born again! I'd heard the term bandied about often enough, but I'd never really thought much about it. Now I had a thousand questions for Charlotte, and she was happy to supply the answers, overjoyed herself that one more lost soul had found a path to the God she'd worshipped all her life.

The last thing I did before I laid my exhausted head down to sleep that night was to talk to God and say thank you a zillion times over, and to pray for his guidance, the way I'd seen McCauley do a few hours earlier.

I slept better that night than I had since ... well, ever, really.

CHAPTER 25

My classmates at the Tech commented, in those first weeks, on how happy I looked and how much I'd changed, not just because I quit smoking overnight and threw out the quarter-full, five-litre box of wine in the kitchen and flushed the baggie of weed down the toilet, but because I was showing up for classes with a renewed sense of optimism. The doubts I had about my place in the acting world persisted, but I was content to push ahead anyway, confident that, however things played out, God had a plan for me. It was all going to be okay, praise the Lord.

I joined Charlotte on the drive to Randburg every Sunday, and we'd talk about the power of prayer and the meanings of various Bible passages and the many traps laid down by Satan to snare the unwary. She introduced me to a bunch of gospel bands and singers, foremost of which was a long-haired hippie guy from America called Don Francisco, a talented guitarist and songwriter who undoubtedly could have been a huge star if he'd gone mainstream, but had instead chosen a life in service to the Lord. We'd drive back to Pretoria afterwards, topped up with the power of the Holy Spirit and ready for another week of spreading the Word.

Rhema, like most revivalist churches, was big on casting out demons and at some point in every service McCauley would call on anyone with a troubled mind or a mental issue of some kind to come on up to the stage. He would walk among the small crowd that invariably assembled and he would pick out an individual and stand before them and place a heavy hand on that person's head and close his eyes and say a prayer, and the whole flock would join in.

The band would play and the chorus would sing and he would suddenly strike out, fast as a rinkhals, tapping the worshipper's forehead with the thumb and index finger of his other hand and commanding the demon to FLEE that body, in the name of JESUS, and to scuttle all the way back into the bowels of HELL from whence he'd come.

The worshipper would stagger backwards, sometimes falling all the way over, but there were always stewards on hand to catch them, and a moment later he or she would jump to their feet, clear-eyed again and freed forever of whatever malign spirit had been nesting within. The crowd would roar its appreciation and McCauley would turn to the next worshipper.

Faith healing was also high on the agenda. I watched a crippled man roll up to the stage in his wheelchair one Sunday; McCauley prayed for him and he suddenly jumped from that chair and raised his eyes to the heavens and cried with happiness. The following week a middle-aged woman took the stage and told of how the cancer in her belly had shrivelled up and then vanished, banished forever by the power of prayer. The next week a younger woman said she'd been told by doctors that she'd never have children, then pointed to her swollen, heavily pregnant belly and sobbed with gratitude.

Charlotte told me on the drive home one night that she herself simply refused to get ill, ever; that the regular winter coughs and colds we were all subject to were merely Satan's way of entering the body, and that if you prayed hard enough you were able to cast them out yourself. God had given us all that power but very few of us ever used it.

I thought about that long and hard. I thought about keratoconus. Could God cure that too? Were my eye problems the handiwork of Satan – and, if so, could the bulging in my corneas be vanished and banished, like the cancer in that woman's belly, by the awesome power of prayer? I suspected it might. The Bible, after all, told us that Jesus had healed several people who were blind, and some of those may very well have been suffering with keratoconus.

I was already in the habit of praying every night, but I redoubled my efforts, adding an hour in the mornings, an hour in the afternoons, another hour before bedtime, seeking guidance from on high. Charlotte had spoken often about the practice of talking in tongues; simply opening your mouth and giving voice to your faith without thinking about whatever words would come out. It usually sounded like gibberish but after a while you would start to recognise some of those alien sounds, and start to repeat them, slowly building a language that only God above was able to understand. I tried that too.

A few Sundays later I was ready, and I knew God was too because He'd been ready the day the first symptoms of keratoconus had manifested themselves. They were the work of Satan, and God could very easily undo that work. All I'd had to do all along, if only I'd known it, was to ask Him for healing.

At some point in every service McCauley would hold his Bible close to his chest and appeal to the Heavenly Father to help everyone in the congregation that night who was hurting, who was ill, or who might be suffering in silence. The singers would start up with another of those gentle, heavenly choruses while a thousand people swayed and prayed and whispered a fervent "Jesus" to themselves.

I bent my head one night, sitting alongside Charlotte as usual, and I sent up an impassioned prayer for healing, an intense and emotional plea that came from the very depths of my soul and which I had no doubt at all was about to be answered, right here, right now. The joy was already building in my heart as I opened my eyes and plucked out my contact lenses, the left and then the right, then lifted my head and looked towards the stage, fully expecting – *knowing* – that I'd be able to see with crystal clarity for the first time since my mid-teens. Hallelujah! Praise the Lord!

I was so sure of it that I actually rose halfway out of my seat

... before I blinked and paused. Things were still a bit fuzzy. I blinked again, a bit harder, and I looked down to my feet and up again. I rubbed my eyes a bit then closed them and opened them again, cautiously this time, and I stared again towards the stage ... but all I could see were the old, familiar frosted-glass shapes and shadows. Nothing had changed. My vision was as poor as ever.

I sat back down.

Charlotte touched me on the shoulder. "Are you okay?" she asked.

Bewildered, I held up my contact lenses to her, one in each palm. "I tried to ... It didn't work. I prayed, just like you said. Like *he* said" – I motioned towards McCauley. "But it didn't work."

Charlotte dropped me off at my parent's flat in Benoni that night because she was heading on to *her* parents' place in nearby Kempton Park, rather than returning to Pretoria as usual. There was none of the usual bubbly, post-Rhema chatter and we drove mostly in silence.

I asked her at one point if I'd been wrong to appeal for God's healing; if maybe part of that plan he had for me depended on me having bad eyesight, and she told me that she didn't know, but that she would pray on it and that I should too. I said I would, but my spirits had plunged and I felt as depressed as I ever had on my very worst high school day.

One thing I did discover that night was that, while the jury is still out on whether faith and happiness can make you healthy, the opposite is certainly true: bad news and bitter disappointment can make you ill, and quickly too. Within an hour my nose was streaming and my head was aching and I was cold and shivery all over, suffering all the symptoms of a hefty bout of flu.

I have a clear memory of me sitting on the carpeted lounge floor in my parents' flat that night, huddling as close to the gas heater as I could get, staring at the TV but not seeing or hearing whatever show it was that my mother and father were watching. I had weightier matters on my mind.

CHAPTER 26

Toni may have been a tiny bit crazy but he was certainly living life to the full, and so too were my other Pretoria Tech classmates. There were two more guys in the group: Sid H, a clean-cut and witty surfer boy from Durban, and Willie F, an intelligent and highly creative soul who was able to turn his hand to just about anything he pleased. There were three girls, all of them bright and vivacious: Jenny B was warm-hearted and fun-loving and she threw a series of memorable parties for the gang at her nearby parent's home; Kerryn H was a gentle blonde, although she did break the heart of one of the Year Two guys; Fiona M had that English-rose appeal, and she was one of those girls I talked about before who I fancied but who didn't fancy me.

I mentioned earlier that there was another group of Year One drama students at the Tech, doing an Afrikaans version of the same course at the same time? Well, one of that cohort, a tall and handsome young buck by name of Arnold Vosloo, would go on to realise the dreams of drama students everywhere, not just in Pretoria but across South Africa and probably farther afield too.

After graduating he appeared in a few local movies and then relocated to California and began living the Hollywood dream, winning starring roles in a couple of big-budget blockbusters. The most memorable was probably *The Mummy*, in which he played a vengeful Egyptian priest called Imhotep who rises from the dead filled with hatred and bile, grimly intent on wiping all of humanity from the face of the planet. Arnold himself, by contrast, was a nice guy.

He and the seven or eight other Afrikaans students, and my classmates on the English side, and even Graham and Christine and Bruce, all had two things in common: a love of acting and at least some talent to go with it. It was becoming ever more apparent that I had neither, and by August I'd pretty much decided that there was no point in me carrying on for the rest of the year, because whatever plan God had for me – and He was being annoyingly vague on the details – it almost certainly did not involve Oscars, Baftas or even Golden Globes. It was time to bring down the curtain on my Pretoria misadventure.

I sold up my bed and my bean bag and I bade farewell to the cockroaches and I headed back to Benoni, another eight months older but still no wiser about what life path to pursue than when I'd left Rhodes or, indeed, Gramco the year before that.

I remember my mother greeting me at the front door with a cold, hard stare.

I continued going to church every Sunday with Charlotte but the honeymoon phase had passed and the effort of presenting a brave face to the world every day began to make itself felt. It's not easy being a reborn Christian in a world filled with sceptics, vulnerable 24 hours a day to the sort of worldly temptations or nagging doubts that inevitably begin to creep in. Also, I began to notice certain similarities in the sermons being presented each week, with the same themes being repeated – casting out the demons, healing the sick, converting a new batch of sinners – and the band playing the same songs, and McCauley offering up the same prayers.

I held fast to my faith for as long as I could, but like the REM song that would hit the charts a decade later I was losing my religion.

The crunch came when I watched the same drama being played out on the Rhema stage for three weeks in a row, with virtually no variation at all. On Week One a stranger limped up to the stage saying that his left leg was shorter than the right. He begged to be healed. McCauley sat the guy down on a chair centre-stage and bent over him, praying and clutching his ankles before suddenly jumping up and declaring that a miracle had taken place; the stranger's leg had grown an inch before his very eyes! The two were now a perfect match! Praise the Lord! Alleluia! Alleluia!

"What? I didn't see it? Did you?" I asked Charlotte.

"Of course! Praise Jesus!" she sang back. Probably my bad eyes, I thought, so I applauded and sang out a chorus of thank-you-Lords and amens along with everyone else as the man hopped down from the stage and walked off with a newly confident, finely balanced gait.

On Week Two the exact same thing happened, with a different guy, only it was his right leg that was apparently shorter than the left, and he wept with joy when McCauley did his thing and – *boinggg* – the problem leg grew an inch. I applauded a bit but I didn't join in when the praise the Lords and Alleluias rang out.

On Week Three yet another guy got up from a seat near the front and hobbled towards the stage with a tragically short right leg, and I muttered under my breath: "Oh come on!" ... which didn't go down especially well with Charlotte. He too was healed, bounding up and away on his perfectly re-aligned pins, holding his arms aloft and singing the Lord's praises as he went. I sat on my hands while the rest of the crowd whooped and prayed.

On Week Four I told Charlotte I had a family engagement that I couldn't get out of and I wouldn't be able to make it to church that night.

I never went back to Rhema, but to this day I still feel a certain enviousness whenever I encounter a recently born-again Christian; the genuine ones, those happy few who give off an inner glow that comes from *knowing* that they have a loving and all-powerful force watching over them, protecting and guiding them on a meaningful life path and even carrying them across thin air should they step out over an icy crevasse they hadn't known was opening underfoot. I imagine that's what a happy toddler in a loving household must feel as they wake up each morning to the warm embrace of a doting parent and a new day filled with small but exciting and always manageable challenges. It's a wonderful state of existence.

Most people saved at a revivalist church tend to backslide later and give it all up, but I think it's fair to say that if everybody on the planet lived their lives the way genuine Christians do, we'd have a far happier world.

Me, I think all the churches have taken the Bible way too literally, particularly the bit that suggests that 80 or 90 billion or so of the 100 billion people I joked about at the start of this tale were, in effect, given zero chance of avoiding an eternity burning in Hell just because they had the poor judgment to be born before Christ arrived to unlock the doors to Heaven, or because they happened to be born into a Muslim or Jewish or Buddhist family (most of whom have probably also taken their scriptures way too literally).

That doesn't mean I don't believe in God; it's just that I have no idea in what form or shape He exists. I've spent many late nights debating the topic with my son Jordan, a very bright young man who holds a Master's degree in theoretical physics, and who consequently takes a scientific view of things.

I had a general idea, before those conversations began, that the universe was a big place, but it was only when he showed me a couple of YouTube videos that I realised just *how* big. There's a video by somebody who calls himself RealLifeLore; call it up and you'll see what I'm talking about. It's titled How the Universe is way bigger than you Think. It runs for about nine minutes and there's a fact listed at about the 4.30min mark that really blew my little mind.

After endless debate about the true meaning of life and whether or not there's a purpose to anything at all that we do, Jordan and I decided that there were two things we could agree on: first, that nobody can prove conclusively either that God exists or that he doesn't, and second, that we humans simply don't have all the information we need to see the Big Picture, nor the brain power to comprehend it even if we could.

We're the frog at the bottom of the well with no concept of the immensity of the sky; the ant scampering across a computer keyboard with no notion of the internet.

Call me naïve, but I pray anyway, because watching those videos served only to reinforce my belief that there simply has to be some higher power at work. Surely something as profoundly complex as this universe – even just this world and the astonishing variety of life that exists upon it – cannot simply magic into existence with a Big Bang and a series of chemical reactions.

Surely the immense, incalculable weight of suffering endured by humans across time has to mean something, particularly in the few thousand years since we began cramming ourselves into cities, setting ourselves up as kings and peasants, warlords and victims, unleashing our innate cruelty on each other on an industrial scale. The joy and love we've shared, the art and the music and the literature we've created, our mass consciousness, and that of all other living creatures ... all of that has to mean something. All of it must be building towards something.

I can't see the Big Picture so I focus on the single pixel I can see, and I live by a simple code: I try to always do right by the people I love, and to never do wrong to anybody who didn't do wrong to me first. Very basic, I know, but hopefully I won't have strayed too far from God's path if there is, indeed, some kind of afterlife and a judgment waiting for me on the day I die.

And if there isn't? Well, the great thing about oblivion is that I'm not going to know that I no longer exist. Simples, as Sergei the Meerkat says.

And with that bit of armchair philosophy out the way – my last digression, I promise, because we're almost at the end of this tale – let's return to Benoni, September 1981.

CHAPTER 27

I spent the next four months pretty much alone, living a hermitic existence from my bedroom in my parents' flat, reading an endless succession of novels borrowed from the Benoni library. I slept all day and read all night, starting at maybe 6pm and continuing through to the dawn, often finishing a book in a single session, breaking off at regular intervals for huge piles of toasted cheese and tea. At least once a week I'd take a walk down to the library for fresh supplies, usually searching for the thickest, chunkiest books I could find, by authors I'd never heard of before. Not such a bad life, to be perfectly honest, albeit a bit pointless.

At some point towards the end of the year I shucked off my pyjamas and took a train into Johannesburg one day to meet up with Toni for a few drinks, and to cheer him on in his role in *Evita*, which had been playing at the Civic Theatre for a month or so (and for which he'd gotten me a free ticket). I thoroughly enjoyed the show, and afterwards, when I was having those few drinks with my old buddy and a couple of his fellow performers, somebody mentioned that they were looking for helpers backstage.

I volunteered, not so much for the modest pay but because I thought it would be interesting to see how it all worked back there, and because I'd be able to, in effect, see the show and listen to the music over and over again, free of charge.

They signed me up and I changed my routine accordingly, riding the train to Joburg six afternoons a week and heading back to Benoni late at night, often having a whole train carriage to myself. That felt a bit creepy, to be honest, but I was perfectly safe doing that back in 1981.

In later years, of course, as the security situation deteriorated, only a madman would have considered riding that late train alone, and today it's simply not possible, because the trains have stopped running altogether. All the overhead cables have been looted and even some portions of the steel tracks have vanished. The station buildings themselves, at George Goch and Benoni and every stop in between, have been reduced to derelict piles of bricks and mortar, picked clean of anything of value, even the rusting old window frames. A very sad situation.

Anyway, on a Saturday afternoon a couple of weeks after I began helping out backstage I found myself with an hour to kill between the matinée and the evening performances. One of my fellow workers said he'd heard that somebody was holding auditions for a new production of *Joseph and the Amazing Technicolour Dreamcoat* in one of the rehearsal rooms behind the main stage, so I decided to wander over to watch for a bit.

I slipped in at the back and found a stray chair up against the wall and looked around me. The set up was similar to the *Evita* auditions I'd bombed out of in Pretoria earlier in the year, with a table in the middle for a couple of judges and a piano to one side, but the room wasn't exactly overcrowded. In fact, there were no more than 35 or 40 people milling about. They'd been at it all day apparently, and things were about to wrap up. They had just a few more singers to get through.

I watched a balding and overweight guy take his place before the judges and muddle through some song I'd never heard of, and then two other hopefuls mauled a couple of tunes from *Joseph*, one of them forgetting the words and the other straying horribly off-key. I was thinking to myself: wow, even I could do better than *that* when one of the judges, a man aged about 40 and with a kindly but care-worn face, cast a despairing look around the room and called out: "Anybody else?"

They were still one brother short of a dozen, it transpired.

I sat forward in my chair. I chewed my lower lip. Yes, the only thing I had learnt from eight months of drama studies was that I belonged on a stage the way a walrus belongs among the condors soaring gracefully through the skies above the Andes ... but hell, *these* people didn't know that. Yet.

"Anybody? Anybody at all?" the judge called, a note of desperation in his voice.

I stood up quickly and walked towards the piano.

"Ah! Do you have your sheet music?" the judge asked.

"No – but I know all the songs from *Joseph*. I can do *One More Angel in Heaven*, if you like? The one you've just finished playing," I added, turning to the pianist.

"No problem," the pianist answered – so I took a minute to fill out a form and then find a spot ten feet in front of the judges, and then I began trilling out the aforementioned song, one of many that I remembered word for word from the Protea production a few years earlier. I wasn't nervous at all, because I'd barely had time to think about what I was doing, and I remembered to move around a bit this time, rather than standing stock-still as I had at the *Evita* audition. I even added a couple of hammy gestures at what seemed to be appropriate moments:

> "*There's one more angel in heaven...*" (point to the ceiling)
> "*There's one more star in the sky...*" (splay them fingers)
> "*Joseph, we'll never forget you...*" (clasp o'
> the hands, shake o' the head)
> "*It's tough but we're gonna get by*" (nod, very sadly).

The judge called a halt before the second verse began but he wasn't looking unhappy. He announced to the room that he and his colleague were wrapping things up, and taking a quick break, so I strolled back to my chair and sat down again, checking my wristwatch to make sure I still had a bit of time before I was due back at the main theatre.

Barely ten minutes later the pair of them returned and

invited everyone to gather around while they read out a bunch of names – one of which was mine.

I'd be playing the role of Levi, one of Joseph's brothers, and doubling as one of the Ishmaelites, they told me. Rehearsals would start within the week. We'd be paid a small fortune (by my standards, at least, at the time), and we'd start with a four-week run in Johannesburg, at this very same Civic Theatre, before heading down to Durban for three weeks and then setting off on a nationwide tour, with additional accommodation and travel expenses paid, of course.

I nodded. They produced a contract. I signed on the dotted line, then I hurried back next door to begin my backstage shift with the *Evita* cast, in a state of shock.

It was only later, on the train ride home, that I dared to read the contract again and allow myself to begin to believe that it was all real; that I hadn't dozed off at some point in my shift and dreamt the whole thing. I had won a part in a real-life, professional production! I really had! Me!

I had the train carriage to myself, as usual. So I stood in the centre of the aisle and belted out *There's One More Angel in Heaven* again at the top of my voice, throwing in every hammy gesture I could think of and jumping up and down on the seats every now and then in sheer unbridled joy.

The judge that day, I learnt later, was Geoffrey Sutherland, one of South Africa's leading directors at the time and the same man who had brought the first professional performance of *Joseph* to South Africa, in 1974. It just so happened that I'd seen that show, along with my family, at a Johannesburg theatre. Like audiences around the world we'd loved it (though the highlight for 12-year-old me, watching avidly from the front row, had been the sight of the go-go girls in their bikini tops and miniskirts, standing with jaunty hands on hips between dances).

The singer Alvon Collison had shocked and thrilled conservative South Africa with his butt-thrusting performances as Pharaoh in 1974, and Sutherland was able to convince him to return for this new season at the start of 1982. He proved to be a wild and exuberant character who turned out to be every bit as outrageous off the stage as he was on it.

The narrator was Marloe Scott Wilson, a local celebrity who styled herself as The Pink Lady, and who dressed accordingly, with a punk, pink haircut and a matching fast car. Joseph was a young singer called Michael Tellinger, who would go on to have a few hit songs in South Africa before, disappointingly, in recent years, becoming better known for pushing a variety of weird and increasingly absurd conspiracy theories online.

Aged 19, I was the youngest member of the cast but playing the third oldest of Joseph's brothers because Sutherland had arranged us from tallest to shortest, and at a string-bean 6ft 2in, I was third in that descending line. I was given two lines to sing solo during the *Benjamin Calypso* number, which I did with gusto, adding a couple more of those hammy gestures during the first rehearsal which Sutherland greeted with an uncertain nod but didn't tell me to stop doing.

The show opened in Joburg to rave reviews and packed houses, and those four weeks performing at the Civic turned out to be a lot of fun; so much so that I was even beginning to wonder if maybe I'd been a bit hasty in giving up on the acting life. Should I have stayed on that path? Didn't somebody famous say that a journey of a thousand miles starts with a step in the wrong blerry direction? Something like that?

We finished up in Joburg and headed for the holiday surf city of Durban for a three-week run at the beautiful old Alhambra theatre, but things started to turn sour when Marloe Scott Wilson fell ill under mysterious circumstances, meaning that an understudy had to be rushed in to learn the part of the narrator. Far, far worse news came a day later when we learnt that two of the cast members had been killed in a car crash on the drive south from Joburg.

Tradition dictates that the show must go on, and the curtain rose on the Durban opening night anyway, with another couple of understudies brought in from Joburg, but a pall of gloom had descended behind the scenes that could not be lifted.

A week later the producers of the show, a glamorous couple whose names I can't remember, were robbed and beaten outside a bank as they went to deposit a substantial amount of cash taken at the box office, adding weight to the whispers that had begun circulating that the whole production was cursed. Another week after that the couple assembled the cast after the Saturday night show to tell us that they had, in effect, gone bust because a sleeping partner had siphoned off all their funds when no one was looking – leaving them with no option but to cancel the show.

And just like that the nationwide tour was over, after just seven short weeks. The curtain had fallen on my fledgling acting career. I hadn't misread those signs from God after all, it seemed.

I had enough money, at least, to buy a train ticket back to Benoni and of course my mother was there to greet me at the front door with a cold, hard stare ... which, frankly, felt a bit unfair this time round. For once, it wasn't my fault that I'd be starting my journey of a thousand miles all over again!

CHAPTER 28

I still had no clue what direction that journey would take nor what the destination might be, so for want of anything better to do I fished out the old library card from my bedside table drawer and returned to the sleep-all-day, read-all-night routine. There were many more piles of toasted cheese, many more cups of tea. The days turned to weeks. I suggested to my mother at one point that maybe I should study music and become a rock star? The pay was pretty good, I'd heard?

There was no response other than a low growl but my question must have stirred her to action because on an evening soon after, just as I was waking up and stretching luxuriously after a solid eight-hour nap, she came stomping into my room with a newspaper in one hand. It was folded open to the Jobs section. One of those jobs had a series of angry red circles scratched all around it, along with half a dozen giant exclamation marks, almost as if she'd been using her fist rather than her fingers to hold the pen. The ad read: "SPORTS REPORTER WANTED".

She said: "You're applying for this."

"I am? Sports reporter? SPORTS?"

"Tomorrow. First thing."

"But – no! Hey! Can we talk about this? I don't know anything about sports –"

"10am. And – good grief, what's that smell? When last did you shower?"

"Tuesday."

"Four days???"

"Tuesday laaast week."

The newspaper in question was the *Germiston City News*, the offices of which were located halfway between Benoni and Joburg. The editor, a gruff, foul-tempered, ginger-bearded man by name of Kevin Keogh, must have been truly desperate to fill the vacancy, because he didn't ask any questions about why I'd flunked out of university, or even how interested I was in sports. The answers to which would have been: a) "I'm inherently lazy", and b) "Not at all – is that going to be a problem for a sports reporter?"

His only question was: how soon can you start? The beginning of the month, I told him.

April 1, 1982 was a Thursday, if I remember right, and I very, very nearly didn't survive in my first real job beyond that same weekend. Keogh handed me a sheet of paper on the Friday with a list of sporting events that I would be covering: football and badminton on the Saturday, and hockey and a powerboating competition on the Sunday. He shoved a camera into my hands.

"EVER USED ONE OF THESE?" he screamed in his gentle, compassionate way.

"Nah."

"YOU PRESS THIS BUTTON! YOU FIDDLE THIS THINGMAJIG! YOU SQUEEZE THIS KNOB! I'LL SEE YOU BACK HERE ON MONDAY MORNING!"

"Wait ... this button? And how do I attach this flash thingie –"

But he lumbered into his office without a backward glance.

I borrowed my sister's old Volkswagen Passat and drove out to the local football club on the Saturday with serious misgivings about the whole idea ... but things actually went off rather well, I thought. I knew a bit about football, of course, so I was able to talk confidently to the coach of the home team, making astute observations about offside traps and diamond formations and things. From time to time I hoisted the camera to eye level and pressed the button, squeezed the thingmajig, fiddled the knob as instructed and it made a satisfying whirring noise every time I did so. Fantastic! I was a natural!

I got through the badminton tournament and the hockey game without incident too, taking a bunch of pics and filling a few pages of my notebook with cryptic notes I'd struggle to decipher later, but it all started to fall apart when I arrived for the powerboating competition on the Sunday.

The organiser, rather surprisingly, waved me away with an angry, impatient gesture when I tried to introduce myself – could be he was just a miserable shit, or it could be that, yes ok, I was an hour late, and the race was about to start within a few seconds – but either way I was left to wander over to the side of the dam by myself.

I squinted out to where the boats were screaming across the water at a hundred miles an hour and decided to take a couple of pics. I hoisted the camera. Pressed the button. Fiddled the thingmajig. Squeezed the knob. But nothing happened.

I pressed harder, fiddled faster, squeezed tighter, and tighter, and tighter, until suddenly there was a loud, snapping noise from somewhere inside the camera body. I thought: "Hmmm. I think I'll open up the back of this camera and see if I can work out what's gone wrong."

And I'm ashamed to admit that that is exactly what I did next, flipping the camera open and drawing out the long roll of film and holding it up to the light to check for obvious signs of damage – completely erasing, of course, every one of my photos from the football, the badminton and the hockey! Aarghh! Noooo! Say it ain't so!

But it was. It was so, and it dawned on me that I'd messed up rather handsomely, and that my budding career as a newshound was probably over. I tossed the now-useless roll of film into a nearby bin and drove back to Benoni in a state of wretched despair, followed by an angst-filled, sleepless night.

Keogh was all smiles and sympathetic hugs and warm twinkles in the eye when I got into the office on Monday morning and told him what had happened ... but no, no of course I'm lying. In fact, he roared out the word "F***!!!" – true story; just that one word, delivered at ear-popping levels – and then turned and stomped back into his office, slamming the door behind him.

And that, dear reader, was one of those sliding-door moments in which your entire life path hangs in the balance, though you don't realise it at the time. A very, very big part of me wanted to simply set the camera down somewhere and slink off towards the exit and never set foot in the offices of the *Germiston City News* ever again – and who knows what course my life would have taken and what line of work I would have ended up in if I had done that? It certainly wouldn't have been journalism. There would have been no coming back from that.

But the thought of notching up yet one more failed enterprise, of making one more drive back to Benoni where my mother would be waiting to greet me at the front door with one more cold, hard stare ... well, that was enough to get me walking in the opposite direction, away from the exit and towards my desk and typewriter instead.

As it happened I didn't last long in that job anyway, me being quick to take offence and Keogh quicker still to offer it, but when I moved to *The Springs Advertiser* six months later I found an editor with a talent for mentoring rather than a foul temper (and a better beard than Keogh's too, now that I think about it). His name was Bruce Bennett, a man of integrity and compassion, and he taught me more about reporting and photography and, later, sub-editing than the professors at Rhodes ever could have.

That in turn laid the groundwork for a 40-year career (and counting) in newspapers that led eventually to *The Times*, which I like to think is still the most prestigious paper on the planet.

My career has allowed me to live and work on three continents, with the added bonus of the occasional press trip to unforgettable places I'd never have had the chance to visit otherwise – but most importantly of all, it was through my job that I met the woman who would turn out to be my wife and soulmate for 30 years (and counting), now quite literally half my life.

Asha is also, of course, the mother of our son Jordan, who surely has the purest heart of any of those 100 billion humans I mentioned earlier … and I'm going to suggest, half-seriously, that simply by raising him to be part Gandhi, part Jesus and part Albert Frickin Einstein, Asha and I, together, have atoned for all the sins of my misspent youth that I've told you about here (and a few others that I haven't).

But that, my friends – the career, the wife, the son – all of that is a story for another day …

The End